The RAPTOR

Guide

of Southern Africa

Ulrich Oberprieler

Burger Cillié

GAME PARKS PUBLISHING

© 2009
© Text: Ulrich Oberprieler and Burger Cillié
© Photographs: Various photographers as indicated

© Publication:
Game Parks Publishing
PO Box 12331
Hatfield 0028
Pretoria
www.gameparkspublishing.co.za
info@gameparkspublishing.co.za

Edited by Johan Steenkamp and Ulrich Oberprieler
Illustrations in Sections 1 and 2 by Marietjie Steyn and Ulrich Oberprieler
Illustrations of flight patterns in Sections 3, 4 and 5 by Marietjie Steyn
Illustrations of perched raptors in Section 4 by Heidi Greeff
Project coordinater: Johan Steenkamp
Distribution maps by Guy Gibbon / S.A. Birding cc
Design ,layout, colour reproduction and cover design by Niel Cillié, DC Graphics, Pretoria

Photographic credits where not otherwise indicated:

Front cover:	African Fish-Eagle / Albert Froneman
Title page:	African Crowned Eagle / Chris van Rooyen
Content page:	Secretarybird / Marietjie Oosthuizen
Acknowledgement page:	Juvenile Yellow-billed Kite / Johann Knobel
Preface page:	Juvenile Southern Pale Chanting Goshawk / Niel Cillié
Back cover:	Lesser Kestrel / Mark Anderson
	Jackal Buzzard / Johann Knobel
	Pearl-spotted Owlet / Albert Froneman
	Bateleur / Niel Cillié

Printed by	Craft Print International Ltd. 9 Joo Koon Circle, Singapore 629041

First edition 2009

ISBN: 978-0-6204-3223-8

THE RAPTOR GROUPS

Secretarybird (p. 33, 48)
This is the only very large raptor with very long legs. It is further characterised by its crest of long feathers on the back of the head and long central tailfeathers. The plumage is grey and black.

Fish-eating raptors (p. 34, 50–53, 217)
The Osprey and African Fish-Eagle are both large raptors that catch fish and are therefore associated with water. Both have long broad wings which enable them to carry even heavy fish. The unfeathered lower legs distinguish them from the true eagles and hawk-eagles.

Vultures (p. 35, 54–71, 218)
These large to very large raptors are adapted to a scavenging life style. The head and neck of most species are partially or wholly naked and the weak feet are not suited to killing prey. Vultures have long broad wings and short tails for soaring flight. The Palm-nut and Bearded Vultures are not typical vultures.

Eagles and hawk-eagles (p. 36, 72–93, 224)
These medium to very large raptors are immediately distinguished by their fully feathered legs. They are powerful and aggressive hunters but are not averse to carrion. Their wings are long and broad, but the tails vary from shortish to medium, depending on the preferred hunting technique of the particular species.

Snake-eagles (p. 37, 94–103, 232)
Although resembling true eagles, snake-eagles are easily distinguished by their large heads, large yellow eyes and unfeathered lower legs. As the name indicates, they feed mostly on snakes. As they soar often and well, their wings are broad and long, while the tail is of medium length. The Bateleur is not a typical snake-eagle as indicated by its dark eyes.

Buzzards (p. 38, 104–115, 236)
Buzzards resemble small eagles, but have unfeathered lower legs. They are medium to medium-large, robustly built raptors that hunt mostly from a perch. They soar well as the wings are long and broad while the tail is shortish to medium in length. The European Honey-Buzzard is not a typical buzzard.

Goshawks and sparrowhawks (p. 39, 116–137, 241)
These very small to medium-sized raptors usually occur in well-wooded habitats where their secretive life style makes them difficult to observe. Their wings are short, while the tail is long: an adaptation for fast but manoeuvrable flight. They have long legs. The two chanting goshawks, the Lizard Buzzard and the African Harrier-Hawk are not typical goshawks.

Harriers (p. 40, 138–147, 250)
Harriers are medium-sized, slenderly built raptors with long narrow wings, long tails and long legs. They occur in marshes or open habitats where they fly low over the ground, quartering to and fro, and dropping onto their prey on the ground.

Kites (p. 41, 148–157, 254)
Kites are a diverse collection of small to medium-sized raptors with long wings, and are excellent flyers. In spite of their names, the African Cuckoo-Hawk and Bat Hawk also belong to this group.

Falcons and kestrels (p. 42, 158–189, 257)
These very small to medium-small raptors inhabit open country and are adapted for fast (falcons) or hovering (kestrels) flight. Their wings are long and pointed while the tail is long.

Owls (p. 44, 190–213, 268)
Owls are very small to very large raptors adapted to a nocturnal life style.

SPONSOR'S FOREWORD

Vodacom South Africa is acutely aware that the future health of humanity depends on the sustainable use of resources and the preservation of our natural heritage. This heritage includes the eleven groups into which the authors classify the raptors. As is the case with the rest of the world, short-term changes such as habitat destruction, and long-term trends such as global warming, are impacting on natural areas in our region, and raptor numbers are slowly but surely decreasing.

An obvious way in which Vodacom expresses its commitment to the environment is through camouflaging its base stations in environmentally-sensitive areas so that they blend in with the natural environment. Many of the network of masts in South Africa's world-famous Kruger National Park are disguised as indigenous trees, for example. This is also the case in many other of the country's national parks, whose base stations blend in with their environments, remaining unnoticed by visitors and pro-viding minimal disruption to the natural wildlife in the parks.

Other base stations are designed to aesthe-tically enhance an environment. These take the form of windmills and a lighthouse, as well as several masts disguised as palm trees. The first such 'tree' in the world – a *Cocos plumosa*-palm – was 'planted' in Cape Town in March 1996.

Vodacom has also installed environmentally friendly cooling systems in some of its base stations that now use solar or wind power to generate their own electricity.

Vodacom's commitment to the environment extends beyond the physical structure of its base stations to the protection of birds of prey that nest on its mast structures. Raptors sometimes choose the cellular mast structures as permanent nesting sites due to their height and safety from natural and unnatural threats. In response, Vodacom has introduced procedures in respect of these structures, and implements a specific environmental policy to ensure that such birds are not disturbed during critical periods of their breeding seasons.

Vodacom is proud of the high standards of environmental protection that we strive to maintain in our operations, as a result of which we received the ISO 14001 environ-mental management certification in July 1999 – one of the few GSM operators in the world to have received this certification.

It is therefore with great pleasure that we are the proud sponsors of this new publication dedicated to the beautiful raptors of our region. We trust that it will prove a useful resource to help our bird-loving public identify these magnificent birds, thereby enhancing their understanding of raptors, and the pleasure derived from the rewarding pursuit of raptor watching. We are also confident that it will play an important role in increasing public awareness of the diversity and behaviour of Southern Africa's raptors.

SHAMEEL JOOSUB
Managing Director
Vodacom South Africa

CONTENTS

ACKNOWLEDGEMENTS

We wish to express our sincere gratitude to our sponsor – Vodacom. Without their financial support it would not have been possible to publish this unique book on the raptors of Southern Africa. We extend our thanks specifically to Dr. Alan Knott-Craig, Vodacom's former CEO, who facilitated the sponsorship. We also thank Vodacom's CEO Pieter Uys, Shameel Joosub: Managing Director and Romeo Kumalo: Commercial Director of Vodacom SA for their involvement in this project.

Our special thanks to Johan Steenkamp, our project coordinator. Thank you for the countless hours spent on coordinating the compilation of this book, and for your friendship.

The success of this publication does not only depend on the accuracy and readability of the text, but to a large extent on the quality of the photographs used. We are thus extremely grateful to all the photographers, both local and international, as well as the various agencies that kindly made their images available.

We would like to thank Guy Gibbon of Birding SA for providing up-to-date distribution maps.

We, the authors and artists, wish to acknowledge *Birds of Prey of Southern Africa – their identification and life histories* (David Philip, 1982) by Peter Steyn and Graeme Arnott as a major source of reference for the illustrations in this publication.

We extend our thanks to the Endangered Wildlife Trust's Bird of Prey Working Group for endorsing this publication.

Thank you, Niel Cillié of DC Graphics, for doing such an outstanding job with the design and layout of this book, as well as the editing of images.

Many thanks to our families and friends, especially Willa, for their ideas, constructive suggestions and patience while we were working on this book.

Most of all we wish to thank our Creator that we are able to share a wonderful part of His creation with other people in this way.

Ulrich and *Burger*

This book is dedicated to

Dr. Alan Knott-Craig
an entrepreneur and nature lover par excellence

Dawid Kunneke
in memory of an extraordinary friend

PREFACE

Raptors are the most magnificent of birds. Who is not impressed by the power and strength of an eagle, the agility and aggression of a sparrowhawk, the spectacular speed of a falcon stooping at its prey, or the silent flight of an owl? As top predators, raptors not only play a special role in nature but are also immensely popular among birdwatchers.

Raptors are not easy to identify. In spite of a number of excellent field guides to the birds of Southern Africa, most birdwatchers experience difficulties with this group.

The Raptor Guide of Southern Africa is a user-friendly identification guide to the diurnal birds of prey and the owls of Southern Africa. Its easy layout, clear photographs, helpful illustrations, readable text and cross-references enable birdwatchers to identify raptors with confidence.

The Raptor Guide is divided into five sections. Section 1 introduces you to the general biology of Southern African raptors. This information will give you a better understanding of the various adaptations and life styles of raptors. Section 2 emphasises the different groups of raptors, as it is of prime importance to first place a raptor within a certain group before attempting to identify the species. Section 3 deals with the species of Southern African raptors. The text is divided into a number of topics and is cross-referenced to Sections 2 and 4.

As most birdwatchers are in possession of one or more of the well-illustrated field guides to the birds of Southern Africa, the authors decided to show the various species by means of photographs. In a few cases photos of captive birds have been used as clear identification photographs of wild birds could not be obtained. As diurnal raptors are often seen in flight, illustrations of the flight patterns are included. The sonograms are an important aid to identify owls by their calls. The simplified drawings in Section 4 enable you to compare similar species and confirm the identification of a specific raptor. The book ends with Section 5, the references. This section includes a number of helpful pages: photo's of raptors in flight, 12 colour plates of the flight patterns, an overview of the raptor groups and a quick index to the species.

Birdwatchers will find this book an indispensable guide to the raptors of Southern Africa.

HOW TO USE THIS BOOK

The Raptor Guide has been designed to be user-friendly. Its easy and logical layout will facilitate the identification of any Southern African raptor. Cross-references on the margin of pages with photographs and in the text will allow you to compare similar birds and to double-check your identification. The book has been divided into five sections:

Section 1: General biology (p. 14)

Read through this section carefully as it will provide a deeper understanding and appreciation of the various adaptations and life styles shown by Southern African raptors. The different topics are illustrated by means of black-and-white drawings and colour photographs.

Section 2: Raptor groups (p. 28)

It is of prime importance to first place a raptor within a smaller group (such as the eagles, buzzards, harriers or falcons) before attempting to identify the species. This section, illustrated by means of black-and-white drawings and colour photographs, allows you to familiarise yourself with the 11 groups of Southern African raptors. This section is cross-referenced to Sections 3 and 4.

Section 3: Species accounts (p. 46)

The 83 species of Southern African raptors are described in a logical way. This section is cross-referenced to Sections 2 and 4. The layout of each double page is as follows:

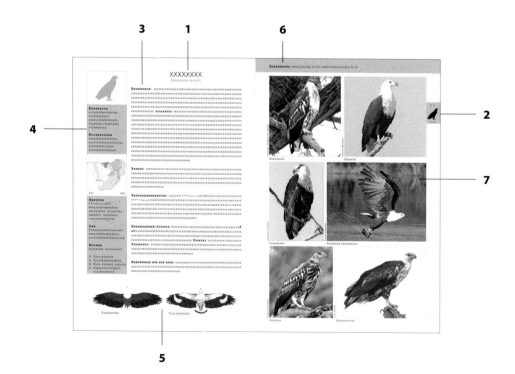

1 **Name**: The English name in common use in Southern Africa is given, together with the scientific name. (For raptor names in South African indigenous languages, please consult *www.fitzpatrick.uct. ac.za/docs/birdname.html*)

2 **Colour-coded group icon and cross-reference:** Each of the 11 raptor groups is indicated by a specific colour. The top page number on the colour block refers to the relevant group in Section 2 and the bottom page number to the group in Section 4 that this species belongs to.

3 **Text:** The description of each raptor is divided into a number of topics:
a. **Field recognition:** This gives a concise description of how to identify the raptor in the field.
b. **Voice:** This topic is only given for owls as it is an important feature in their identification.
c. **Behaviour:** Interesting behaviour which will often aid identification is described here.
d. **Feeding methods:** Raptors use different techniques to capture prey or to obtain food.
e. **Breeding:** Basic information on the breeding biology is given here.
f. **Origin of name:** The scientific names and some English names are explained.

4 **Basic information:** The following information is given:
a. **Comparative sizes:** The size of each raptor (black silhouette) is compared to one of three well-known birds (blue silhouette): the Feral Pigeon for small raptors, the Helmeted Guineafowl for medium raptors and the African Fish-Eagle for large raptors.
b. **Measurements: Length:** The measurement of a dead bird lying flat on its back, from the tip of its bill to the tip of the tail or toes, whichever is the longest. **Wingspan:** The measurement from wing tip to wing tip across the bird with its wings fully extended. Where possible the minimum, maximum and mean (in brackets) of a sample are given. **Weight:** Where possible the minimum, maximum and mean weight (in brackets) of a sample are given. **Sexes:** The symbols are ♂ for the male and ♀ for the female.
c. **Distribution:** A description of the larger distribution as well as a map indicating the Southern African distribution is given. The darker shade indicates where the bird is most common. The colours on the map indicate the following: **Green** (Resident); **Blue** (Summer resident); **Yellow** (Visitor or vagrant). The number on the left is the Southern African number as used in Roberts VI while the number on the right is the one used in Roberts VII.
d. **Habitat:** The preferred habitat is indicated.
e. **Food:** The preferred food is indicated.
f. **Status: Endemic:** A species whose distribution is confined to Southern Africa. **Resident:** A species that breeds in Southern Africa and remains here throughout the year. **Summer resident:** A species that breeds in Southern Africa but occurs here during the summer months only. These are mostly migratory raptors that spend the southern winter in central and northern Africa. **Visitor:** A migratory species that does not breed in Southern Africa. These are mostly raptors breeding in the northern hemisphere and visiting Southern Africa during the southern summer season. **Vagrant:** A species not normally recorded here.
g. **Other names:** S: English synonyms; A: Afrikaans name; F: French name; G: German name; P: Portuguese name.

5 **Flight pattern or sonogram:** Illustrations of the various colour forms of diurnal raptors are given here. Compare these to the photographs on the adjacent page as well as pages 274-295. The calls of the owls are illustrated by means of a sonogram. Compare this to the information given under 'Voice' above and see page 21.

6 **Possible confusion:** Similar species are listed here.

7 **Photographs:** These show variations of a specific raptor, such as male and female, adult and juvenile, as well as melanistic and other colour forms. Compare these photographs to the illustrations given in some of the excellent field guides to the birds of Southern Africa.

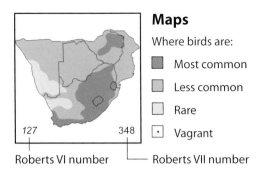

Maps

Where birds are:

- ■ Most common
- ▥ Less common
- □ Rare
- ⊡ Vagrant

127 Roberts VI number

348 Roberts VII number

Resident (green)
A species that breeds here and occurs in Southern Africa throughout the year.

Summer Resident (blue)
A species that breeds in Southern Africa during the summer season, but migrates north in winter, usually to other regions of Africa.

Visitor or Vagrant (yellow)
Most visitors occur in Southern Africa during the summer season and migrate north during winter to breed, usually in Europe or Asia. Vagrants are not usually recorded here.

Section 4: Confusing birds (p. 214)

Similar species are compared by means of black-and-white drawings on which the diagnostic features are highlighted. This section is cross-referenced to Section 3.

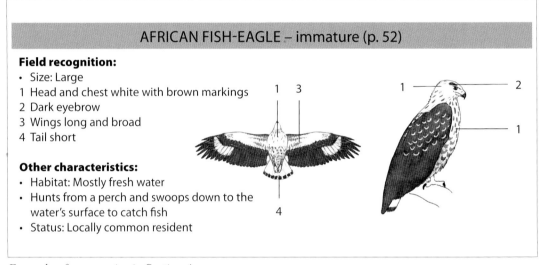

Example of one species in Section 4

Section 5: References (p. 272)

The book ends with a bibliography and index as well as a number of quick references: photographs of raptors in flight, 12 colour plates of the flight patterns, selected bibliography, a comprehensive index, an overview of the raptor groups and a quick index to the species.

Summary

1. Place the raptor within a group as indicated in Section 2. Use the cross-references to go to Sections 3 and 4 in order to identify the species.
2. If you already know which group the raptor belongs to, go immediately to Section 3 by using the colour codes for the different groups. Check your identification by referring to Section 4.
3. Make use of the quick references in Section 5.

TERMINOLOGY

A RAPTOR'S BODY PARTS

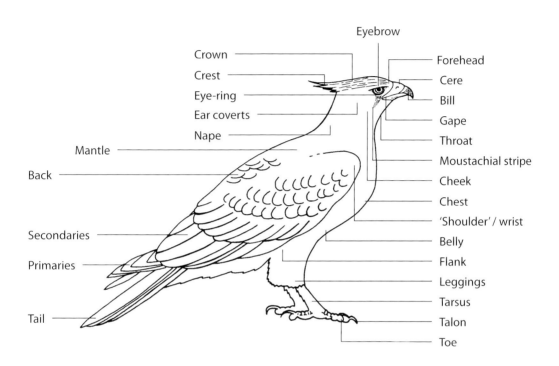

Eyebrow

Crown — — Forehead

Crest — — Cere

Eye-ring — — Bill

Ear coverts — — Gape

Nape — — Throat

Mantle — — Moustachial stripe

Back — — Cheek

— Chest

— 'Shoulder' / wrist

Secondaries — — Belly

Primaries — — Flank

— Leggings

— Tarsus

Tail — — Talon

— Toe

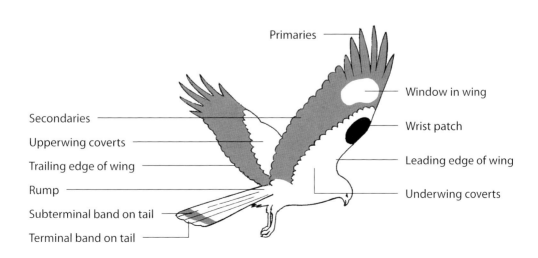

Primaries —

— Window in wing

Secondaries — — Wrist patch

Upperwing coverts —

Trailing edge of wing — — Leading edge of wing

Rump — — Underwing coverts

Subterminal band on tail —

Terminal band on tail —

THE MARKINGS OF RAPTORS

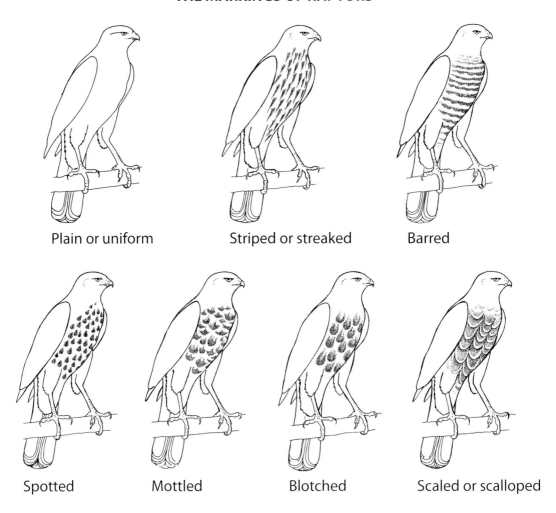

Plain or uniform   Striped or streaked   Barred

Spotted   Mottled   Blotched   Scaled or scalloped

THE SIZES OF RAPTORS

The following three species are used as reference:

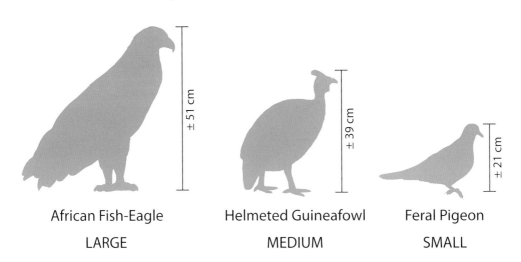

± 51 cm

± 39 cm

± 21 cm

African Fish-Eagle   Helmeted Guineafowl   Feral Pigeon

LARGE   MEDIUM   SMALL

GLOSSARY

Accipiter	True goshawk or sparrowhawk belonging to the scientific genus *Accipiter*
Arboreal	Living in trees
Cainism	The process in which the first-hatched chick kills its younger sibling
Colonial	Associating in groups, especially while breeding
Conspecific	Belonging to the same species
Crepuscular	Active at dusk and dawn
Diurnal	Active during the day
Endemic	A species whose distribution is confined to Southern Africa
Fledgling	A young bird that has just acquired its first proper feathers
Form	An alternative but permanent plumage colour (also refered to as a colour morph)
Gregarious	Living together in groups or flocks
Immature	In the context of this guide, a young bird that has moulted its juvenile plumage but has not yet attained its adult plumage
Juvenile	In the context of this guide, a young bird in its first fully feathered plumage
Length	The measurement of a dead bird lying flat on its back, from the tip of the bill to the tip of the tail or toes, whichever is the longest
Melanistic	A dark or black form of a particular species, resulting from a high production level of the black pigment melanin
Migration	The regular movement of birds between their breeding and non-breeding areas
Miombo	A broadleaved woodland (common in Zimbabwe) which is dominated by trees of the genus *Brachystegia*, *Julbernardia* and *Isoberlinia*
Nocturnal	Active at night
Nomadism	An irregular movement of birds, usually in response to changing conditions
Resident	A species that breeds in Southern Africa and remains here throughout the year
Rufous	Reddish
Sub-adult	In the context of this guide, a young bird which will attain its full adult plumage during its next moult
Summer resident	A species that breeds in Southern Africa but occurs here in the summer months only. These are mostly migratory raptors that spend the southern winter in central and northern Africa
Visitor	A migratory species that does not breed in Southern Africa. These are mostly raptors breeding in the northern hemisphere and visiting Southern Africa during the southern summer season
Vagrant	A species not normally recorded in Southern Africa
♂	Male
♀	Female

VEGETATION MAP

▢ Desert	▨ Coastal bush and lowland forest
▨ Karoo-like vegetation	▨ Montane forest
▨ Arid savanna and bushveld	▨ Fynbos
▨ Moist savanna, bushveld and woodland	▨ Grassland

Shikra / Alan Knott-Craig

SECTION 1
GENERAL BIOLOGY

WHAT IS A RAPTOR?

The word 'raptor' is derived from the Latin *raptare*, meaning 'to seize'. Although a number of other bird groups, such as the shrikes, rollers and hornbills, take live or even warm-blooded prey, raptors are characterised by their hooked bills and keen eyesight as well as their powerful feet with sharp talons.

Southern Africa is blessed with a rich diversity of raptors. Scientifically these are divided into the 71 diurnal bird of prey species of the order Falconiformes and the 12 species of owl belonging to the order Strigiformes. The Falconiformes are made up of the Secretarybird in its own family, the Sagittariidae, the falcons and kestrels in the family Falconidae and all the other diurnal raptors that are included in the family Accipitridae. Owls are divided into two families, namely the Barn and African Grass-Owl of the family Tytonidae and the 10 typical owls of the family Strigidae. The scientific classification system is, however, of limited practical use to the average birdwatcher and will not be further emphasised in this book.

Owl

Typical diurnal raptor

Lappet-faced Vulture

The smallest Southern African raptor is the Pygmy Falcon, which has a total length of ± 19 cm, a wingspan of 37 cm and weighs about 60 g. The Lappet-faced Vulture is usually considered the largest raptor in Southern Africa. It measures over 1 m in length, has a wingspan of ±2,7 m and weighs about 6,5 kg. Between these two extremes, raptors show a variety of adaptations, occur in diverse habitats and feed on virtually any conceivable prey.

Pygmy Falcon

The female is larger than the male in most raptor species. The size difference between the sexes correlates with the agility of the preferred prey. It is thus largest in sparrowhawks and falcons, where the female may be twice as heavy as the male. The female is responsible for the incubation of the eggs and care of the young while the male feeds her and the nestlings on small birds caught in flight. At the other end of the spectrum are the vultures, which show no or very little size difference between the sexes. Here both sexes are involved in the incubation of the eggs and the care of the offspring. Although the reason for the size difference is a much debated topic, the improved ability of a small male to pursue agile prey clearly plays a role. A larger female on the other hand is able to invest more energy in the production and incubation of eggs.

Female sparrowhawk

Male sparrowhawk

BILLS

The hooked bill of a raptor seems a dangerous weapon. In spite of this outward appearance the bill is never used to catch prey and very rarely in defence. Its main purpose is to cut and tear prey into sizeable chunks for swallowing. Only some raptors, such as falcons and kestrels, also use the bill to kill prey after having caught it with their feet. The size and shape of the bill reflect its function in the feeding habits of each species.

The Lappet-faced Vulture has a huge bill to tear open the skin of a carcass and to feed on the tougher parts.

Hooded Vultures use their delicate bills to probe for small pieces of meat left on the carcass after other vultures have had their share.

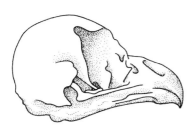

The bill of an owl is quite long. It usually appears short as the base is covered by stiff feathers.

The Bat Hawk has a large gape as it swallows its prey whole.

Eagles have large bills in order to deal with larger prey such as mammals and birds.

The bill of a falcon or kestrel is characterised by a prominent notch or 'tooth' behind the pointed tip. This is used to dislocate the neck vertebrae of prey and also helps in cutting off a billful of flesh. Cuckoo-hawks have two such 'teeth' on either side of the bill.

Goshawks and sparrow-hawks have small bills in relation to their heads.

LEGS AND FEET

The legs, toes and sharp talons of most raptors are used first to capture and subsequently to subdue struggling prey. Although the lower leg and toes often look thin and weak, they are connected via tendons to, and operated by, large muscles in the upper part of the leg. Even the minute Little Sparrowhawk therefore has an extremely powerful grip, as anybody who has handled one will well know.

Legs and feet show large variation in design, depending on the main food and hunting method of each species.

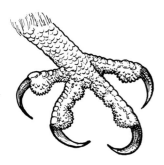

Fish-eating raptors, such as the African Fish-Eagle, have spiny soles and extremely long talons which help them to hold onto their slippery prey.

Shortish legs with short thick toes belong to those raptors that specialise in killing mammals or other larger ground-living prey. The legs of both true eagles and hawk-eagles are fully feathered down to the toes.

Snake-eagles have short toes. The feet are covered with thick scales, that protect them from being bitten by their prey, which include venomous snakes.

The feet of vultures are not adapted to grasp or kill prey. Their talons are short and blunt.

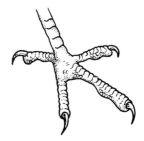

Raptors, such as sparrowhawks and falcons, that specialise in catching birds have long legs and long thin toes. These enable them to reach forward when grasping their prey in flight.

WINGS AND TAILS

Most raptors are excellent flyers. Some have to cover large areas in search of prey. Others are fast and agile in pursuit.

The flight silhouette gives an indication of a raptor's hunting method.

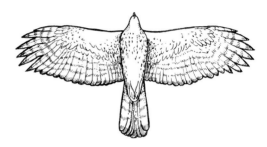

Vultures, eagles, snake-eagles, buzzards and some other large raptors have long broad wings for soaring flight. The long primaries which protrude like fingers from the tip of the wing are designed to reduce air turbulence and so increase the efficiency of the wing in carrying a heavy bird. The short tail is used to steer. Most soaring raptors make use of thermals of air or updraughts in front of cliffs.

Raptors that inhabit forests or dense woodland, such as sparrowhawks, goshawks and the African Crowned Eagle, have short rounded wings but long tails. These give them manoeuvrability while pursuing their prey through dense vegetation.

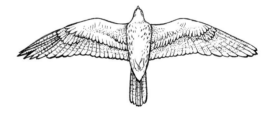

Harriers have long narrow wings and long tails which enable them to quarter up and down while flying low over open ground. They suddenly twist and turn to drop onto their prey.

Falcons have long pointed wings and long tails for high-speed flight and aerial manoeuvres. Kestrels also use similarly shaped wings for hovering motionless above the ground.

The fringed trailing edge and downy upper surface of each primary on the wings of owls reduce air turbulence, thus enabling the birds to fly noiselessly.

EYES AND VISION

The keen eyesight of raptors is legendary. The retina of a raptor is more densely packed with light-sensitive cells, called rods and cones, than in any other vertebrate. As the retina of diurnal raptors consists mostly of cones, these birds have excellent colour vision, but their vision at night is probably equal to that of humans.

Owls, on the other hand, have many more rods in their retina, which gives them outstanding night vision. The bony eyebrow which often gives raptors a fierce appearance, probably helps to protect the eyes from being damaged by struggling prey.

SECTION THROUGH A RAPTOR'S EYE

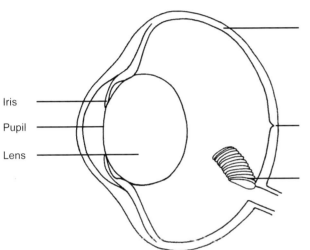

Iris

Pupil

Lens

The retina is densely packed with light-sensitive cells. These give raptors about eight times more detailed vision than humans.

As light strikes the slanting walls of the foveal pit at an angle, the image may be magnified as much as 30%.

The large pecten provides the eye fluids with nutrients via its well-developed blood supply.

BINOCULAR VISION

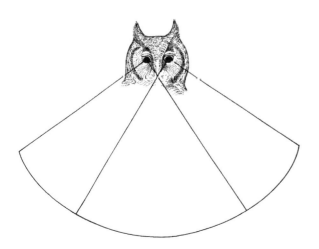

The forward-facing eyes of an owl give it excellent binocular vision, i.e. the fields of view of the two eyes overlap. This allows it to judge depth and distances, an ability of prime importance to any predator trying to catch prey. The eyes of diurnal raptors are situated slightly more towards the sides of the head than those of an owl.

CALLS AND HEARING

All raptors have excellent hearing. Although they hunt mostly by sight, sounds such as the squeaking of mice inform them of the presence of potential prey.

Most diurnal birds of prey have a variety of simple calls. These may be given to demarcate the territory, during the courtship display, at the nest or to act as an alarm call. As most of the calls are fairly similar, but difficult to describe in words, only the more characteristic calls are mentioned in the species accounts. The calls of owls, on the other hand, are much easier to recognise. For this reason they are not only described in the text, but a sonogram is also given for each species.

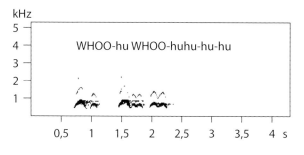

Sonogram of an African Wood-Owl's call

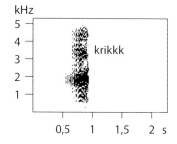

Sonogram of a Marsh Owl's call

A sonogram is a visual presentation of a series of sounds, in this case the 'WHOO-hu, WHOO-huhu-hu-hu' call of an African Wood-Owl and the tearing 'krikkk' of the Marsh Owl. It shows four sound characteristics.

1. The frequency is indicated in kiloHertz on the vertical axis. This represents the pitch of the call – the higher the pitch the higher the frequency and vice versa.
2. The length of the call (time) is indicated in seconds on the horizontal axis.
3. The amplitude or loudness of the call is indicated by the density of the tracing. This ranges from grey (a soft sound) to black (a loud sound).
4. The quality of the call is indicated by the range of frequencies covered. The 'WHOO' call of the African Wood-Owl covers a narrow range of frequencies and is thus heard as a pure sound, whereas the call of the Marsh Owl, which covers a wide range of frequencies, has a tearing quality.

The flattish facial disc of an owl (such as this Barn Owl) fulfils a similar function to the external ear of a mammal, i.e. to focus sounds onto the ear opening. It is most highly developed in Barn, African Grass- and Marsh Owls, but even harriers have a well-defined facial disc, emphasising the importance of hearing in locating prey. Experiments have shown that Barn Owls are able to catch prey even in a pitch dark room, being guided by sounds alone.

Graham Kearney

21

COLOUR

Raptors are not particularly colourful birds when compared to such groups as bee-eaters or sunbirds. Their plumage colour usually serves the function of camouflage. Communication between members of a species is achieved by contrasting patterns on the wings, tail and rump, which are mostly hidden but clearly visible in flight or during the display.

Chris van Rooyen

Burger Cillié

The bright colours of the bare parts in raptors such as those of the Southern Pale Chanting Goshawk play a role in communication. These areas are usually dull in immatures. Also note the white rump which is highly visible in flight.

Juvenile raptors often differ dramatically from the adults. The immature African Fish-Eagle is mainly brown and may be confused with a variety of other large brown raptors, while the adult is unmistakable.

Niel Cillié

Richard du Toit

Geoff McIlleron

Melanistic Gabar Goshawks are quite rare, as are the melanistic (black) forms of some of the other goshawks, sparrowhawks and harriers.

Some species have dark and pale colour forms which may not be associated with age, sex or subspecies but are just individual variations. The pale and dark forms of the Wahlberg's Eagle are a good example.

Odd-looking individuals, such as this sub-adult African Harrier-Hawk, which is not depicted in any field guide, are sometimes encountered. These are usually immature birds moulting from one plumage into the next.

HABITAT AND DISTRIBUTION

Southern African habitats cover the whole spectrum from deserts to forests, from mountains to swamps. This diversity in habitats is reflected by the rich variety of raptors occurring in this region. Most are resident or locally nomadic, but some species visit us from the north.

Isolated habitats, such as high mountains or indigenous forests, are home to a few more specialised raptors.

The woodland-savanna-grassland mosaic supports the largest variety of raptors.

Even the arid western regions are not devoid of raptors. A few generalists such as the Southern Pale Chanting Goshawk occur here.

Vagrant species:

- Egyptian Vulture
- Eleonora's Falcon
- Long-legged Buzzard
- Rüppell's Vulture

Species that breed in Eurasia, but visit Southern Africa during our summer months:

- Amur Falcon
- Booted Eagle (partially)
- European Honey-Buzzard
- Montagu's Harrier
- Pallid Harrier
- Red-footed Falcon
- Western Marsh-Harrier
- Black Kite
- Eurasian Hobby
- Lesser Spotted Eagle
- Osprey
- Peregrine Falcon (partially)
- Steppe Buzzard

Species that breed in Southern Africa, but spend the winter months elsewhere in Africa:

- African Hobby
- Wahlberg's Eagle
- Yellow-billed Kite

FOOD AND HUNTING METHODS

Raptors are predominantly carnivores although a few species, such as the Palm-nut Vulture, feed primarily on vegetable matter. The specific food or prey taken differs from species to species, but includes such diverse items as carrion, small and medium-sized mammals, birds, reptiles, frogs, fish as well as a variety of invertebrates such as insects.

Raptors use various techniques to capture their prey. Compare these to the wing and tail shapes on page 19.

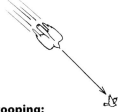

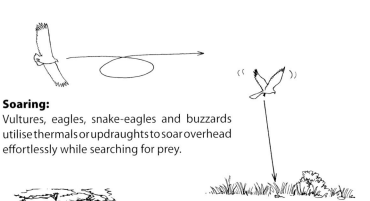

Soaring:
Vultures, eagles, snake-eagles and buzzards utilise thermals or updraughts to soar overhead effortlessly while searching for prey.

Stooping:
Some falcons are well known for their spectacular stoops. They rise above their flying prey, then accelerate and fold their wings to hurtle down at a tremendous speed. The prey is usually killed on impact with the slender yet powerful feet.

Hovering:
Kestrels, the Black-shouldered Kite and even the much larger Black-chested Snake-Eagle hover regularly. This allows them to scan the ground below.

Perch-hunting:
Many raptors forage patiently from a perch, either scanning the ground below or waiting for suitable prey to fly past. Raptors as diverse as some eagles, snake-eagles, fish-eagles, buzzards, sparrowhawks, falcons, kestrels and owls use this method.

Quartering:
Harriers cruise low over open areas, flying to and fro and then suddenly twisting and dropping onto prey they may surprise on the ground.

Surprise attack:
Goshawks, sparrowhawks and even some larger raptors make use of natural barriers such as reedbeds, hedges and ridges to hide their approach towards unsuspecting prey.

Foraging on the ground:
Some raptors, such as chanting goshawks and some owls, may forage for small prey by walking around on the ground.

BREEDING BEHAVIOUR

The majority of raptor species breed within a well-defended territory, although their larger hunting range may overlap with those of adjacent pairs. The size of the hunting range varies between and within species, depending on the preferred prey and its availability in a particular area. A pair of Pygmy Falcons would be able to live within a square kilometre, while Martial Eagles might require over 300 km^2 to support themselves and their offspring.

Raptors time their breeding cycle in order for the hatching of the chicks to coincide with the maximum availability of prey. The courtship behaviour at the beginning of the breeding season includes not only mutual calling and the feeding of the female by the male, but often also spectacular aerial displays such as the cart-wheeling behaviour of the African Fish-Eagle. The function of these behaviour patterns is to strengthen the bond between the sexes and thus prepare them for the responsibilities of breeding.

The typical nest of a raptor (Jackal Buzzard above) consists of a platform of twigs or sticks. The central cup is usually lined with greenery but also with a variety of other material. Falcons and kestrels, and also owls, do not build their own nests. They either use an old nest of another bird or lay their eggs in a slight depression in the ground, on a cliff ledge, in a hollow tree trunk or other such suitable site. Generally speaking, larger raptors lay smaller clutches of eggs and invest more time in the rearing of young than smaller species. This means that the larger species may not breed annually, whereas smaller species may raise more than one clutch during a season when prey is abundant.

Cainism (or the 'Cain and Abel syndrome') describes the sibling aggression frequently found in broods of large raptors such as the African Crowned Eagle shown below. Here the older chick kills its smaller sibling within a few days of hatching.

It is usually the female's responsibility to incubate the eggs and to brood and feed the chicks. The male helps building the nest, but his main task is to bring food to his mate and later their offspring. This system does not apply to vultures and the Secretarybird.

Because of factors such as inexperience and competition with other members of their species, the vast majority of young raptors do not survive to breeding age.

CONSERVATION PROBLEMS

Raptors are, as carnivores, at the end of the food chain and thus at the top of the ecological pyramid. As such they are excellent ecological indicators of environmental health: if raptors are rare or even absent from an area it means that the ecological balance of that area has been severely disturbed. Only healthy environments can support healthy populations of raptors.

The irresponsible and indiscriminate use of poison is of major conservation concern. Not only vultures but most larger raptors, e.g. Tawny and Verreauxs' Eagles, regularly feed on carrion. Consequently they are often killed by poisons which are aimed at controlling mammalian predators such as jackals. Owls, such as this Spotted Eagle-Owl, are often killed by feeding on poisoned rats or mice.

The alteration or destruction of their habitat plays a major role in causing raptors to decrease in numbers. So-called 'afforestation', i.e. the large-scale planting of exotic trees, affects both forest species such as the African Crowned Eagle and grassland species such as the Pallid Harrier.

Other conservation problems affecting raptors are collisions with or electrocution by electricity lines, drowning in farm reservoirs, indiscriminate shooting as well as the use of body parts in traditional medicine. Owls are often killed by cars when they perch on roads at night. This Marsh Owl became entangled in a barbed wire fence.

CONSERVATION SOLUTIONS

The long-term survival of our raptor species needs the input of every nature lover. Always remember the slogan: 'Think globally – act locally.'

Protect or rehabilitate natural habitats. No major development should be allowed before a proper environmental impact assessment has been done.

Vulture restaurants, areas where carcasses of farm animals are dumped on a regular basis, have not only proved to be a major success in the conservation of vultures, but also allow farmers to dispose of carcasses in an easy and hygienic way.

New designs of power pylons have greatly reduced the risk of collisions and electrocutions, as illustrated by this juvenile Martial Eagle.

Raptors rarely kill young livestock such as lambs. Ascertain the cause of death before accusing an eagle of being the culprit. Natural mortality, poor husbandry or mammalian predators play a far greater role than raptors.

The Endangered Wildlife Trust's Birds of Prey Working Group focuses on the conservation of diurnal and nocturnal raptors and their habitats. A strong scientific component adds authority to the dedicated efforts of the large network of field coordinators. The Group currently manages 35 projects across southern Africa, which cover a range of species and areas. Methodologies are shared, ideas communicated and solutions reached through collaborative efforts that combine science with practical efficiency. In this way key concerns re the conservation of raptors are identified, informed conclusions are reached and decisive action may be implemented.

For more information, please visit our website *www.ewt.org.za*

Endangered Wildlife Trust

birds of prey working group

Male Lesser Kestrel / Mark Anderson

SECTION 2
RAPTOR GROUPS

THE RAPTOR GROUPS

The key to raptor identification is the ability to place a bird in one of the 11 groups indicated in this section.

It is thus of the utmost importance to be familiar with the characteristics of these groups before attempting to identify a species in Sections 3 or 4.

1 Secretarybird (p. 33)

Secretarybird (p. 48)

2 Fish-eating raptors (pp. 34, 217)

Osprey (p. 50)   African Fish-Eagle (p. 52)

3 Vultures (pp. 35, 218)

4 Eagles and hawk-eagles (pp. 36, 224)

5 Snake-eagles (pp. 37, 232)

HOW TO IDENTIFY RAPTORS

Raptors are not easy to identify! Like all carnivores they are not only rare by nature, but they also occur in a bewildering variety of species and variations. As they are shy but active birds, good sightings are hard to come by.

In spite of the difficulties, raptors are not impossible to identify. A birder should note the following:

1. **Which group does the raptor belong to?** Before attempting to identify the species, first place the raptor in a smaller group. For example, is the raptor an eagle, a snake-eagle, a falcon or an owl? Southern African raptors may be divided into 11 groups as indicated in this section. This is the most important step when identifying a raptor.
2. **Note the distribution and habitat.** Although some raptors are widely distributed and occur in various habitats, most are confined to a specific habitat and thus have a limited distribution. Similar species often differ in the habitat they prefer.
3. **Note the size and body shape.** Although one must be aware that the female is generally larger than the male and species may thus overlap in size, this remains an important feature. The general body shape will also help you to narrow the choice down to a few species.
4. **Note the behaviour.** Even general behaviour, such as whether the raptor is perching on a telephone pole, soaring overhead, cruising over an open habitat or hovering, will give you clues to its identity. Also be aware of special behaviour such as courtship, hunting and the like.
5. **Note the colour of the plumage and the soft parts.** First note the general colour and then any specific pattern; for example, does the bird have a moustachial stripe, is the belly barred or is the rump white? The colour of the eyes, cere and legs often differs between species.
6. **Be aware of colour variations.** Raptors are well known for the fact that immatures usually differ from adults. Juveniles often have paler tips to the feathers of the upperparts, which gives them a scaled appearance. Even in adult birds there may be differences between the sexes. In addition, some raptors have a variety of colour forms, such as very pale or melanistic (black) individuals.
7. **Be aware of moulting birds.** A juvenile or immature bird may have very mottled plumage when it is moulting into the next stage. As it is virtually impossible to illustrate these temporary conditions, you will rarely find such unusual-looking birds in any book on raptors. Try to imagine what the bird looked like before it started moulting or what the plumage will be like after moulting. Again concentrate on other features such as size and shape.
8. **Listen to the calls.** Most diurnal raptors have simple calls that are difficult to distinguish from each other. Start by familiarising yourself with more characteristic calls like that of the African Fish-Eagle, the two banded snake-eagles and the chanting goshawks, then gradually progress to the more difficult calls. The calls of owls are highly distinctive and are an important aid in their identification. The sonograms in the species accounts of the owls as well as the variety of tapes, CDs and software available are of great help.
9. **Study raptors whenever and wherever possible.** As raptors are not often encountered, make use of every sighting to study them in minute detail. Even if you are familiar with a specific species, look at it again and again as this will help you with similar species. Study *The Raptor Guide* whenever possible. It will enable you to build up a mental picture which will greatly facilitate any practical identification. Familiarise yourself with the raptors of an area and draw up a checklist before a visit.

SECRETARYBIRD
(PAGE 48)

ONE SPECIES:

• Secretarybird (p. 48)

The Secretarybird is a very large and unmistakable raptor characterised by its very long legs. Although at a distance it might be confused with a large heron, stork or crane, the hooked bill immediately distinguishes it as a raptor. It prefers open veld where it can be observed walking around slowly in search of prey.

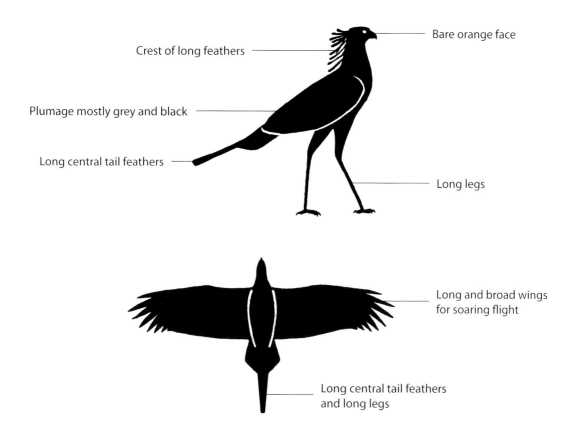

Crest of long feathers

Bare orange face

Plumage mostly grey and black

Long central tail feathers

Long legs

Long and broad wings for soaring flight

Long central tail feathers and long legs

Albert Froneman

Secretarybirds walk purposefully across open veld while foraging.

Ulrich Oberprieler

Secretarybirds feed on a variety of small animals, not only snakes such as this Snouted Cobra. Prey is stamped to death with the short thick toes.

FISH-EATING RAPTORS
(PAGES 50–53, 217)

The unrelated Osprey and African Fish-Eagle belong to this group. Both specialise in catching fish and are therefore associated with water. They have long broad wings which enable them to lift even heavy fish from the water. The Osprey is a medium-large raptor which occurs in Southern Africa as an uncommon non-breeding summer visitor only. It resembles a smallish eagle but has bare lower legs. Fish are caught by plunge-diving into the water. The well-known African Fish-Eagle is large and eagle-like, but also lacks feathers on the lower legs. It feeds mostly on fish caught by swooping down to the water's surface. The long broad wings and short tail distinguish it from similar raptors in flight.

2 SPECIES:

- Osprey (p. 50)
- African Fish-Eagle (p. 52)

An African Fish-Eagle calls to proclaim its territory.

OSPREY

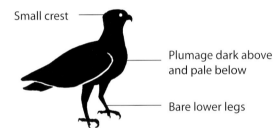

Small crest

Plumage dark above and pale below

Bare lower legs

Dark wrist patch

Very large wings in relation to body

Tail longish

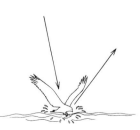

Ospreys usually hover over the water and then plunge down to catch their prey.

AFRICAN FISH-EAGLE

Distinctive shape of head and bill

Colour depends on age

Bare lower legs

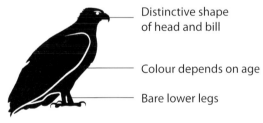

Wings long and broad with 'fingers' at the tip for soaring flight

Tail short

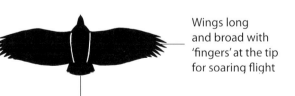

The African Fish-Eagle swoops down from a perch to catch fish just below the water's surface.

VULTURES
(PAGES 54–71, 218)

9 SPECIES:

These large to very large, robustly built raptors are well known for their scavenging habits. The sexes are alike in colour and size, except in the White-headed Vulture. They depend on soaring flight to a larger degree than most other raptors and often congregate in large numbers at a suitable carcass. In addition to the seven typical vulture species which may be seen in Southern Africa, the Palm-nut and Bearded Vultures, which have fully feathered heads, also belong to this group. Those vultures that resemble the Cape, White-backed and Rüppell's Vultures in shape and habits are often referred to as griffons.

Head and neck partially or wholly devoid of feathers for easy cleaning

Bill shape varies from slender to massive, depending on what type or part of a carcass is preferred

Typical hunched posture when perched

Toes comparatively weak, not used to kill prey

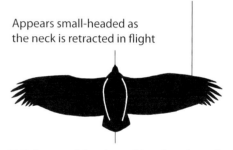

Wings very long and broad with long 'fingers' at the tip for soaring flight

Appears small-headed as the neck is retracted in flight

Tail short and fan-shaped (wedge-shaped in Egyptian and Bearded Vultures)

Albert Froneman

Vultures locate carcasses by scanning the ground while soaring high in the air. As vultures also watch each other, an individual descending to a carcass will soon be followed by others. (Cape Vulture shown.)

Ulrich Oberprieler

Vultures usually spend considerable time on safe perches to ascertain that their intended food is dead. Only after a particularly brave bird has taken the initiative, will others come down to feed.

EAGLES AND HAWK-EAGLES
(PAGES 72–93, 224)

Eagles and the similar hawk-eagles are medium to very large raptors. The fully feathered legs immediately distinguish them from similar birds of prey. They are powerful and aggressive hunters that prey on medium-sized and small mammals, birds and reptiles, but are not impartial to carrion. Although eagles may search for prey from a perch, they often hunt on the wing, soaring effortlessly for hours. Hawk-eagles are smaller than most other eagles and are active, fast flyers.

11 SPECIES:

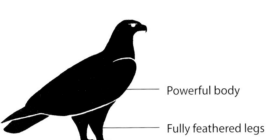

Powerful body

Fully feathered legs

There is one unsubstantiated record of the Greater Spotted Eagle (*Aquila clanga*) for Southern Africa.

Wings long and broad with obvious 'fingers' at the tip for soaring flight

Tail shortish to medium in length

Clem Haagner

The Martial Eagle, like most eagles, is a powerful hunter that often takes large prey.

Alan Knott-Craig

The long broad wings and shortish tail enable eagles, such as this Martial Eagle, to soar for most of the day while looking for food. They also often hunt from a perch.

SNAKE-EAGLES

(PAGES 94–103, 232)

5 SPECIES:

These medium-large to large raptors can easily be mistaken for true eagles, but their lower legs are unfeathered. They are characterised by large heads with large yellow eyes. They hunt from a perch or in soaring flight. The food consists mostly of snakes which are grasped in the short but powerful toes and usually swallowed whole. The Bateleur is an aberrant snake-eagle which feeds on a variety of small animals and even carrion. Adults are unmistakable, but the brown juvenile is distinguished from typical snake-eagles by its dark eyes.

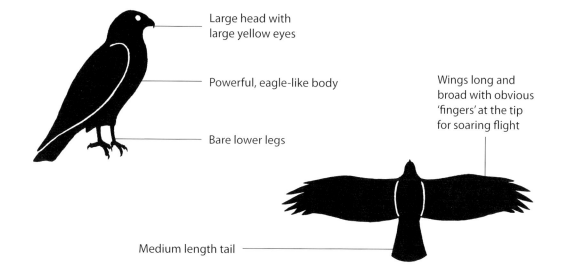

Large head with large yellow eyes

Powerful, eagle-like body

Bare lower legs

Wings long and broad with obvious 'fingers' at the tip for soaring flight

Medium length tail

Ron Hartley

The short powerful toes enable this adult Black-chested Snake-Eagle to grasp and kill its prey.

Bredan Ryan

Snake-eagles (such as this Brown Snake-Eagle) regularly hunt from a perch, but prey may also be detected while soaring overhead.

BUZZARDS
(PAGES 104–115, 236)

Buzzards are basically smaller versions of eagles, but have unfeathered lower legs. They are medium to medium-large, robustly built raptors that soar well but hunt mostly from a perch. Although some species are easy to recognise, others have drab brown plumages and much individual variation. Adults have dark, and immatures pale, eyes. Honey-buzzards are not true buzzards. They are characterised by their pigeon-like heads and bills, and their eyes which are bright yellow in adults and dark in immatures. The Lizard Buzzard is not included in this group as it has many goshawk-like features.

6 SPECIES:

• Augur Buzzard	(p. 104)
• Jackal Buzzard	(p. 106)
• Steppe Buzzard	(p. 108)
• Forest Buzzard	(p. 110)
• Long-legged Buzzard	(p. 112)
• European Honey-Buzzard	(p. 114)

Wings long and broad with 'fingers' at the tip for soaring flight

Tail shortish to medium in length

Powerful, eagle-like body

Bare lower legs

Albert Froneman

Alan Knott-Craig

Buzzards, like this Jackal Buzzard, usually take smaller prey than similar eagles.

Buzzards (such as the Steppe Buzzard shown here) hunt mostly from a perch, although some prey is detected from soaring flight.

GOSHAWKS AND SPARROWHAWKS

(PAGES 116–137, 241)

11 SPECIES:

Hawks are very small to medium-sized raptors, the female generally significantly larger than the male. Most occur in well-wooded habitats where their short rounded wings but long tails, give them great manoeuvrability when pursuing prey in short dashing flights. They are usually secretive birds and not easily identifiable. Sparrowhawks specialise in catching birds in flight, while goshawks take a fair number of ground-living prey as well. The Gabar Goshawk is an intermediate species between true goshawks and chanting goshawks. The latter are medium-sized raptors which often occur in more open savanna. Their call is loud and chanting. The Lizard Buzzard, which is more aptly called a Lizard Hawk, is not a buzzard but rather a specialised goshawk. The African Harrier-Hawk is also best placed in this group.

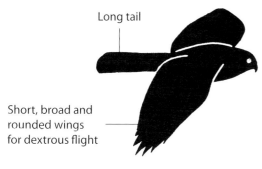

Long tail

Short, broad and rounded wings for dextrous flight

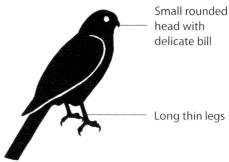

Small rounded head with delicate bill!

Long thin legs

Graham Kearney

Niel Cillié

Lizeth Cillié

Sparrowhawks and goshawks are well adapted to hunt among trees and other dense vegetation. Like most species, the African Goshawk spends most of the day perched well concealed in a tree and is thus difficult to see.

The African Harrier-Hawk, the Lizard Buzzard and the chanting goshawks are not typical hawks, but may be regarded as specialised goshawks.

HARRIERS
(PAGES 138–147, 250)

Harriers are a group of medium-sized raptors with slender bodies, long narrow wings and long tails and legs. They inhabit marshes or open country where they fly low over the ground, quartering to and fro, and drop onto their prey on the ground. The wings are often held in a shallow V in flight. The owl-like facial disc serves to indicate a well-developed sense of hearing, which is used to locate prey. They feed on a variety of small animals, including frogs and rodents. The nest is hidden among vegetation on the ground. Most harriers are brown, but the males of some species are predominantly grey. The Black Harrier is black and white.

5 SPECIES:

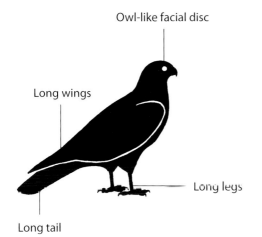

Owl-like facial disc

Long wings

Long legs

Long tail

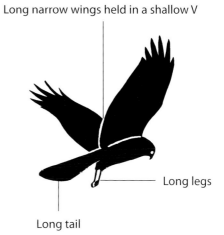

Long narrow wings held in a shallow V

Long legs

Long tail

Chris van Rooyen

Harriers are excellent flyers, as indicated by their long wings and tails. They are usually seen in flight, less often on the ground and rarely on a perch. (Sub-adult male Montagu's Harrier)

Chris van Rooyen

Harriers, such as this African Marsh-Harrier, often hold their wings in a shallow V while searching for prey on the ground. They course slowly just above the ground, flying to and fro.

KITES
(PAGES 148–157, 254)

5 SPECIES:

Kites (some of which are actually called hawks) are a diverse collection of small to medium-sized raptors. All have long wings and are excellent flyers.

The Black and Yellow-billed Kites are often called *Milvus* kites, referring to their scientific genus name. Their plumage is mostly brown. The wings are long and characteristically angled in flight while the long and forked tail is constantly twisted. They are excellent and agile flyers which feed on almost any animal material, both alive and dead.

The Black-shouldered Kite is a small, mostly grey-and-white raptor with black markings on the 'shoulder' of the upper wing. It inhabits open country where it often perches on telephone poles or tall trees, dropping on small mammals or insects in the grass. It hovers frequently on gently fanning wings as it searches for prey.

The colour pattern of the African Cuckoo-Hawk resembles that of a cuckoo – hence the name. The wings are fairly long and pointed; the tail is long. The flight is slow and buoyant. This raptor feeds mostly on insects.

The Bat Hawk is a unique raptor with large yellow eyes, long and pointed wings, and a long tail. It resembles a large falcon when it hunts at dusk over open areas. Prey consists mostly of bats, but it also catches swallows and swifts in flight.

FALCONS AND KESTRELS
(PAGES 158–189, 257)

Falcons and kestrels are both very small to medium-small raptors; the female is much larger than the male, especially in the falcons. They usually inhabit open country and are built for fast flight: their wings are long and pointed and the tail is long. The eyes are dark except in the adult Greater Kestrel. The head is slightly pug-faced due to the powerful jaw muscles which, together with the characteristic notch ('tooth') in the upper jaw, are used to kill prey. Most species have moustachial stripes on the cheeks. As none build their own nests, these raptors breed on cliff ledges or on the platform nests of other birds. Falcons make use of fast flight to catch their prey, while kestrels hover more often.

16 SPECIES:

FALCON

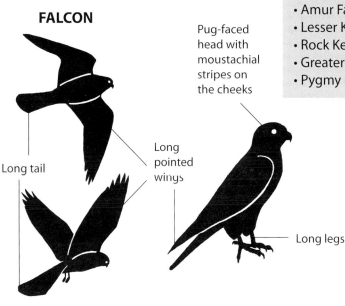

Pug-faced head with moustachial stripes on the cheeks

Long tail

Long pointed wings

Long legs

KESTREL

Chris van Rooyen

Kestrels, such as this Greater Kestrel, hover regularly as they search for prey.

Alan Knott-Craig

The head has a characteristic shape due to the bird's powerful jaw muscles. Note the moustachial stripe.

Ulrich Oberprieler

The long, pointed wings and the long tail enable falcons to fly fast. This makes birds such as this juvenile Lanner Falcon ideal for the sport of falconry.

The division of the family Falconidae into falcons and kestrels is an oversimplification. Its 16 species are best divided into a number of smaller groups based on physical characteristics and general habits.

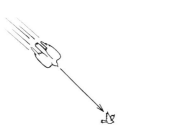

Large true falcons, such as the Peregrine and Lanner Falcons, are stocky, powerful birds and excellent flyers. They stoop at their prey, usually birds, in exceptionally swift flight, either killing them outright by striking them with a foot or seizing the prey and dropping to the ground with it. In addition to birds, they may occasionally eat small mammals or insects. Although only half its size, the Taita Falcon is very similar to the Peregrine in its habits.

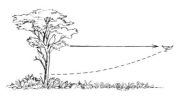

The Red-necked Falcon (sometimes called a Red-necked Merlin) is similar to the Merlin of the northern hemisphere. It is a dashing, fast-flying falcon, that waits for prey inside the canopy of a small tree. Once a suitable small bird passes, the falcon launches itself out on a high-speed chase, pursuing its prey in level flight.

Hobbies, such as the Eurasian and African Hobbies, are exceedingly swift falcons with long narrow wings. They often hunt at dusk and catch almost all their prey on the wing. These are usually insects, but also small birds, including swifts. Very similar in habits are the Sooty Falcon and Eleonora's Falcon. All four species are uncommon in Southern Africa.

The Grey Kestrel and Dickinson's Kestrel are not true kestrels. They hunt from a perch, killing a variety of prey such as small mammals, lizards and insects on the ground, but can also fly swiftly to pursue birds. They sometimes hover like true kestrels.

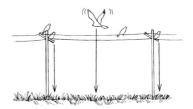

The Red-footed and Amur Falcons as well as the Lesser Kestrel, are migratory birds, occurring in flocks on both their breeding grounds in the northern hemisphere and while overwintering in Southern Africa. These kestrels hover regularly. They feed on insects and are fond of flying termites. The males and females are differently coloured.

True kestrels, such as the Rock Kestrel, hover frequently, dropping onto prey by parachuting in stages. They feed on a variety of small animals. The Greater Kestrel is best placed in this group, although it hunts mostly from a perch and hovers less often.

The Pygmy Falcon has a close relative in Asia. It is a dashing little predator, feeding mostly on insects, but capable of killing small mammals and birds. The male and female differ from each other.

OWLS
(PAGES 190–213, 268)

Owls are very small to large birds of prey that are well known for their nocturnal life style, although some species are also partially diurnal.

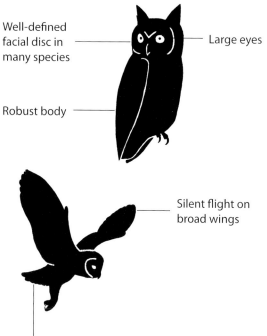

Well-defined facial disc in many species

Large eyes

Robust body

Silent flight on broad wings

Short tail in most species

Albert Froneman

The 'ears' of some owls are not ears at all, but tufts of feathers which are used in communication and camouflage.

Calls play an important role in communication. Some species, such as this Spotted Eagle-Owl, display their conspicuous white throat while calling.

Nico Myburgh

Nico Myburgh

Owls (such as the African Wood-Owl) do not build their own nests, but utilise either natural sites such as cliff ledges or tree holes, or they breed on the platform nests of other birds.

The large eyes are an adaptation to gather as much light as possible, enabling an owl to see at night. The flattish facial disc of this Barn Owl functions in the same way as the external ear of a mammal: to gather sound waves and direct them towards the ear openings.

As owls are active at night, calls play an important role in their communication. The distinctive call of each species may be used in their identification. To visually identify owls, the 12 species may be divided into three groups according to their size. The silhouettes indicate the relative sizes.

SMALL OWLS

1. Pearl-spotted Owlet (p. 198)
2. African Barred Owlet (p. 200)
3. African Scops-Owl (p. 202)
4. Southern White-faced Scops-Owl (p. 204)

MEDIUM OWLS

5. Barn Owl (p. 190)
6. African Grass-Owl (p. 192)
7. Marsh Owl (p. 194)
8. African Wood-Owl (p. 196)

LARGE OWLS

9. Verreaux's Eagle-Owl (p. 206)
10. Spotted Eagle-Owl (p. 208)
11. Cape Eagle-Owl (p. 210)
12. Pel's Fishing-Owl (p. 212)

1 **2** **3** **4**

SMALL OWLS (1–4)

The Pearl-spotted Owlet (1) and African Barred Owlet (2) are very similar in size, colour pattern and body shape. They have large rounded heads and fairly long tails. The African Scops-Owl (3) is immediately distinguished from other small owls by its ear-tufts and yellow eyes. The Southern White-faced Scops-Owl (4) is larger than the others. It also has ear-tufts, but the eyes are orange and it has a distinctive white face bordered with black bands.

MEDIUM OWLS (5–8)

The elongated body shape and well-defined facial disc distinguish the Barn Owl (5) and African Grass-Owl (6) from all other owls. Although looking very similar, they occur in different habitats. The African Grass-Owl shares its moist grassland habitat with the Marsh Owl (7), which has a rounder facial disc. The small ear-tufts may sometimes be visible. Its forest habitat and the large rounded head make the African Wood-Owl (8) a highly distinctive species.

5 **6** **7** **8**

LARGE OWLS (9–12)

The three species of eagle-owl are immediately recognised by their large size and prominent ear-tufts. The Verreaux's Eagle-Owl (9) is the largest and the Spotted Eagle-Owl (10) the smallest. The Cape Eagle-Owl (11) is intermediate in size. Pel's Fishing-Owl (12) is easily recognised by its large size, rufous brown colour, dark eyes and the absence of ear-tufts.

9 **10** **11** **12**

Martial Eagle / Chris van Rooyen

SECTION 3
SPECIES ACCOUNTS

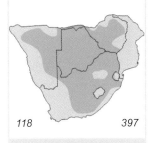

Measurements
Length: 125-150 cm
Wingspan: ±212 cm
Weight: 2,3-4,27 kg
Males are somewhat
larger than females.

Distribution
Widespread in Africa.

118   397

Habitat
Prefers open country,
especially grassland, but
also mountain slopes,
semi-desert, savanna,
farmland and open
woodland.

Food
A variety of small animals,
mostly insects, such as
grasshoppers and beetles.

Status
Uncommon to locally
common resident.

A: Sekretarisvoël
F: Messager serpentaire /
    Messager sagittaire
G: Sekretär
P: Secretário

SECRETARYBIRD
Sagittarius serpentarius

Field recognition: Very large. Unmistakable: the only raptor with very long legs, standing ± 1,3m tall. From afar it may be confused with a crane or even a stork or large heron, but the hooked bill, long erectile crest of feathers on the nape and long projecting central tail feathers are characteristic. The plumage is mostly grey with black flight feathers, crest, rump, belly, leggings and subterminal band on the elongated central tail feathers. The bare face is red to orange. In flight the black flight feathers and characteristic shape, with the long central tail feathers and legs protruding behind, are easily recognised. The sexes are alike. **Juv.** The plumage of the juvenile is slightly browner. It has a yellow face, pale (not brown) eyes, and shorter central tail feathers.

Behaviour: The pair usually roosts on a tree, often the nest tree, at night. Starts foraging 1–2 hours after dawn, then spends most of the day walking slowly across open veld at a speed of 2,5–3 km/h. Flies seldom, but soars well. The pair usually separates during the day, but family groups of 3–4 birds and even larger aggregations at waterholes are sometimes seen. Usually silent.

Feeding methods: Catches all prey on the ground, usually in the bill, and then swallows it whole. Stamps the ground to disturb prey that is then killed by hard downward blows of the feet. In spite of popular belief, snakes are only rarely eaten. This, however, has contributed towards the Secretarybird's conservation, as 'anything that eats snakes is worth protecting'.

Breeding: Season: Any time of the year when food is abundant, peaking in July to January. **Nest:** A large flat platform of sticks 1–1,5 m across at first, but up to 2,5 m after repeated use, and 30–50 cm deep. The central depression is lined mainly with grass. Although the nests are built on top of trees 2–12 m (average 5 m) above the ground, the height is less important than the dense, thorny nature of the tree or bush. **Clutch:** 1–3 eggs, usually 2 and rarely 4. In a clutch of 3, one egg is often infertile. **Incubation:** 40–46 days, mostly by female. **Nestling:** Usually 75–85 days, but may range from 65–106 days. Fed by both parents. Although there is no or little aggression between siblings, 3 chicks are only rarely raised as the smallest chick usually dies of starvation.

Origin of name: The name 'Secretarybird' might refer to the crest's resemblance to old-time quill pens, which a secretary often stuck behind his ear. On the other hand, it might also be derived from the Arabic *saqr et-tair*, a 'hunter-bird'. *Sagittarius* is Latin for 'bowman' or 'archer' (referring to its upright carriage), while *serpentarius* means 'interested in snakes'.

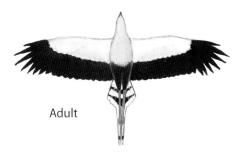

Adult

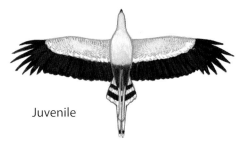

Juvenile

Possible confusion: This unique raptor may only be confused with a crane, stork or larger heron

p. 33

Niel Cillié

Adult

Niel Cillié

Juvenile

Geoff McIlleron

Adult

Albert Froneman

Adult

Measurements
Length: 55-58 cm
Wingspan: 145-170 cm
Weight: ♂ 1,2-1,6 (1,4) kg
♀ 1,25-1,9 (1,57) kg

Distribution
Occurs almost throughout
the world. In Southern
Africa more common
in the east and south,
especially along the coast,
and rare in the dry west.

170   344

Habitat
Mostly freshwater and
estuaries, rarely at sea.

Food
Fish.

Status
Uncommon non-breeding
summer visitor. Young
birds may overwinter.

S: Fish Hawk
A: Visvalk
F: Balbuzard pêcheur
G: Fischadler
P: Águia-pesqueira

OSPREY
Pandion haliaetus

Field recognition: Medium-large. The aquatic habitat, where it may be confused with a large immature gull, is distinctive. The upperparts are brown, the underparts mostly white. The chest is streaked, often more prominently in females than males. The yellow eye, dark band through the eye and shaggy crest on the nape give the head a characteristic appearance. It is large-winged with a slow but powerful flight action. The underwing shows dark wrist patches and a dark central bar, i.e. the last row of underwing coverts. The flight feathers and tail are faintly barred. Sexes very similar. May be confused with an immature African Fish-Eagle, which is larger with broad wings and a short tail. **Juv.** Juvenile Ospreys resemble the adults, but are paler. The upperparts are streakier; the feathers have a broader buff tip. Adult plumage is acquired after ±18 months.

Behaviour: Occurs in Southern Africa mainly from October to March, although immatures often overwinter. Usually solitary on a prominent perch near or above water, but flies well and soars easily. Silent.

Feeding methods: Hunts in flight over water rather than from a perch as fish-eagles do. It flies 20–30 m above the water (sometimes higher), alternately flapping and gliding. On sighting fish it often hovers briefly, then dives down. Moments before hitting the water the wings are thrown back and it plunges in feet first. Smaller fish are sometimes caught with hardly a splash, but it may submerge completely, only the wingtips showing above the water. Rising, it flaps energetically, gives a characteristic shake to dry itself and flies off to a perch where it will feed. The fish is carried in both feet with the head pointing forward. Often loses its prey to pirating African Fish-Eagles.

Breeding: Ospreys visiting Southern Africa breed in Eurasia. Only two breeding records are accepted for Southern Africa: one on the Limpopo River near Messina, Limpopo, in December 1933 and one in Ndumo Game Reserve, northern KwaZulu-Natal, in October 1963. Any suspected nest should be carefully authenticated. **Nest:** A large collection of sticks and flotsam, usually wedged high in an exposed tree, but also on cliffs or other structures. **Clutch:** 1–4 eggs, usually 3. **Incubation:** 35–43 days, mostly by female. **Nestling:** ± 50 days.

Origin of name: Pandion was a legendary king of Athens, who was believed to have been changed into an Osprey. *Haliaetus* is derived from the Greek words *halieos*, 'fisherman', and *aetos*, 'eagle'.

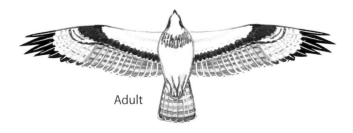

Adult

p. 34

p. 217

Adult

Adult

Markus Varesvuo

Markus Varesvuo

Adult

Juvenile

Markus Varesvuo

Conrad Greaves (Aquila)

Adult fishing

Markus Varesvuo

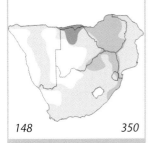

Measurements
Length: 63-73 cm
Wingspan: ♂ ±191 cm
♀ ±237 cm
Weight: ♂ 1,99-2,5 kg
♀ 3,17-3,63 kg

Distribution
Africa south of the Sahara. Throughout Southern Africa except in waterless regions.

148   *350*

Habitat
Mostly larger bodies of fresh water, but also coastal lagoons and estuaries. Very rarely at sea.

Food
Mostly fish. Also feeds on carrion and may catch a variety of small animals.

Status
Locally common resident.

A: Visarend
F: Pygargue vocifère
G: Schreiseeadler
P: Águia-pesqueira-africana

AFRICAN FISH-EAGLE
Haliaeetus vocifer

Field recognition: Large. Adults of Africa's best-known raptor are unmistakable; it can only be confused with the Palm-nut Vulture, which is much whiter. In flight the conspicuous white head, short white tail, broad wings with dark flight feathers and chestnut underwing coverts are characteristic. The sexes are alike, but females are 10–15% larger than males and have a broader white chest. **Juv.** Young birds may easily be confused with other large raptors, but the unfeathered lower legs, the body and head shape, as well as the habitat and behaviour, are good pointers. The first-year juvenile is mostly brown (also see page 22). The neck and chest are white and heavily streaked brown and black. The cere is grey and the lower legs dirty yellow. In flight the underwing coverts are mostly white. The flight feathers are dark with large white windows on especially the primaries. The off-white tail is slightly longer than that of the adult and has a broad terminal band. The second-year immature is much paler and is often mistaken for an Osprey: the head is mostly white with a dark eyebrow, the brown streaks on the white chest are much reduced, while the upperparts are distinctly mottled with white. From the third year on the immature gradually changes into the adult plumage, which is attained after at least five years.

Behaviour: Pairs are highly territorial. Groups seen are either parents and their youngsters, or immature and sub-adult birds that have not yet established their territories. Perches for hours, but soars regularly. The loud, ringing call is well known, that of the male being higher in pitch than the female's.

Feeding methods: Usually hunts from a perch, gliding down towards a surface-feeding fish, grabbing and lifting it from the water, and then returning to a perch. Although preferring fish of less than 1 kg, fish up to 2 kg are easily carried. Heavier fish are either planed along the water surface or the Fish-Eagle submerges and paddles to the shore using its wings. Also feeds on carrion and various small animals it may catch. Often pirates prey from other birds.

Breeding: Season: March to September, peaking June to August. **Nest:** A large platform of sticks, initially 20–30 cm thick, but up to 2,2 m after long use. Lined with grass, papyrus heads and some green leaves. Usually in trees, sometimes on cliffs. **Clutch:** 1–4 eggs, usually 2. **Incubation:** 42–45 days by both sexes. **Nestling:** 70–75 days, fed mostly by female on prey brought by male. Dependent on parents for another ± 60 days.

Origin of name: *Haliaeetus* is derived from the Greek words *halieos*, 'fisherman', and *aetos*, 'eagle'. *Vociter* refers to its loud, vociferous call.

Adult   Immature

bl. 34

bl. 217

Johan & Louise van Heerden

Graham Kearney

Immature

Adult

Graham Kearney

Sub-adult

Albert Froneman

Adult fishing

Ulrich Oberprieler

Juvenile

Niel Cillié

Immature

53

PALM-NUT VULTURE
Gypohierax angolensis

Measurements
Length: ±60 cm
Wingspan: 130-140 cm
Weight: ♂ ± 1,5 kg
♀ ± 1,7 kg

Distribution
Widespread in tropical Africa. In Southern Africa largely confined to northern KwaZulu-Natal. Vagrants, usually immatures, occur widely.

147   *351*

Habitat
Forest, mangroves, woodland and coastal regions, always in association with Raffia Palms.

Food
In Southern Africa mostly the fruit of Raffia Palms.

Status
A small but stable population in northern KwaZulu-Natal.

S: Vulturine Fish-Eagle
A: Witaasvoël
F: Palmiste africain
G: Palmengeier
P: Abutre-das-palmeiras

Field recognition: Large. Adults may be confused with the adult African Fish-Eagle or adult Egyptian Vulture. Plumage is black and white, but the wing coverts and belly may be stained orange-brown during the breeding season. The bare red to orange face is characteristic. The eyes are yellow. The stout bill is pale yellowish, the cere a pale blue. The bare legs vary from pinkish to dull orange or yellow. In flight it is distinguished from the Egyptian Vulture by the white primaries, which are only tipped black, and the tail that is mainly black with a white tip. The tip of the tail is square or slightly rounded. **Juv.** The juvenile is brown with yellowish to orange facial skin, dark eyes and whitish legs. It may be confused with brown eagles, but the legs are not fully feathered. Its large size, bare face and characteristic shape of the bill and head distinguish it from other similar species, such as the Brown Snake-Eagle or the immatures of the African Harrier-Hawk, and Hooded and Egyptian Vultures. It acquires adult plumage after 3–4 years.

Behaviour: Adults live a sedentary life in areas where there are Raffia Palms, even if these have been cultivated, as in Mtunzini. Vagrants have been widely recorded. Mostly solitary, sometimes in pairs. Usually seen perched in a tree, or while soaring, but spends some time on the ground. Usually silent.

Feeding methods: Although it feeds on the fruit of the Oil Palm (*Elaeis guineensis*) in the rest of Africa (hence its name), its main diet in Southern Africa consists of the fruit of the Raffia Palm (*Raphia australis*). These are held down with a foot while the protein-rich husk is torn off. Both the kernel and the hard outer scales are rejected. It also feeds on dates, grain, seeds of the introduced *Acacia cyclops*, small fish (which are caught in the manner of a fish-eagle), crabs, frogs, molluscs, small birds and mammals, as well as carrion.

Breeding: Although this vulture used to occur along much of the southern Mozambique coast, breeding in Southern Africa now seems to be limited to Kosi Bay and Mtunzini in KwaZulu-Natal. **Season:** Peaking August to September, but as early as May. **Nest:** A large platform of sticks, lined with grass, leaves, sisal fibre and dung. Built high up in trees, often palms. **Clutch:** 1 egg. **Incubation:** 42–47 days, mainly by female. **Nestling:** 85–91 days.

Origin of name: *Gypohierax* (*gups* is Greek for 'griffon vulture' and *hierax* for 'hawk') indicates that this is not a typical vulture. The fact that it resembles a fish-eagle is also emphasised by the alternative name of Vulturine Fish-Eagle. The first specimen was collected in Angola.

Adult

Juvenile

p. 35

p. 218

Adult

Juvenile

Immature

Adult

EGYPTIAN VULTURE
Neophron percnopterus

Measurements
Length: 58-71 cm
Wingspan: 164-168 cm
Weight: 1,58-2,40 (2,0) kg
Females are slightly larger than males.

Distribution
Northern and eastern Africa, southern Europe, Middle East and central Asia. Mostly a vagrant to Southern Africa.

120   353

Habitat
Semi-desert, open plains and arid savanna.

Food
Carrion, but also birds' eggs, insects and refuse.

Status
Used to breed regularly in Southern Africa, but is now a rare vagrant from the north.

S: Scavenger Vulture / White Vulture
A: Egiptiese Aasvoël
F: Vautour percnoptère / Percnoptère d'Egype
G: Schmutzgeier
P: Abutre do Egipto

Field recognition: Large. Mainly white or buffy with black flight feathers. The bill is long and thin, the face orange-yellow, the eye dull red. Long feathers cover the back of the head, which gives it a crested appearance. The legs are yellow to pinkish. In flight the wedge-shaped tail and black primaries distinguish it from the Palm-nut Vulture. **Juv.** Juveniles are dark brown. The bare face and legs are dull greyish. The eye is dark. The slender bill distinguishes it from similar raptors, except the Hooded Vulture, which lacks the long feathers on the back of the head. In flight it may only be confused with a juvenile Bearded Vulture, which also has a wedge-shaped tail, but is much larger.

Behaviour: Reports from the 19th century claim that this vulture was once common in Southern Africa's arid regions. Why it has become virtually extinct in the subregion is a mystery. Vagrants from the north, often immature or sub-adult birds, are seen every few years. Usually solitary. Soars easily, often to great heights, as it is not dependent on thermals. Usually silent.

Feeding methods: Feeds mainly on carrion, but also insects (such as termites), refuse and dung. The slender bill is ideally adapted for picking small remnants off bones and collecting scraps. Flamingo and similar eggs are picked up and then thrown down. Ostrich eggs are cracked in a different manner: a stone is picked up in the bill and then hurled repeatedly at the egg.

Breeding: In Southern Africa breeding has only been recorded once since 1923, namely in the Kaokoveld, Namibia, in the 1990s. **Season:** Presumed August to December. **Nest:** A large platform of sticks, with a central depression lined with skin, hair, wool, dung and other items such as bones, pieces of carcasses, paper or old rope. It becomes plastered with droppings. Built in small caves or under overhanging ledges on cliffs. Pairs may breed in loose associations. **Clutch:** 1–3 eggs, usually 2. **Incubation:** ± 42 days by both sexes. **Nestling:** 71–85 days, fed by both parents.

Origin of name: Neophron, a character in the pseudomythological stories of Antoninus Liberalis, was changed into a vulture by Zeus because of trickery. The Greek words *percnos* ('dusky') and *pterus* ('wing') refer to the dark flight feathers. Egyptian Vultures used to be abundant along the Nile River and were even depicted by ancient Egyptians. Their close association with people earned them the name 'Pharaoh's chicken'.

Adult   Juvenile

Adult

Adult

p. 35

p. 218

Adult

Juvenile

Juvenile breaking egg with stone

HOODED VULTURE
Necrosyrtes monachus

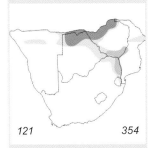

Measurements
Length: 65-75 cm
Wingspan: 170-182 cm
Weight: 1,8-2,6 (2,1) kg
Male and female are
similar in size.

Distribution
Africa south of the Sahara.
In Southern Africa mainly
in the north and east.

121   354

Habitat
Well-developed woodland
and savanna.

Food
Mostly carrion, but also
bones, refuse, insects and
dung.

Status
Rare to locally common
resident. Numbers have
declined and the range
contracted in recent times.

A: Monnikaasvoël
F: Vautour charognard
G: Kappengeier
P: Abutre-de-capuz

Field recognition: Large. Could be confused with the other two dark vultures, namely the White-headed and Lappet-faced Vultures, but the smaller size, very slender bill and white down on the back of the head distinguish this vulture. The plumage is dark brown, with some white feathers on the crop and the leggings. These are the only white patches seen in flight. The bare face and throat are pink, but flush red to purplish in excitement. The legs are pale blue-grey. The tail is almost square in flight. **Juv.** The juvenile is darker than the adult and lacks the white patches on the underparts. The down on the back of the head is dark brown. The bare face is grey at first and gradually becomes reddish. The slender bill distinguishes it from all similar raptors, except the juvenile Egyptian Vulture, which has long feathers on the back of the head and shows a wedge-shaped tail in flight. In flight the juvenile Hooded Vulture also resembles a small version of juvenile Lappet-faced or White-headed Vultures, but the slender bill aids identification.

Behaviour: Although Hooded Vultures in the northern parts of Africa are often associated with people and are a common sight in villages, those in Southern Africa are shy and retiring in their habits. They are nowhere plentiful, but prefer well-developed woodland and savanna. Here they regularly perch inside the canopy of a tree and are easily overlooked. They are not as dependent on thermals as larger vultures and soar less often. This enables them to fly earlier in the morning and they are often the first to arrive at a carcass, where they may gather in small groups. Otherwise mostly solitary. Usually silent.

Feeding methods: The slender bill indicates that this vulture cannot compete with larger vultures at a carcass, but rather feeds on scraps, pieces of skin and small bones. It also regularly scavenges on the carcasses of small animals or fish, digs for insects in the soil and even feeds on dung and refuse.

Breeding: Season: June to August, preferring the end of the dry season. **Nest:** A small platform of sticks, lined with green leaves, grass, hair and skin. Built in the main fork below the canopy of a tree, preferably tall and thorny. Well hidden. Often associates in loose groups. **Clutch:** 1 egg. **Incubation:** 46–54 days by both parents. **Nestling:** 90–130 days (mostly 100–120 days), fed by both parents. Dependent on parents for another 4 months.

Origin of name: The genus name is derived from the Greek words *nekros* ('corpse') and *surtes* ('to pull') and refers to the feeding habits of vultures. *Monachus* is Latin for 'monk', referring to the hooded appearance.

Adult

Juvenile

Possible confusion: Juvenile Egyptian Vulture p. 56, White-headed Vulture p. 60, Lappet-faced Vulture p. 62

Adult blushing

p. 35

p. 218

Adult

Juvenile

Sub-adult

WHITE-HEADED VULTURE
Aegypius occipitalis

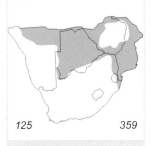

Measurements
Length: 78-85 cm
Wingspan: 202-230 cm
Weight: 3,30-5,30 (4,26) kg
Females are larger
than males.

Distribution
Africa south of the Sahara.

125   359

Habitat
Prefers broadleaved
woodland, but also
savanna, lightly wooded
grassland and semi-
desert.

Food
Carrion; often scraps
or small animals. Also
insects. Regularly pirates
food.

Status
Uncommon resident.
Rare outside major
conservation areas.
Numbers have declined in
recent years.

A: Witkopaasvoël
F: Vautour à tête blanche
G: Wollkopfgeier
P: Abutre-de-cabeça-
   branca

Field recognition: Very large. May be confused with the other two dark vultures, namely the Hooded and Lappet-faced Vultures but is intermediate in size. The head is triangular in shape. Conspicuous white down covers the back of the head, while the bare face and throat are pink, blushing red in excitement. The cere is blue, the bill red to orange. The legs are pinkish to red. The plumage is mainly black with a white belly, leggings and crop patch. These colours may be seen in flight, including the off-white or grey secondaries of the male, or the white secondaries of the female. **Juv.** The juvenile lacks the white plumage. The head is covered with brown down, but the pink face, blue cere and red bill remain diagnostic. The legs are brownish-pink. It may be confused with juvenile Hooded and Lappet-faced Vultures, but the shape and colour of the head and bill prevent confusion. In flight the narrow whitish line running along the base of the flight feathers is also a useful identification pointer. It takes about six years to moult into full adult plumage.

Behaviour: Pairs are territorial, occupying areas of 50–430 km^2 and thus no more than two adult birds are ever seen at a carcass. Roosts on trees, usually at or near the nest site. Starts flying early in the morning and thus has a better opportunity to spot carcasses. Never very numerous, but prefers areas with Baobab or large acacia trees as these make excellent nest sites. Usually silent.

Feeding methods: Often arrives first at a carcass, but cannot compete with larger vultures when they arrive. Dropped scraps, tougher material, such as sinews and skin, as well as insects are therefore an important part of its diet. It also feeds on the dead bodies of smaller animals, such as hares, antelope lambs, guineafowl and mongooses, and is suspected of killing some of them itself. It may kill flamingo chicks and capture barbel in a drying pool. More important, however, is that it often pirates food from other raptors.

Breeding: Season: May to August, peaking in June. **Nest:** A large platform of sticks, lined with grass and hair. Built on top of preferably flat-topped trees. Breeds singly. The nests are widely spaced, as pairs are territorial. **Clutch:** 1 egg. **Incubation:** 55–56 days by both sexes. **Nestling:** ±100 days, fed by both parents. Fledgling dependent on parents for another few months.

Origin of name: In the pseudomythological stories of Antoninus Liberalis, both Neophron (see the Egyptian Vulture) and Aegypius were changed into vultures by Zeus. The Latin *occipitalis* is a reference to the back of the head.

Male

Female

Juvenile

Burger Cillié

Female

Dave Richards

Adult

p. 35

p. 218

Albert Froneman

Juvenile

Philip van den Berg

Male

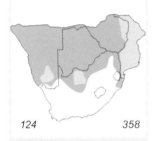

Measurements
Length: 98-115 cm
Wingspan: 258-280 cm
Weight: 5,9-7,9 (6,6) kg
Females are slightly
larger than males.

Distribution
Africa south of the Sahara,
Arabia and Israel.

124   *358*

Habitat
Prefers semi-arid habitats,
from desert to savanna.

Food
Carrion, often the tougher
parts. Also feeds on
insects and may kill its
own prey.

Status
Uncommon resident.
Rare outside major
conservation areas.
Numbers have declined in
recent years.

S: African Black Vulture /
   African King Vulture /
   Nubian Vulture
A: Swartaasvoël
F: Vautour oricou
G: Ohrengeier
P: Abutre-real

LAPPET-FACED VULTURE
Aegypius tracheliotus

Field recognition: Huge. The largest of the three dark vulture species, the other two being the Hooded and White-headed Vultures. The heavy, yellowish bill and bare red head with its conspicuous skin folds are diagnostic. The underparts are white, but boldly streaked brown on the chest. The legs are blue-grey. In flight the colour of the underparts, as well as a narrow white bar running along the forepart of the underwing, from the body to the wrist joint, will be seen. The tail is slightly wedge-shaped.
Juv. The young takes 5–6 years to reach adult plumage. In the first-year juvenile the plumage appears almost wholly black, the bare head is dull pinkish, the bill is horn-coloured and the legs are dull grey. At the end of the first year the bill starts changing to yellow; at the end of the second, the white colour on the leggings gradually appears. At the end of the first year the immature also acquires a characteristic pale dappling on the mantle and upperwing coverts that gradually disappears over the years. In flight it is difficult to distinguish from juvenile Hooded and White-headed Vultures, except by size and the characteristic shape of the head and bill.

Behaviour: Often the most common vulture in semi-arid regions. Occurs solitarily or in pairs and is never very numerous at a carcass. Roosts in trees at night and starts soaring well after sunrise as its huge body makes it very dependent on thermals. Aggressive at a carcass. Normally silent.

Feeding methods: Feeds on carrion: mainly flesh, but the huge bill enables it to feed on tougher material such as skin, sinews and bones. Arrives later than other vultures, but is often the first to break into the carcass. Dominates all other vultures. It may kill flamingo chicks and barbel, and is suspected of occasionally killing other small animals. Also feeds on insects, such as termites.

Breeding: Season: April to September, peaking May to June. **Nest:** A huge platform of sticks up to 3 m in diameter and 0,5–1 m thick, lined with dry grass, hair and skin. Built on top of a flat-topped bush or tree. Solitary, but may breed in loose groups if trees are scarce. **Clutch:** 1 egg, very rarely 2. **Incubation:** 55–56 days by both sexes. **Nestling:** 125–130 days, fed by both parents. Partially dependent on parents for the rest of the 12 months' breeding cycle.

Origin of name: In the pseudomythological stories of Antoninus Liberalis, both Neophron (see the Egyptian Vulture) and Aegypius were changed into vultures by Zeus. The Greek words *trachelos* ('throat') and *otos* ('ear') draw attention to the naked throat and head as well as to the characteristic skin folds (lappets) on the ear region.

Adult

Juvenile

p. 35

p. 218

Immature

Juvenile

Adult

Adult

WHITE-BACKED VULTURE
Gyps africanus

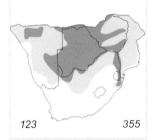

Measurements
Length: 90-100 cm
Wingspan: 212-228 cm
Weight: 4,15-7,2 (5,46) kg
The sexes are similar
in size.

Distribution
Widespread in Africa
south of the Sahara.

123   355

Habitat
Savanna and dry, open
woodland.

Food
Carrion, especially softer
parts of large mammalian
carcasses.

Status
Locally common resident.
The most frequently
seen vulture in bushveld
conservation areas, but
numbers have declined in
some regions.

S: African White-backed
   Griffon
A: Witrugaasvoël
F: Vautour africain
G: Weissrückengeier
P: Grifo-de-dorso-branco

Field recognition: Large. May be confused with Cape and even Rüppell's Vultures, but is smaller. The adult's characteristic white rump is only visible when the wings are spread or the flying bird is seen from above. The overall plumage is buffy-brown, although very old birds may be much paler. The eyes, bill and legs are blackish. The face appears black, but the head and neck are sparsely covered in white down, unlike the Cape Vulture, in which the face appears pale blue and the neck is mainly naked. In flight the dark flight feathers contrast strongly with the paler leading edge of the wing. **Juv.** The juvenile is dark brown with narrow pale streaks on the underparts and wing coverts. The head and neck are covered in dense woolly white down, only the face being naked. In flight it is difficult to distinguish from the juvenile Cape Vulture as it appears dark brown with pale streaks on the body and underwing coverts. A narrow white bar runs near the leading edge of the wing. The adult plumage is acquired over six years, although the bird may start breeding when four years old.

Behaviour: Although not the most widespread vulture in Southern Africa, it is certainly the most numerous, especially in savanna and dry, open woodland. Gregarious at the roost and at a carcass, but less so when breeding. Roosts in trees at night and starts soaring as soon as thermals form. Often rests on the ground and bathes regularly after feeding. Hisses and squeals at a carcass as it squabbles aggressively with other vultures.

Feeding methods: Specialises in carrion, mainly the soft flesh and intestines of large mammals. Also eats bone fragments. Often the most numerous vulture at a carcass in its preferred habitat. Follows other scavengers, such as vultures and hyenas, to a carcass.

Breeding: Season: May to July, corresponding with the beginning of the dry season. Breeding starts later in the south of the range. **Nest:** A large platform of sticks, lined with grass and sometimes with green leaves. Built in trees (not cliffs), tall thorny ones being preferred. Breeds singly or in loose colonies. **Clutch:** 1 egg. **Incubation:** 56–58 days by both sexes. **Nestling:** 120–125 days, fed by both parents. Partially dependent on parents for food for about 4 months.

Origin of name: *Gups* is Greek for 'griffon vulture', while the Latin word *africanus* refers to its distribution, thus distinguishing it from the Asian White-rumped Vulture.

Adult   Juvenile

p. 35

p. 218

Adult

Adult

Adult showing white rump

Juvenile

Pale adult

65

Measurements
Length: 100-120 cm
Wingspan: ±255 cm
Weight: 7,3-10,9 (8,6) kg
Birds of the Drakensberg
are larger than elsewhere.

Distribution
Endemic to
Southern Africa.

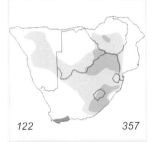

122   357

Habitat
Prefers mountainous
country or open veld
with scattered mountains
or escarpments, but
immatures wander wldely.

Food
Carrion, preferably the
softer parts of large
mammals.

Status
Resident. Rare, except
in the Drakensberg and
Eastern Cape. Numbers
have declined in recent
years.

S: Cape Griffon
A: Kransaasvoël
F: Vautour chassefiente
G: Kapgeier
P: Grifo do Cabo

CAPE VULTURE
Gyps coprotheres

Field recognition: Very large. Similar to White-backed and Rüppell's Vultures, but is larger. The overall plumage is pale to whitish, but the flight feathers and tail are dark. The pale yellowish eye and the black spots on the last row of upper- and underwing coverts are diagnostic. The back is mottled, although it may be nearly white in very old birds. The face is pale bluish, not dark as in the White-backed Vulture. The head is covered with white down, but the blue neck is mainly naked. The naked blue patches on either side of the crop are not always visible. In flight the secondaries appear much paler than the dark primaries. **Juv.** The juvenile has a dark eye. It resembles the juvenile White-backed Vulture as it is also streaked on the underparts and wing coverts, but is a more rufous, warmer brown. The naked patches on the neck and on either side of the crop are red. In flight it lacks the white bar on the underwing of the juvenile White-backed Vulture and is not as dark in appearance. The full adult plumage is reached after six years.

Behaviour: Endemic to Southern Africa, although vagrants are sometimes seen in Zambia. Prefers mountainous country, or open country with escarpments and inselbergs and is thus less often seen in savanna and bushveld than the White-backed Vulture. Adults are tied to their breeding colony on a cliff for most of the year, seldom venturing far to forage, usually 10–20 km, at the most 150 km away. Immatures may wander widely and have been recorded up to 1 200 km from their natal colony. They roost on trees or power pylons at night, often in groups. Hiss, grunt and squeal at a carcass.

Feeding methods: Specialises in carrion, especially the softer parts of large mammalian carcasses. Bone fragments are an important source of calcium, especially for chicks. Very gregarious and aggressive at a carcass, often mixing with the White-backed Vulture in areas where their ranges overlap.

Breeding: Season: March to July. **Nest:** A platform of sticks, stems, brush, bracken and grass, lined with grass and leaves. Varies in size from merely a scrape surrounded by a few sticks to substantial. Built colonially on cliff ledges. **Clutch:** 1 egg, very rarely 2. **Incubation:** 55–58 days by both sexes. **Nestling:** ±140 days, fed by both parents. Dependent on parents for another ±114 days.

Origin of name: The Greek word for 'griffon vulture' is *gups*. The specific name *coprotheres* is also derived from Greek (*kopros* is 'dung', *theres* means 'hunting') and is based on the earlier belief that vultures feed mainly on dung.

Adult   Juvenile

Ulrich Oberprieler

Adult

Albert Froneman

Dirty adult

p. 35

p. 218

Ulrich Oberprieler

Juveniles

Ulrich Oberprieler

Adult

Clem Haagner

Adults on nests

Marietjie Oosthuizen

Adult

RÜPPELL'S VULTURE

Gyps rueppellii

Measurements
Length: 95-107 cm
Wingspan: 230-250 cm
Weight: 6,8-9,0 (7,57) kg
The sexes are similar
in size.

Distribution
Western and eastern
Africa, usually as far south
as central Tanzania.

356

Habitat
Mainly mountainous
country and lowlands with
inselbergs, but may occur
in savanna.

Food
Carrion. Adapted to eat
soft flesh and intestines of
large mammals.

Status
A rare vagrant to Southern
Africa, but common in its
normal range.

S: Rüppell's Griffon
A: Rüppell-aasvoël
F: Vautour de Rüppell
G: Sperbergeier
P: Grifo de Rüppell

Field recognition: Very large. May be confused with Cape and White-backed Vultures, but is intermediate in size. Adults are distinctive. The bill is strikingly yellowish-orange, the cere black. The eye is pale yellow, but not as conspicuous as that of the adult Cape Vulture. The neck is mostly naked, coloured greenish-grey (as are the patches on either side of the crop), but flushes mauve when the bird is excited. Most of the body feathers have a pale edge, giving the bird a diagnostic speckled or scaled appearance. In flight the flight feathers and tail appear dark, but the underwing coverts are mottled. **Juv.** The juvenile is so similar to the juvenile Cape Vulture that they may not safely be separated in the field. It has a dark eye and bill. The bare patch on the neck is reddish-pink. It is darker than the juvenile Cape Vulture and the underparts and wing coverts are more broadly streaked. The adult plumage is acquired over six years.

Behaviour: Rüppell's Vulture is the equivalent of the Cape Vulture in suitable habitat (mountains and open country with inselbergs) of western and eastern Africa, where it is a well-known bird. The large-scale clearing of miombo woodland in south-central Africa may have aided this vulture in reaching Southern Africa, where it has been observed at various Cape Vulture colonies since 1989, from Wabai Hills in Zimbabwe to Potberg in the Western Cape. Its habits are similar to those of the Cape Vulture.

Feeding methods: Specialises in carrion, namely the soft flesh and intestines of larger mammalian carcasses.

Breeding: The presence of Rüppell's Vultures at Cape Vulture breeding colonies raise the possibility that they may breed here and even hybridise with Cape Vultures. In its normal range the following applies: **Season:** Variable, but usually at the beginning of the dry season. **Nest:** A platform of sticks, lined with grass and green leaves. Built on rock ledges or in niches on cliffs. Colonial. **Clutch:** 1 egg. **Incubation:** ±55 days, by both sexes. **Nestling:** ±150 days.

Origin of name: *Gups* is Greek for 'griffon vulture'. Dr Eduard Rüppell (1794–1884), a German zoologist, travelled extensively in north-eastern Africa while collecting specimens for the Senckenberg Museum. Rüppell's Korhaan and Rüppell's Parrot were also named after him.

Adult

Juvenile

p. 35

p. 218

Kobus Fourie (Photo Access)

Adult

Steve Garvie

Adult

Ron Eggert

Juvenile

BEARDED VULTURE
Gypaetus barbatus

Measurements
Length: ±110 cm
Wingspan: 263-282 cm
Weight: 5,20-6,25 (5,76) kg
Females are slightly larger than males.

Distribution
Occurs in the high mountains of Africa, Europe and Asia. In Southern Africa confined to the Drakensberg, although vagrants may be recorded elsewhere.

119   352

Habitat
The Drakensberg massif and foothills, above 1 800 m.

Food
Carrion, especially bones and marrow.

Status
Rare and endangered resident.

S: Lammergeier (outdated)
A: Baardaasvoël / Lammergier (outdated)
F: Gypaète barbu
G: Bartgeier
P: Quebra-ossos

Field recognition: A very large raptor of the Drakensberg. The long body shape, with the wings giving it a hunched appearance and almost reaching the tip of the long tail, as well as the baggy leggings, make it unmistakable. The black face mask and the bristly beard of feathers are characteristic, although these might only be seen at close range. The eye is yellow with a red sclerotic ring. Plumage is mainly dark with rufous to yellowish underparts. The amount of white on the head is variable. In flight the long, narrow and pointed wings as well as the long wedge-shaped tail seem falcon-like. **Juv.** The juvenile has a similar silhouette, but is browner all over with a blackish-brown head. The adult plumage is acquired after about seven years.

Behaviour: Solitary. May associate with other individuals or other vultures at a carcass. Roosts on cliffs, often on or near the nest. Starts flying early in the morning and soars for long periods, usually fairly close to the ground and rarely flapping its wings. May forage up to 90 km from the nest. The rufous colour of the underparts is caused by iron oxide (rust), acquired from either dusting on ledges or from bathing in the iron-rich water of streams. Usually silent.

Feeding methods: Feeds on carrion – scraps of meat, skin and bone inedible to other birds. Carries food in the feet, sometimes in the crop. Although long bones may be swallowed whole, the Bearded Vulture has the remarkable habit of dropping bones on flat rocks to break them, then swallowing the fragments and marrow. These rocks, called ossuaries, are probably used for centuries and become littered with bleached bones. The vulture, carrying the bone in its feet and approaching in a fast glide, releases the bone 50–150 m above the ossuary and hits it with great accuracy. This behaviour may be repeated several times.

Breeding: Season: May to July. **Nest:** A huge flat platform of sticks up to 2 m across, lined with grass, moss, skin, hair, bones, dry dung and even old clothing. Built mainly in caves high up on large cliffs, sometimes on ledges under overhangs. **Clutch:** 1–3 eggs, usually 2. **Incubation:** 55–58 days by both sexes. **Nestling:** 124–128 days, fed by both parents. Only 1 chick survives, the second dies of starvation. Dependent on parents for another ±60 days.

Origin of name: The scientific name emphasises the bearded appearance (*barbatus* is Latin for 'bearded') and the fact that this is not a typical vulture (*gups* is 'griffon vulture' and *aetos* 'eagle' in Greek). The outdated name Lammergeier refers to the erroneous belief that this bird is able to catch lambs.

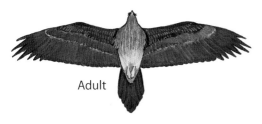

Adult

Juvenile

Possible confusion: Juvenile Egyptian Vulture (in flight) p. 56

p. 35

p. 218

Albert Froneman

Adult

Albert Froneman

Adult

Albert Froneman

Immature

Dup du Plessis

Juvenile

Measurements
Length: 80-96 cm
Wingspan: ±200 cm
Weight: ♂ 3,0-4,15 (3,7) kg
♀ 3,1-5,8 (4,45) kg

Distribution
Southern to eastern Africa and Arabia.

131 *389*

Habitat
Rocky hills, mountains, gorges and isolated koppies from near sea level to the high Drakensberg.

Food
Mostly dassies (both Rock and Yellow-spotted Dassies). Also other small mammals and larger birds. Sometimes reptiles and carrion.

Status
Locally fairly common resident.

S: Black Eagle
A: Witkruisarend
F: Aigle de Verreaux
G: Felsenadler
P: Águia-preta

VERREAUXS' EAGLE
Aquila verreauxii

Field recognition: Very large. The typical large eagle of mountains. Adults are unmistakable: jet black with a white V on the upper back and a white lower back. (The latter is only visible when the wings are spread. In the female this white area is larger than in the male.) The cere and feet are yellow. In flight the wings have a characteristic narrow base and broad tip. The primaries are mainly white, showing as large white windows towards the tip of the wing. **Juv.** The juvenile may easily be confused with other brown eagles, but the large size, characteristic wing shape and habitat help to identify it. It has a mottled light and dark brown plumage with black chest and cheeks. The diagnostic feature is the rufous crown and nape. More and more black feathers start appearing from the age of about one year, until the sub-adult has only a few brown feathers. Full adult plumage is acquired over a period of 4–5 years.

Behaviour: Usually occurs in pairs or a pair with a juvenile. Starts flying soon after dawn. Spends long periods on the wing, gliding along ridges and cliffs or sometimes soaring on thermals to great height. Sits for hours in the shade of a tree or rock face during the heat of the day. Usually silent.

Feeding methods: Dassies usually make up more than 90% of its prey. Hunts mostly on the wing (less often from a perch), by stooping from a height or swooping around a corner of a cliff or hillside, thereby surprising its prey. Pairs often hunt co-operatively: one draws the prey's attention while the other attacks. Rarely pirates prey from other raptors or feeds on carrion.

Breeding: Season: April to June or even August. **Nest:** A huge platform of sticks, lined with green leaves. Usually built on cliffs and may become tower-like after decades of use, up to 4 m high. Pairs have more than one nest, although one is preferred above others. **Clutch:** 1–2 eggs. **Incubation:** 43–48 days, mainly by female. **Nestling:** 90–98 days, fed by female on food brought by male. Only 1 chick survives, the younger being killed by the older within 3 days. Dependent for another 13–19 weeks after leaving nest.

Origin of name: *Aquila* is the Latin word for 'eagle'. Jules (1808–1873) and Edouard Verreaux (1810–1868) visited Southern Africa to collect birds. They then returned to Paris to run a taxidermy and natural history specimen business. Jules joined the Paris Museum in 1864 and later became its director.

Juvenile

Adult

p. 36

p. 224

Juvenile

Adult

Juvenile

Immature

Adult

73

TAWNY EAGLE
Aquila rapax

Measurements
Length: 65-73 cm
Wingspan: ±182 cm
Weight: ♂ 1,85-1,95 kg
♀ 1,57-2,38 kg

Distribution
Throughout Africa in suitable habitat. Also southern Arabia and India.

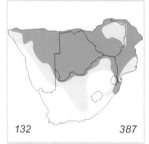

132   387

Habitat
Mostly woodland and savanna. Also grassland and Karoo with scattered trees.

Food
Very opportunistic: eats anything from flying termites to the remains of dead elephants.

Status
Common resident in large conservation areas. Elsewhere rare and declining in numbers.

A: Roofarend
F: Aigle ravisseur
G: Raubadler / Savannenadler
P: Águia-fulva

Field recognition: Large. The body shape of a classic eagle with a shaggy appearance and rounded head. Legs fully feathered. Smaller than the similar juvenile Black Eagle, but larger and more powerfully built than Wahlberg's, Booted or Lesser Spotted Eagles. Similar to the Steppe Eagle (a non-breeding summer visitor) in shape and size. Although the plumage is variable from streaked dark brown to pale buff (blond), all but very pale individuals have some tawny (rufous-brown) colour. In this way it differs from the Steppe Eagle, which is a plainer, darker brown. It further differs from the Steppe Eagle in that the gape extends to below the centre of the eye only, the tail is not (or only faintly) barred and adults have dull yellow to pale brown (not dark) eyes. In flight the trailing edge of the wing is S-shaped. The broad rounded tail is usually spread. Colour variations reflect sex and age to a certain degree. Most adult males are tawny, while females are often dark brown and streaked. **Juv.** Juveniles are usually a warm rufous-tawny colour at first, but then fade to a pale brown. They gradually moult into adult plumage over 3–4 years. The juvenile resembles the juvenile Steppe Eagle, but is paler and more rufous, with less distinct pale markings on the wing. (The gape distinction still applies.) In flight it lacks the white rump of the latter. The eye is brown, changing to dull yellow after two years.

Behaviour: Mostly solitary, but somewhat gregarious at a good food source. Often seen roosting on trees, especially during rainy or overcast weather. Prefers flying only when thermals assist soaring. Usually silent.

Feeding methods: Obtains its food in three ways: by pirating food from other birds, by scavenging and by actively hunting. The latter is done either by diving from a perch or by stooping from a soaring flight. Unlike the Steppe Eagle, it rarely takes prey while walking around on the ground.

Breeding: Season: March to September, peaking in April to July. **Nest:** A large, flat platform of sticks, lined with grass and green leaves. The only African eagle to build its nest regularly on the crown of a thorny tree. **Clutch:** 1–3 eggs, usually 2. **Incubation:** 39–44 days, mainly by female. **Nestling:** 77–84 days, fed by both parents, but mainly by female. Only the oldest chick survives as it kills the younger ones. Dependent on the parents for at least another 6 weeks after leaving the nest.

Origin of name: Tawny is a brownish-orange to rufous-brown colour. *Aquila* is Latin for 'eagle'. *Rapax* (Latin) means 'grasping' or 'rapacious'.

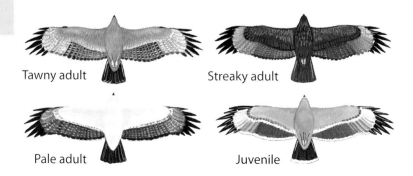

Tawny adult   Streaky adult

Pale adult   Juvenile

Lizeth Cillié

Streaky adult

Geoff McIlleron

Juvenile

p. 36

p. 224

Richard du Toit

Moulting sub-adult

Clem Haagner

Pale adult

Ulrich Oberprieler

Tawny adult

Niel Cillié

Tawny adult

STEPPE EAGLE
Aquila nipalensis

Measurements
Length: 70-84 cm
Wingspan: 174-260 cm
Weight: ♂ 2,25-3,11 (2,5) kg
♀ 2,6-3,8 (3,03) kg

Distribution
Breeds in eastern Europe and Asia. Migrates to southern and eastern Africa, the Middle East and southern Asia.

133   386

Habitat
Woodland, thornveld and arid savanna.

Food
Mostly flying termites. Also feeds on Red-billed Quelea nestlings at nesting colonies.

Status
Common but erratic non-breeding summer visitor.

A: Steppe-arend
F: Aigle des steppes
G: Steppenadler
P: Águia-das-estepes

Field recognition: Large. Legs fully feathered. The powerful body shape of a classic eagle distinguishes it from the smaller Lesser Spotted, Wahlberg's or Booted Eagles. The juvenile Black Eagle is larger and has a distinct pattern. Similar to the Tawny Eagle (a breeding resident) in shape and size. Of the two Steppe Eagle subspecies which visit Southern Africa, the western *A. n. orientalis* is by far the commoner (see 'Breeding'). Both are uniform dark chocolate brown, the rare eastern *A. n. nipalensis* being larger and darker. A small ginger patch on the nape may be visible. The eye is dark brown. The gape is much more prominent than in the Tawny Eagle and extends to behind the eye in *A. n. nipalensis* and nearly to the back of the eye in *A. n. orientalis*. In flight it is similar to the Tawny Eagle, but the tail is distinctly barred. **Juv.** Young Steppe Eagles, clay-brown in colour, are much more common in Southern Africa than the dark chocolate brown adults. They are similar to the more rufous juvenile Tawny Eagle, but the gape distinction applies as in the adults. The pale buff feather edges may give a scaled or even mottled appearance. Two pale bars on the wing are often very prominent. These are also distinctive in flight, as are the pale tip to the tail, the white, broadly U-shaped rump and pale windows in the innermost primaries.

Behaviour: The behaviour of this migratory eagle in Southern Africa is closely linked to its main prey, termite alates. Flocks are nomadic and follow rain fronts. They often associate with other raptors, especially Lesser Spotted Eagles and Black Kites. More often seen feeding or perched on the ground than the similar Tawny Eagle. Usually silent.

Feeding methods: The Steppe Eagle takes a large variety of prey in its breeding range, feeding mainly on flying termites in Southern Africa. A single bird requires between 1 600 and 2 000 of this tiny but highly nutritious prey per day. These could be obtained in three hours' feeding. The only other prey of importance is Red-billed Quelea nestlings taken at nesting colonies.

Breeding: The subspecies *A. n. orientalis* breeds from eastern Europe east to Kazakhstan in mountainous regions up to 2 300 m, while *A. n. nipalensis* breeds more to the east (Altai and Tibet east to Manchuria) in lowlands and low hills. The latter migrates mostly to southern Asia when not breeding.

Origin of name: The steppe is a level grassy plain with few trees, especially in south-eastern Europe and Siberia. *Aquila* is the Latin word for 'eagle'. *Nipalensis* means 'from Nepal'.

Adult   Juvenile

Adult

Adult

p. 36

p. 224

Juvenile

Immature

Sub-adult

Juvenile

LESSER SPOTTED EAGLE
Aquila pomarina

Measurements
Length: 61-66 cm
Wingspan: 134-159 cm
Weight: ♂ 1,05-1,51 (1,2) kg
♀ 1,19-2,16 (1,5) kg

Distribution
Breeds in eastern Europe, western and southern Asia. Migrates to southern and eastern Africa when not breeding.

134   388

Habitat
Woodland and savanna.

Food
Mostly termites. Also feeds on Red-billed Quelea nestlings, small birds, rodents and frogs.

Status
Locally common but regular non-breeding summer visitor.

A: Gevlekte Arend /
 Klein Gevlekte Arend
F: Aigle pomarin
G: Schreiadler
P: Águia-pomarina

Field recognition: Large. A brown eagle with long, thin-looking 'stove-pipe' but fully feathered legs. Although similar to all other brown eagles, it is most easily confused with Steppe and Wahlberg's Eagles. It is distinguished from the Steppe (and Tawny) Eagle by its smaller, more buzzard-like proportions (not a classic eagle shape). A number of features distinguish it from Wahlberg's Eagle: its larger size, tightly feathered legs, yellowish eye and short, rounded tail. In flight the trailing edge of the wing is nearly straight and the unmarked tail is usually spread slightly. From above one may see small white windows at the base of the primaries. Less than 5% of adult Lesser Spotted Eagles are pale yellowish instead of brown. Young birds are far more common in Southern Africa than adults. **Juv.** The juvenile is warm brown with a ginger patch on the nape, two pale bands on the folded wing, pale spots on the wing coverts and pale streaks on the head and underparts. The eye is brown. In flight it is most easily confused with the juvenile Steppe Eagle, although it is not quite as boldly patterned. From below there is a white line between the underwing coverts and the flight feathers, and the undertail coverts are white. A white line between the upperwing coverts and the flight feathers, white windows on the base of the primaries and a white U-shaped rump may be seen from above. Some birds have a white patch on the back. The immature gradually loses its distinctive markings until adult plumage is reached at an age of 4–5 years.

Behaviour: The behaviour is similar to that of the Steppe Eagle in that it often feeds on the ground and follows rain fronts in search of its termite prey. It is, however, less gregarious and prefers moister habitats. Usually silent.

Feeding methods: Although taking a variety of prey in its breeding range, this eagle preys mainly on flying termites while visiting Southern Africa. Red-billed Quelea nestlings are also an important food source, while other small birds, rodents and frogs are taken occasionally. Most food is taken while walking about on the ground, but it may hunt from a perch or on the wing.

Breeding: Migratory birds breed from eastern Europe to the southern Caspian lowlands. A resident subspecies occurs in southern Asia.

Origin of name: In Eurasia and northern Africa the Lesser Spotted Eagle may be confused with the Greater Spotted Eagle (*Aquila clanga*). (There is only one unsubstantiated record of this eagle for Southern Africa.) *Aquila* is Latin for 'eagle'. Pomerania was a province of Prussia.

Adult

Juvenile

Dirk Verwoerd

Juvenile

Burger Cillié

Adult

p. 36

p. 224

Niel Cillié

Sub-adult

Ulrich Oberprieler

Sub-adult

Niel Cillié

Adult

Niel Cillié

Sub-adult

79

WAHLBERG'S EAGLE
Aquila wahlbergi

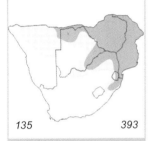

Measurements
Length: 55-60 cm
Wingspan: ±141 cm
Weight: 0,44-1,4 kg
Females are larger than males.

Distribution
Africa south of the Sahara. Bulk of population breeds south of the equator and winters in north-eastern Africa.

135   393

Habitat
Woodland and savanna.

Food
Very varied: small mammals up to size of hare, birds up to size of guineafowl, reptiles and insects.

Status
Common breeding summer resident.

A: Wahlberg-arend / Bruinarend
F: Aigle de Wahlberg
G: Silberadler / Wahlbergs Adler
P: Águia de Wahlberg

Field recognition: Medium-large. Although most individuals are brown, a confusing variety of colour forms occur. The body shape is thus the easiest way to distinguish it from other brown eagles with fully feathered legs. It is a small, slenderly built eagle, not showing the powerful classic eagle shape of Tawny and Steppe Eagles. The face is small and pointed with a slight crest on the back of the head, although this is not always visible. The dark eye, together with the dark patch in front of the eye, gives it a characteristic expression. The leggings are fairly baggy, not thin-looking 'stove-pipes' as in the Lesser Spotted Eagle. Individuals may vary from dark chocolate brown to very pale, some looking rather patchy, but none have the broad buff band on the wing of the Booted Eagle. Very pale birds appear nearly white, while pale Booted Eagles also have darker heads. The flight pattern looks like two crossed planks as the leading and trailing edges of the wing are nearly parallel and the long square tail is usually held closed. **Juv.** Juveniles and immatures resemble adults, but their backs and upperwing coverts have a slightly scaled pattern and the crest is less obvious.

Behaviour: Usually the most common small eagle in wooded country during the summer season, but solitary, unobtrusive and easily overlooked in a leafy tree. Soars regularly, often to great height. Very vocal. Whistles a fluty 'kleeeeu' while soaring or utters a rapid 'kyip-kyip-kyip' contact call.

Feeding methods: This agile raptor hunts mostly on the wing, only rarely from a perch. Most of its varied prey is taken on the ground, but some may be caught in aerial pursuit.

Breeding: Season: Mainly September to October, but sometimes up to January. **Nest:** A small platform of sticks, lined with leaves. Built below the canopy in a tall tree, often along watercourses, or on a hillside or along the edge of woodland. **Clutch:** Usually 1 egg, very rarely 2. **Incubation:** 44–46 days, mostly by female. **Nestling:** 70–75 days, fed mostly by female on food brought by male. In contrast to other *Aquila* eagles, the chicks are not white, but covered in chocolate brown or pale brown down, which determines the eventual colour form when adult. Dependent on the parents for another few weeks.

Origin of name: *Aquila* is the Latin word for 'eagle'. Johan August Wahlberg (1810–1856) was a Swedish naturalist and explorer who travelled widely in Southern Africa. 'Wahl' is pronounced 'vaal' (as in Vaal River) and not 'wall'.

Brown form

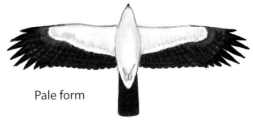

Pale form

Pale brown adult

Dark brown adult

p. 36

p. 224

Brown adult

Pale adult

Pale brown adult

Brown adult

Dark brown adult

BOOTED EAGLE
Aquila pennatus

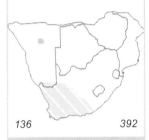

Measurements
Length: 48-52 cm
Wingspan: 110-132 cm
Weight: ♂ 510-770 (712) g
♀ 840-1 250 (975) g

Distribution
Eurasia and Africa.

136 392

Habitat
Wide range of habitats from desert to woodland; absent from forests. Most common in Karoo and fynbos. Breeds on cliffs in hilly country.

Food
Mainly birds up to size of francolin. Also rodents, lizards and insects.

Status
Fairly common breeding resident and non-breeding summer visitor.

A: Dwergarend
F: Aigle botté
G: Zwergadler
P: Águia-calçada

Field recognition: Medium. May be confused with various medium-sized brown raptors, but the fully feathered legs distinguish it as Southern Africa's smallest brown eagle. Two colour forms occur, a pale and a dark, the former being the most common (±80% of all individuals). The pale form has brown upperparts and pale underparts with a variable amount of streaking on the chest. It differs from the pale form of Wahlberg's Eagle in that the head is mostly brown, showing a pale throat only. The dark form is more uniform brown, but both forms are characterised by a broad pale band across the upperwing and white patches ('landing lights') on the leading edge of the wing near the body. The thick leggings distinguish it from the Lesser Spotted Eagle. In flight it differs from Wahlberg's Eagle in the prominent 'landing lights', broader wings and shorter, broader tail. From above the broad pale band across each wing and the pale U-shaped rump are seen. From below the dark form is nearly uniform dark, whereas the pale form has whitish underwing coverts. Both forms have a pale brown tail. **Juv.** The juvenile of the pale form is washed with rufous on the underparts and underwing coverts, thus resembling the juvenile African Hawk-Eagle and juvenile Ayres's Hawk-Eagle. All other young birds resemble the adults.

Behaviour: Solitary or in pairs. Usually seen flying as it is inconspicuous when perched. See also 'Breeding' below. Very vocal when breeding.

Feeding methods: Hunts mostly on the wing, soaring at a height of 200–300 m and stooping at prey on the ground. Less often perch-hunts.

Breeding: There are probably three separate populations in Southern Africa. The first comprises birds that breed in the winter rainfall region of the Northern, Western and Eastern Cape, but move northwards after breeding. The second is a small population breeding in northern Namibia's Waterberg. The third are non-breeding summer visitors from Eurasia and North Africa. **Season:** August to January (peaking September to November) in the Cape, during winter in the Waterberg. **Nest:** A small platform of sticks and twigs, lined with fresh leaves. In Africa usually built on cliff ledges or at the base of a tree on a cliff, very rarely in a tree in flat country as in Eurasia. **Clutch:** 2 eggs. **Incubation:** ±40 days, mostly by female. **Nestling:** 50–54 days, fed mostly by female. Both chicks may be raised. Dependent on parents for at least 47 days after leaving nest.

Origin of name: *Aquila* is the Latin word for 'eagle'. *Pennatus* is Latin for 'feathered', referring to the thick, booted appearance of the legs which, however, is not a good field character.

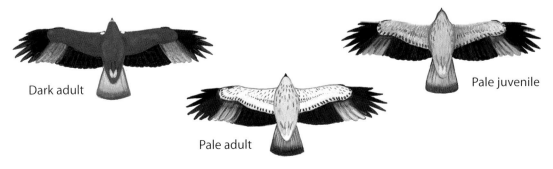

Dark adult

Pale adult

Pale juvenile

Chris van Rooyen

Juvenile

Chris van Rooyen

Pale adult

p. 36

p. 224

Niel Cillié

Dark adult

Ulrich Oberprieler

Juvenile

Christo Joubert

Pale adult

83

LONG-CRESTED EAGLE
Lophaetus occipitalis

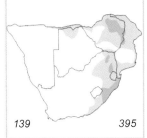

Measurements
Length: 52-58 cm
Wingspan: 112-129 cm
Weight: ♂ 0,91-1,36 kg
♀ 1,37-1,52 kg

Distribution
Africa south of the Sahara.

139   395

Habitat
Closed to well-developed,
moist woodland,
forest edge and exotic
plantations, especially
where these are in
association with wetlands,
marshes and rivers.

Food
Mostly small rodents and
shrews, especially vlei
rats. Occasionally birds,
reptiles and invertebrates.
Rarely fruit.

Status
Locally common resident.

A: Langkuifarend
F: Aigle huppard
G: Schopfadler
P: Águia-de-penacho

Field recognition: Medium-large. Unmistakable and easy to identify, as the long, loose crest of feathers on the head is diagnostic at all ages. The plumage is blackish brown, except for the leggings, which are white in males and dirty white to mottled brown in females. Seen from the front, the shoulders of the wing show a white edge. The eye is yellow to golden, the bill black with a yellow cere. The feet are yellow. In flight the large white windows towards the tip of the wing and the white barring on the black tail are diagnostic from above and below. **Juv.** Juveniles have white leggings, irrespective of sex. They have a shorter crest than adults until they are about five months old. The eye is grey at first, then changes to hazel at the age of about five months and has turned yellow by the time the immature is a year old.

Behaviour: Usually solitary. Perches conspicuously on one of several regularly used posts within its territory, making frequent flights from perch to perch. Does not soar often, seldom higher than 300 m above the ground. A vocal species which calls while perched or during the display flight. The most common call is a clear high-pitched scream 'keeeee-eh' or a long series of sharp 'kik-kik-kik-kik-keee-eh' notes.

Feeding methods: Hunts by perching conspicuously on top of a tree or telephone post, scanning the ground intently and swooping down diagonally to take prey. All prey is caught on the ground. Small animals are swallowed whole (note the long gape which extends almost to the back of the eye), while larger rodents may be transported in the bill. Feeds primarily on vlei rats, *Otomys* spp., although other animals might also be taken. Responds quickly to veld fires that expose rodent prey.

Breeding: Season: Throughout the year, but usually peaking in the wet season. **Nest:** A fairly small platform of sticks, lined with green leaves, in the upper fork of a tall tree on the edge of woodland or forest. **Clutch:** 1–2 eggs, usually 2. **Incubation:** 42 days, mostly by female. **Nestling:** 53–58 days, fed mostly by female on food brought by male. Two chicks are raised regularly. May breed twice in good years. Fledglings dependent on parents for another 3–4 months after leaving nest.

Origin of name: *Lophaetus* is derived from the Greek *lophos*, 'crest', and *aetos*, 'eagle'. *Occipitalis* (Latin) means 'belonging to the back of the head, the occiput'.

Adult

Male

Female

p. 36

p. 224

Female

Female

AFRICAN HAWK-EAGLE
Aquila spilogaster

Measurements
Length: 60-65 cm
Wingspan: ±142 cm
Weight:
♂ 1,22-1,3 (1,25) kg
♀ 1,44-1,64 (1,58) kg

Distribution
Africa south of the Sahara.

137   390

Habitat
Woodland and savanna,
from riverine growth in
arid regions to miombo
and forest edges.
Common in mopane-veld.

Food
Mostly birds, especially
gamebirds, and small
mammals up to size of
hare. Also reptiles and
insects. Prey often heavier
than itself.

Status
Uncommon to locally fairly
common resident.

S: African Eagle
A: Grootjagarend /
   Afrikaanse Jagarend
F: Aigle fascié
G: Afrikanischer
   Habichtsadler
P: Águia-dominó

Field recognition: Large. Above blackish; below white, streaked with black. Very similar to the smaller Ayres's Hawk-Eagle, but the African Hawk-Eagle is larger, more slenderly built. The underparts are streaked, but the leggings are unmarked. (Females are more heavily marked than males.) The lower edge of the black cap on the head is less well defined than in Ayres's Hawk-Eagle, but it is always completely black, without any white on the forehead or eyebrow. In flight this eagle appears white from below, as the underwing coverts are less spotted than in Ayres's Hawk-Eagle and the white flight feathers have a black trailing edge only. From above the characteristic white windows and white shafts to the primaries are diagnostic. The tail has a broad terminal band. **Juv.** The juvenile is brown above and rich rufous below with narrow dark streaks on the chest. The eye is brown (yellow in adults). In flight the underwing coverts are also rufous, while the flight feathers and tail are white, faintly barred black. May be confused with the juvenile Ayres's Hawk-Eagle, which is heavily barred on the flight feathers and tail. (The adult African Hawk-Eagle resembles the pale juvenile Black Sparrowhawk, while the rufous juvenile Black Sparrowhawk may be confused with the juvenile African Hawk-Eagle.)

Behaviour: Solitary or in pairs. Spends much time on the wing, soaring to great height. Perches inconspicuously within the cover of a tree, often near a water-hole. Not shy of people. Usually silent, except when breeding. The typical call consists of mellow, fluting whistles 'klu-klu-klu-kluee'.

Feeding methods: A rapacious, powerful predator taking a wide variety of prey, but preferring gamebirds. It hunts either by dashing from a perch like a sparrowhawk, by stooping from soaring flight, or by quartering low over the ground to surprise prey.

Breeding: Season: May to July, rarely later. **Nest:** A substantial platform of sticks in a prominent upper fork of a large tree, often along rivers; rarely on power pylons or cliffs. **Clutch:** 1–3, usually 2 eggs. **Incubation:** 42–44 days, mostly by female. **Nestling:** 61–71 days, fed mostly by female. The oldest chick kills younger ones within the first few days. Dependent on parents for up to 2 months after leaving nest.

Origin of name: *Aquila* means 'eagle' in Latin. *Spilos* means 'spotted' and *gaster* 'stomach' in Greek, referring to the spotted underparts. Used to be regarded as conspecific with Bonelli's Eagle (*Hieraaetus fasciatus*) of northern Africa and Eurasia.

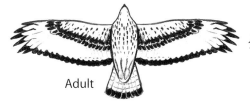

Adult

Juvenile

Possible confusion: Ayres's Hawk-Eagle p. 88, juvenile Black Sparrowhawk p. 136

Graham Kearney

Female

p. 36

p. 224

Richard du Toit

Adult

Bruno Portier

Juvenile

Alan Knott-Craig

Juvenile

Clem Haagner

Female on nest

Graham Kearney

Male

AYRES'S HAWK-EAGLE
Aquila ayresii

Field recognition: Medium. Above slate-black; below white with black blotches. Very similar to the larger, but more slender African Hawk-Eagle to which it should be compared. Ayres's Hawk-Eagle is a small but stockily built eagle with characteristically 'broad shoulders', which indicate powerful flight muscles (see 'Feeding methods'). The underparts, including the leggings, are blotched with spade-shaped markings. As the amount of blotching varies, some individuals seem to have pale and others very dark underparts. (Females are usually more heavily marked than males.) The head has a slight crest, but this is usually not a good field character. The black cap looks like an executioner's mask, as it extends to a line below the eye. The eyebrows may be white and the forehead often has a white patch. The 'shoulders' of the wing have a distinctive white edge, showing as 'landing lights' during flight. It appears much darker than the African Hawk-Eagle in flight, as the underwing coverts are heavily spotted, while the flight feathers are distinctly barred below, but without any white windows from above. A very rare melanistic form exists. **Juv.** The juvenile is grey-brown above and rufous or (rarely) pale below with dark streaks on the chest. It resembles the juvenile African Hawk-Eagle, but is more stockily built, the eye is yellow and in flight the flight feathers and tail are heavily barred below. (See pale juvenile Booted Eagle, p. 82, and juvenile Black Sparrowhawk, p. 136.)

Behaviour: Solitary. Seldom seen as it perches for hours within the canopy of a large leafy tree. Rarely flies above treetops, but often soars to great height, suddenly appearing in swift descending flight. Usually silent.

Feeding methods: A dashing hunter specialising in pursuing birds in flight, combining the speed of a falcon with the agility of a sparrowhawk. Stoops from great height into the forest canopy, wings held in a typical heart-shaped formation, and pursues prey by twisting among branches.

Breeding: Season: April to May, rarely to September. **Nest:** A fairly large nest of sticks, lined with green leaves. Built in a high fork of a large leafy tree in dense woodland. **Clutch:** 1 egg. **Incubation:** 43–45 days by female only. **Nestling:** 73–75 days, fed by female only on food brought mostly by male. Accompanies parents for up to 3 months after first flight.

Origin of name: *Aquila* means 'eagle' in Latin. Thomas Ayres (1828–1918) was one of South Africa's best known ornithologists. The Wing-snapping Cisticola (*Cisticola ayresii*) and the White-winged Flufftail (*Sarothrura ayresi*) are also named in his honour.

Measurements
Length: 46-56 cm
Wingspan: ±124 cm
Weight: 0,71-1,0 kg
Females are larger than males.

Distribution
Africa south of the Sahara. Migrates within Africa.

138   391

Habitat
Dense woodland and forest edge; stands of exotic trees.

Food
Mostly small to medium-sized birds. Occasionally small mammals.

Status
Uncommon to rare. Resident in the north and probably a non-breeding summer visitor to the south of its Southern African distribution.

S: Ayres' Eagle
A: Kleinjagarend
F: Aigle d'Ayres
G: Fleckenadler
P: Águia de Ayres

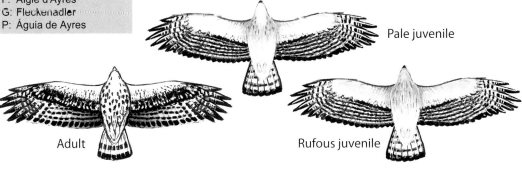

Pale juvenile

Adult

Rufous juvenile

Peter Pickford (SIL)

Dark adult

Ron Hartley

Pale adult

p. 36

p. 224

Ron Hartley

Typical adult

Ron Hartley

Pale juvenile

Ron Hartley

Rufous juvenile

Measurements
Length: 80-92 cm
Wingspan: 152-209 cm
Weight: 2,7-4,12 kg
Females are larger than males.

Distribution
Tropical and Southern Africa.

141   396

Habitat
Mainly forest, but also dense miombo woodland and tall riverine growth.

Food
Mostly mammals such as forest antelope, dassies, monkeys and others. Also medium to larger birds. Occasionally reptiles.

Status
Locally common resident. Numbers declining due to deforestation.

S: Crowned Hawk-Eagle / Crowned Eagle
A: Kroonarend
F: Aigle couronné / Aigle blanchard
G: Kronenadler
P: Águia-coroada

AFRICAN CROWNED EAGLE
Stephanoaetus coronatus

Field recognition: Very large. Africa's most powerful eagle is a typical forest species. Adults are slaty black above and heavily barred with rufous, black and white on the underparts and leggings. (The female is much larger than the male. She is usually more heavily barred with less white on the underparts.) The pronounced crest is not a good field characteristic as it may not be visible. In flight it is hawk-like in appearance, with short, rounded wings and a long tail. The underwing coverts are rufous, while the flight feathers are boldly barred. The tail has three broad dark bars. Perches very erectly. **Juv.** The juvenile is brown-grey on the upperparts, white on the underparts and on the head. The leggings are spotted black. It may have a rufous wash on the chest. In flight it resembles the adult in shape and pattern, as the flight feathers and tail are boldly barred, but the underwing coverts are only pale rufous. It may be confused only with the juvenile Martial Eagle, which is grey on the head and sides of the neck, has unmarked leggings, white underwing coverts, and fine barring on the flight feathers and on the shorter tail. Gradual development into adult plumage takes about four years.

Behaviour: Solitary or in pairs. Usually perches unobtrusively, but may soar above the forest. A very vocal eagle: pairs call during their undulating display flight. The male utters a melodious 'kewee-kewee-kewee-kewee', while the female's voice is lower-pitched and more mellower: 'kooi-kooi-kooi-kooi'.

Feeding methods: A powerful hunter, regularly killing prey in excess of its own body weight – up to 20 kg. Usually hunts from a perch, less often on the wing. Most prey is taken on the ground. Large prey may only be killed after a considerable struggle. It is then dismembered and pieces are cached in tree forks far away to be fed on for the next few days. Pairs may hunt co-operatively and usually feed on each other's kills.

Breeding: Season: Mainly August to October. **Nest:** A huge structure of sticks, lined with green leaves, built in the main fork of a large forest tree. **Clutch:** 1–2 eggs, usually 2. **Incubation:** 49–51 days, mostly by female. **Nestling:** 103–115 days, fed by female on food brought by male. Older chick always kills younger one. Dependent on parents for another 9–11 months after first flight. Breeding usually possible only every alternate year.

Origin of name: *Stephanoaetus* is derived from the Greek *stephanos*, 'crown', and *aetos*, 'eagle'. *Coronatus* is Latin for 'crowned'.

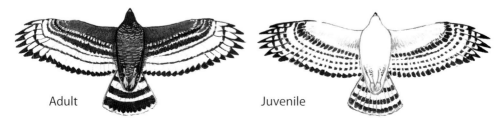

Adult   Juvenile

p. 36

p. 224

Adult

Adult and chick on nest

Juvenile

Juvenile

Adult

91

MARTIAL EAGLE

Polemaetus bellicosus

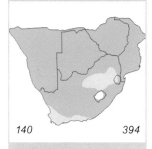

Measurements
Length: 78-83 cm
Wingspan: 195-260 cm
Weight: 3,01-6,2 kg
Females are larger than males.

Distribution
Africa south of the Sahara.

140   394

Habitat
Prefers savanna and bushveld, but occurs in various habitats from semi-desert to woodland.

Food
A wide range of small to medium mammals, medium to large birds, reptiles and even carrion.

Status
Fairly common resident in large conservation areas. Uncommon elsewhere.

S: Martial Hawk-Eagle
A: Breëkoparend
F: Aigle martial
G: Kampfadler
P: Águia-marcial

Field recognition: Very large. The head, upperparts and chest are very dark brown. The rest of the underparts are white with dark brown spots, although these might not be visible at a distance. (Females are more heavily built than males and are more spotted below.) There is a short crest at the back of the large head. The underwings are mostly dark in flight, the tail fairly short and narrowly barred. Similar to the adult Black-chested Snake-Eagle, which is smaller, has unmarked underparts, bare lower legs and mainly white underwings. **Juv.** The juvenile has an overall pale appearance: it is grey above and pure white below. It may be confused only with the juvenile African Crowned Eagle, which prefers forests rather than savanna. It is distinguished from that species by the grey of the upperparts extending onto the sides of the neck and upper chest, and the unmarked leggings. In flight it is mainly white below with fine barring on the wings and tail. The wings are long, whereas the tail is relatively short. The immature retains this plumage until it is about five years old. Over the next two years it then acquires full adult coloration.

Behaviour: A shy, elusive eagle that avoids humans. Solitary or in pairs. Spends most of the day on the wing, often soaring to great height. It is the most aerial of all the large raptors except for vultures and the Bateleur. Sometimes perches on top of a prominent tree or power pylon. Usually silent.

Feeding methods: A versatile hunter whose prey preference varies from region to region. Hunts mostly by soaring high overhead in search of prey, which may be observed at a distance of 5–6 km. Attacks in a long shallow dive, often concealed behind cover to surprise prey. Sometimes hunts from a high, exposed perch, rarely by hovering. Prey too heavy to be lifted to a perch is eaten on the ground. Although small domestic stock is sometimes taken, this eagle has no serious negative impact on farming activities.

Breeding: Season: March to November. **Nest:** A large structure of sturdy sticks, well lined with green leaves. Usually built in the main fork of a large tree, but even on power pylons and cliffs. **Clutch:** 1 egg. **Incubation:** 47–53 days, by female only. **Nestling:** 96–99 days, fed by female only on food brought mostly by male. Dependent on parents for another 3–8 months.

Origin of name: Both the common and scientific names refer to the fact that this eagle is a versatile, aggressive hunter, often taking large prey. *Polemaetus* is derived from the Greek *polemos*, 'war', and *aetos*, 'eagle'. *Bellicosus* is a Latin word meaning 'warlike'.

Adult   Juvenile

Lizeth Cillié

Adult

Niel Cillié

Adult

p. 36

p. 224

Mark Anderson

Juvenile

Graham Kearney

Immature

Burger Cillié

Juvenile

93

BLACK-CHESTED SNAKE-EAGLE
Circaetus pectoralis

Measurements
Length: 63-68 cm
Wingspan: 152-209 (190) cm
Weight: 1,18-2,26 (1,5) kg
Females are larger
than males.

Distribution
From Southern Africa
north to the Congo River
and Ethiopia.

143   360

Habitat
From desert to open
woodland, but preferring
open, arid regions with
scattered trees.

Food
Mostly snakes. Also
lizards, rodents, frogs,
fish, insects and
sometimes birds.

Status
Possibly two populations:
one of nomadic residents
and another of non-
breeding summer visitors.

S: Black-breasted Snake-
    Eagle / Black-breasted
    Harrier-Eagle
A: Swartborsslangarend
F: Circaète à poitrine noire
G: Schwarzbrust-
    Schlangenadler
P: Águia-cobreira-de-
    peito-preto

Field recognition: Large. The head, upperparts and chest are blackish, while the rest of the underparts are white. May be confused only with the adult Martial Eagle, but the white underparts are unmarked, the white lower legs are bare and the underwing is white in flight, with bold barring on the flight and tail feathers. It also differs from the Martial Eagle by being smaller and having the typical body shape and large yellow eyes of a snake-eagle.
Juv. The juvenile is easily confused with other snake-eagles, especially the Brown Snake-Eagle, but has a more rufous brown appearance. The upperparts are darker than the underparts, which vary from pale tawny to dark rufous brown. In flight the underwing coverts are the same rich colour as the underparts, while the flight feathers (which show three indistinct narrow bars) and tail are pale. At about six months a few blackish feathers appear on the chest. By eight months the rufous brown colour, especially of the head and upperparts, changes to grey-brown. From ten months the first white feathers appear on the belly. The immature's colour slowly changes until the last brown spots on the belly and leggings disappear and full adult plumage is attained in the third year.

Behaviour: Usually solitary, but may roost communally when not breeding. Such birds spread out during the day although they may hunt in sight of each other. When breeding, various melodious, fluting calls are uttered, one of which is very similar to the call of the African Fish-Eagle.

Feeding methods: Takes a wider variety of prey than other snake-eagles. Although it perch-hunts for long periods, this snake-eagle spends much time on the wing in search of prey. It soars well and is the largest raptor to hover regularly. Drops down like a parachute, often in stages, until it plunges onto its prey. Smaller snakes are swallowed head first, often in flight, while larger prey is dismembered and eaten on the ground.

Breeding: Season: Any month of the year, peaking August to November.
Nest: A small platform of thin sticks, with a deep cup lined with green leaves. Built on top of flat-crowned tree or euphorbia. **Clutch:** 1 egg. **Incubation:** 51–52 days, mostly by female. **Nestling:** 89–90 days, fed by both parents. Partially dependent on parents for another 6 months.

Origin of name: *Circaetus* is derived from the Greek *kirkos*, 'harrier', and *aetos*, 'eagle'. (Snake-eagles are often called harrier-eagles.) The name *pectoralis* refers to the chest, which distinguishes this species.

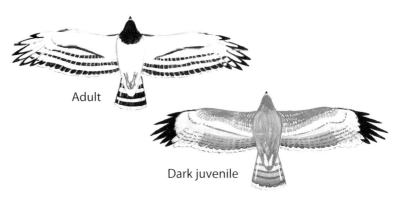

Adult

Dark juvenile

Possible confusion: Martial Eagle p. 92, Brown Snake-Eagle p. 100, juvenile Bateleur p. 102

Adult

Brendan Ryan

Pale juvenile

Geoff McIlleron

p. 37

p. 232

Sub-adult

Niel Cillié

Immature

Niel Cillié

Adult

Burger Cillié

Dark juvenile

Simon du Plessis

SOUTHERN BANDED SNAKE-EAGLE
Circaetus fasciolatus

Measurements
Length: 55-60 cm
Wingspan: ±120 cm
Weight: 0,91-1,11 kg
Females are larger than males.

Distribution
From northern KwaZulu-Natal along the coastal plain to Kenya.

144   362

Habitat
Prefers lowland evergreen forest and dense woodland. Sometimes occurs in adjacent savanna or stands of alien trees.

Food
Mostly snakes and lizards. Very rarely other small animals.

Status
Rare, localised resident.

S: Fasciolated Snake-Eagle / Fasciated Snake-Eagle
A: Dubbelbandslangarend
F: Circaète barré
G. Graubrust Schlangenadler
P: Águia-cobreira-barrada

Field recognition: Medium-large. A small, stockily built snake-eagle. The overall colour is greyish brown with conspicuous white barring from the lower chest to the belly and thighs. The tail shows three dark and two white bars (hence the Afrikaans name), which are clearly visible in flight. At rest the long tail extends well beyond the tips of the folded wings. Could be confused with the Western Banded Snake-Eagle, but the two do not overlap in distribution. (The Western Banded Snake-Eagle is only indistinctly barred on the lower belly and thighs, and its short, dark tail has a single broad white bar.) It could also be confused with the African Cuckoo-Hawk, but is much larger, has the typical large rounded head and large, owl-like yellow eyes of all snake-eagles, and has a shorter tail. The bill is black, the cere yellow and the legs pale yellow. In flight the white underwing is heavily barred with a dark trailing edge. **Juv.** The overall impression of the juvenile is of a snake-eagle with dark brown upperparts and pale underparts and head. The head and chest are streaked brown. The rest of the underparts may be slightly buffy and are barred brown on the flanks. In flight the pattern of barring on the underwings and tail is similar to that of the adult. The cere and legs are a richer yellow than in the adult. The sub-adult probably has a browner head with some white streaks and whiter underparts than the juvenile.

Behaviour: A shy and retiring snake-eagle that usually keeps to the cover of heavy woodland and forest. In the early morning it can sometimes be seen perched conspicuously on a dead tree at the edge of a clearing. When disturbed it flies a short distance to another perch. The main call is a rapid, high-pitched 'ko-ko-ko-ko-kaauw', which betrays its presence.

Feeding methods: It searches for prey, mainly snakes and lizards, by still-hunting from a perch, scanning the ground carefully.

Breeding: Little known. **Season:** August to October. **Nest:** A small platform of twigs, the central cup lined with green leaves. Built in a fork below the canopy of a forest tree. **Clutch:** 1 egg. **Incubation:** 49–51 days, mainly by female. **Nestling:** Unrecorded.

Origin of name: *Circaetus* is derived from the Greek *kirkos*, 'harrier', and *aetos*, 'eagle'. (Snake-eagles are often called harrier-eagles.) *Fasciolatus* is Latin for 'broadly transversely barred', referring to the bands on the tail.

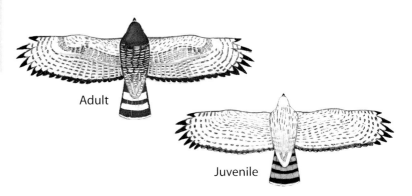

Adult

Juvenile

Possible confusion: Western Banded Snake-Eagle p. 98, African Cuckoo-Hawk p. 150

Johan van Rensburg

Adult

Bazil Boer

Adult

Johan van Rensburg

Adult

Johan van Rensburg

Adult

Bruce Stephenson

Juvenile

p. 37

p. 232

97

WESTERN BANDED SNAKE-EAGLE
Circaetus cinerascens

Measurements
Length: 55-60 cm
Wingspan: ±114 cm
Weight: ±1,13 kg
Females are larger than males.

Distribution
Patches of suitable habitat in tropical Africa. In Southern Africa along the Okavango, Chobe and Zambezi Rivers and some of their tributaries. (Does not overlap with the Southern Banded Snake-Eagle in Southern Africa.)

145   363

Habitat
Riverine woodland.

Food
Mostly snakes. Also a variety of other small animals.

Status
Uncommon resident.

S: Banded Snake-Eagle / Smaller Banded Snake-Eagle / Banded Harrier-Eagle
A: Enkelbandslangarend
F: Circaète cendré
G: Bandschlangenadler
P: Águia-cobreira-de-cauda-branca

Field recognition: Medium-large. A small, stockily built snake-eagle, with an ashy-brown overall colour. (Males are darker than females.) The belly and thighs are faintly barred. The female has less barring on the underparts, but the bars are more distinct. The single broad white band on the dark tail is diagnostic. The tail is short, reaching to the tip of the folded wing. It is similar to the Southern Banded Snake-Eagle, which occurs more easterly in Southern Africa. (The Southern Banded Snake-Eagle has clear barring on the lower chest, belly and thighs, and two white bands across a longer tail.) It may also be confused with the Brown Snake-Eagle, as the barring on the belly may be absent or difficult to see. Then it is distinguished by its overall greyer colour and especially the yellow legs and yellow-orange cere and base of the bill. The flight pattern is similar to that of the Southern Banded Snake-Eagle, but shows less barring on the underwing. Again the tail pattern is diagnostic. **Juv.** The juvenile has brown upperparts with buffy barring on the upperwing coverts. The crown is whitish with darker streaks. The underparts are buffy white. The tail is pale brown with a dark terminal band, but without the broad white band of the adult. The bill is dark, but the cere yellow. Immatures become mottled with brown until sub-adulthood, when they are all dark brown, assuming barring on the belly and thighs only when fully adult.

Behaviour: A secretive bird, perching for hours hidden in the canopy of a tree. Sometimes sits on a dead tree in the open. In spite of this, it is not shy and may be approached quite closely. Does not fly far. The call is like that of the Southern Banded Snake-Eagle, but louder and more staccato: 'kok-kok-kokkok-ko-ho'.

Feeding methods: Perch-hunts for long periods. Swoops down to the ground, but also catches prey in trees. Usually returns to the perch to feed.

Breeding: Little known. **Season:** Probably December to April. **Nest:** A small platform of pliable sticks, with a deep central cup lined with leaves. Built below the canopy of large trees. May use the old nests of other raptors. **Clutch:** 1 egg. **Incubation:** Estimated 36–42 days. **Nestling:** ±56 days.

Origin of name: *Circaetus* is derived from the Greek *kirkos*, 'harrier', and *aetos*, 'eagle'. (Snake-eagles are often called harrier-eagles.) The Latin word *cinerascens* means 'becoming grey or ashy', referring to the bird's colour.

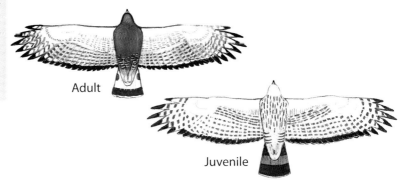

Adult

Juvenile

Albert Froneman

Adult

Henri Royer

Adult

p. 37

p. 232

Ulrich Oberprieler

Adult

Nigel Voaden

BROWN SNAKE-EAGLE

Circaetus cinereus

Measurements
Length: 71-76 cm
Wingspan: ±164 cm
Weight: 1,54-2,47 (2,05) kg
Females are larger than males.

Distribution
Africa south of the Sahara.

142   361

Habitat
Savanna, bushveld and woodland. Prefers more wooded country than the Black-chested Snake-Eagle.

Food
Mostly snakes, including venomous species up to 3 m long. Also lizards.

Status
Resident, somewhat nomadic. Common in the north and northeast. Rare or a vagrant in the south.

S: Brown Harrier-Eagle
A: Bruinslangarend
F: Circaète brun
G: Brauner Schlangenadler / Einfarb-Schlangenadler
P: Águia-cobreira-castanha

Field recognition: Large. The largest snake-eagle. The plumage is dark brown all over. It may be confused with various large brown eagles, but is a typical snake-eagle with a large rounded head, large owl-like yellow eyes and unfeathered lower legs (which are grey-white in colour). It could also be confused with the juvenile Black-chested Snake-Eagle, which is a richer rufous brown colour, the Western Banded Snake-Eagle, which is faintly barred on the belly and flanks, has yellow legs and a yellow-orange cere and base of the bill, or even the immature Bateleur, which has dark eyes and a characteristic stumpy tail. In flight the brown underwing coverts of the Brown Snake-Eagle contrast strongly with the silvery-grey flight feathers. The three narrow pale bars on the tail are not always obvious. **Juv.** Juveniles are very variable. Some are indistinguishable from adults, while others are paler, or have white mottling on the chest and belly, or even have white streaks on the crown. Adults, however, may also appear mottled with white when they are moulting.

Behaviour: Usually solitary, even members of a pair do not stay close to each other. A sluggish bird that is mostly seen perched on a tree or hilltop. A loud 'kok-kok-kok-kok-kaauw' is uttered during the display flight.

Feeding methods: Normally hunts from a perch on top of a tree, rarely by soaring or hovering. Prey is caught and usually eaten on the ground. Snakes are killed by gripping them with the short, strong toes. As even large venomous species are caught, the legs are protected by heavy scales. The snake also harmlessly strikes at the dense belly feathers or at the spread wings. Snakes are transported to the nest in typical snake-eagle fashion, by being swallowed with only the tail tip hanging from the bill. The nestling then pulls the prey from the adult's stomach.

Breeding: Season: Mostly midsummer, especially December to March, but may start breeding in July. **Nest:** A small platform of thin twigs, lined with leaves. Built on top of a flat-crowned tree or euphorbia. **Clutch:** 1 egg. **Incubation:** 48–53 days, by female only. **Nestling:** 97–113 days. The juvenile becomes independent very rapidly, at most after 2 months.

Origin of name: *Circaetus* is derived from the Greek *kirkos*, 'harrier', and *aetos*, 'eagle'. (Snake-eagles are often called harrier-eagles.) The name *cinereus*, meaning 'grey or ashy', is not accurate as the plumage is brown.

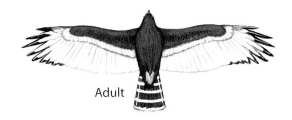

Adult

Burger Cillié

Immature

Albert Froneman

Adult

Sue Robinson

Juvenile

p. 37

p. 232

Ulrich Oberprieler

Immature

Burger Cillié

Adult

Measurements
Length: 55-70 cm
Wingspan: 173-177 cm
Weight: 1,82-2,95 (2,24) kg
Females are larger
than males.

Distribution
Widespread in Africa
south of the Sahara, as
well as in Arabia.

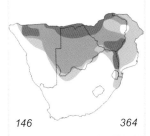

146   364

Habitat
Woodland and savanna.

Food
Mostly birds and small
mammals, but also
carrion, eggs, reptiles,
fish, crabs and insects.

Status
Common resident in
conservation areas, but
rare or even extinct in
developed regions.

A: Berghaan /
   Stompstertarend
F: Bateleur des savanes
G: Gaukler
P: Águia-bailarina

BATELEUR
Terathopius ecaudatus

Field recognition: Large. Adults are easily recognised: black, stockily built, snake-eagle-like raptors with characteristically short tails. The eyes are dark, not yellow as in true snake-eagles. The legs and the bare face are red. The back and tail are usually chestnut, but the back may be cream in a few individuals. The male has black flight feathers while those of the female are pale, showing as a paler window towards the wingtip of the perching bird. In flight the wings are long and tapering; the legs extend beyond the short tail. Again the female can be recognised by the larger white area on the underwing. **Juv.** The juvenile is brown but can be distinguished from similar raptors by its dark eye, bare face and characteristic body shape with a large head and short tail. As full adult plumage is only acquired after 7–8 years, sub-adult birds with mottled plumage are often seen.

Behaviour: Mostly solitary, but sometimes occurs in temporary flocks, especially at water, where it may mix with other raptor species. Spends most of the day in flight, soaring at 50–80 km/h. In this way it can cover several hundred kilometres daily. The flight action, slowly rocking from side to side, is characteristic. Usually quiet, its main call is a barking 'kow-ow'. Sometimes calls softly 'kya-kya-kya-kya' while sitting.

Feeding methods: Catches mostly birds (such as hornbills, rollers, starlings and francolin) and small mammals (such as rats and hares), either by stooping in flight or by parachuting slowly with wings held up and legs extended. Reptiles, crabs, insects and eggs of ground-nesting birds are also eaten. Most prey is caught on the ground, but birds may be taken on the wing. Carrion is an important part of the diet. Although sometimes seen together with vultures at larger carcasses, it regularly feeds on the dead bodies of smaller animals, such as road kills of birds, mammals and reptiles. Unfortunately Bateleurs are attracted to poisoned bait put out for jackals and other 'problem animals' and are unnecessarily killed in this way.

Breeding: Season: Throughout the year, but peaking in January to March. **Nest:** A small platform of sticks, built in the canopy of a large tree. **Clutch:** 1 egg. **Incubation:** 52–59 days, mostly by female. **Nestling:** 111–112 days, fed for another 90–120 days by both parents after leaving the nest.

Origin of name: *Terathopius* means 'pretty face', while *ecaudatus* refers to its tailless appearance. François Levaillant (1753–1824) named it Bateleur (French for 'tightrope walker') in reference to its rocking flight action.

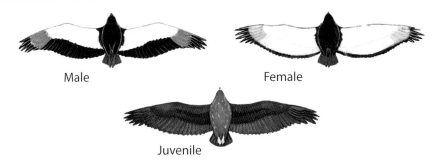

Male   Female

Juvenile

Possible confusion: Jackal Buzzard p. 106, Brown Snake-Eagle p. 100, juvenile Black-chested Snake-Eagle p. 94

Niel Cillié

Male

Albert Froneman

Female

Johan & Louise van Heerden

Cream-backed male

Johan Knobel

Sub-adult

p. 37

p. 232

Niel Cillié

Juvenile

Burger Cillié

Immature

AUGUR BUZZARD

Buteo augur

Measurements
Length: 55-60 cm
Wingspan: ±132 cm
Weight: ♂ 0,88-1,16 (1,0) kg
♀ 1,1-1,3 (1.13) kg

Distribution
From the northern regions of Southern Africa through eastern Africa to Ethiopia.

153   384

Habitat
Mountains, hilly country and granite inselbergs in woodland, savanna and desert.

Food
Mostly snakes and lizards. Also small mammals, birds and insects.

Status
Breeding resident; locally fairly common.

A Witborsjakkalsvoël
F: Buse augure
G: Augurbussard
P: Bútio-augur

Field recognition: Medium-large. A characteristically pied buzzard of mountainous country that may only be confused with the Black Sparrowhawk, but is much larger and differs in habitat and behaviour. The upperparts are slaty black with some white markings. The underparts are completely white in the male, but the female has black streaks on the throat and upper chest. The tail is deep rufous. The eyes are dark brown, the cere and legs yellow. (Melanistic birds occur in eastern Africa and are quite common in some wet, forested mountains of Ethiopia, but only partially melanistic individuals have been seen in Southern Africa. These have some black blotches on the belly and underwing coverts.) In flight the white underparts as well as the white underwing with a black trailing edge and tip contrast with the broad, rufous tail. These characteristics distinguish it from the Bateleur and Black-chested Snake-Eagle. **Juv.** The juvenile may be confused with the juvenile Jackal Buzzard (especially in central Namibia where both species occur). The upperparts are grey-brown with some buff markings. The underparts are buff to nearly white with a variable amount of streaks on the sides of the throat and chest. The tail is a pale rufous brown with indistinct barring. In flight the underwing coverts are also buff, while the white flight feathers have a dark trailing edge and faint bars.

Behaviour: Very similar to that of the Jackal Buzzard. Solitary or in pairs. Perches for long periods on conspicuous posts such as rocks, trees or telephone poles, but soars and hovers often. The call is a yelping 'kow-kow-kow-kow'.

Feeding methods: Hunts from a perch, swooping down onto ground-living prey. Also regularly searches for prey from a soaring or hovering position, then drops down like a parachute, with legs extended.

Breeding: Season: July to November, peaking from August to October. **Nest:** A substantial platform of sticks, the central cup lined with green leaves. Usually built on a cliff ledge, less often at the base or even in the branches of a small tree growing from a cliff, and rarely in trees on wooded hillsides. **Clutch:** 2 eggs, rarely 1 or 3. **Incubation:** 39–40 days, mostly by female. **Nestling:** 48–55 days, fed mainly by female. The older chick kills its younger sibling within the first week. Juvenile dependent on parents for another 6–7 weeks.

Origin of name: *Buteo* is Latin for a kind of raptor. An augur was a prophet or soothsayer in ancient Rome, who interpreted omens from a variety of phenomena, including the behaviour of birds. It is not certain why the buzzard was given this name as it is not used in augury by local people.

Adult   Juvenile

Veronica Roodt

Female

Brendan Ryan

Male

Atle Helge Qvale

Female

p. 38

p. 236

Richard du Toit

Juvenile

Mark Anderson

Immature

105

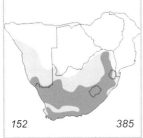

JACKAL BUZZARD
Buteo rufofuscus

Measurements
Length: 55-60 cm
Wingspan: ±132 cm
Weight:
♂ 0,86-1,08 (0,95) kg
♀ 1,15-1,69 (1,3) kg

Distribution
Endemic to Southern Africa.

152   385

Habitat
Mountainous and hilly country, favouring areas covered with grass or other short vegetation.

Food
Mostly small rodents, but also other small mammals up to size of dassie, birds up to size of francolin, reptiles, insects and carrion.

Status
Breeding resident; locally common. May be locally nomadic.

A: Rooiborsjakkalsvoël
F: Buse rounoir
G: Felsenbussard
P: Bútio-de-cauda-
    vermelha

Field recognition: Medium-large. Unmistakable. The plumage is slaty black except for the rufous chest and tail, some white markings on the upperparts, an irregular white band above the rufous chest and a varying amount of white barring or blotches on the dark belly and thighs. The eyes are dark brown, the cere and legs yellow. (Melanistic individuals with completely black underparts are very rare, as are pale individuals, with a dull white chest that merges into the darker belly. The latter resemble the Augur Buzzard, but are distinguished by the distinctive underwing pattern of the typical Jackal Buzzard.) In flight the underwing coverts are dark, while the flight feathers are white with a dark trailing edge and indistinct barring. The broad, rufous tail remains diagnostic and distinguishes it from the Bateleur.
Juv. The juvenile can easily be confused with various brown buzzards, including the juvenile Augur Buzzard in central Namibia. The upperparts are brown with some buff markings, especially on the wing coverts. The underparts are uniform rufous (not buff as in the juvenile Augur Buzzard and lacking the darker markings of the other brown buzzards). The tail is grey-brown with indistinct bars. The underwing resembles that of the adult in flight, but the coverts and the trailing edge of the wing are rufous, not black. Full adult plumage is attained when 2–3 years old.

Behaviour: Solitary or in pairs. Perches inconspicuously on rocks, trees or utility poles. Usually seen in flight. The call is reminiscent of that of the Black-backed Jackal, a yelping 'kyaa-ka-ka-ka', hence the name. Behaviour similar to that of the Augur Buzzard, but the two species overlap only in Namibia.

Feeding methods: Usually catches prey on the ground, either from a perch or from a soaring position. Often hangs on updraughts of air above a hill or hovers while gently flapping its wings, then parachutes down onto prey. Rarely pursues flying prey in a dashing stoop.

Breeding: Season: May to October with a peak from August to September. **Nest:** A large platform of sticks lined with green leaves, usually built on a cliff ledge (often at the base of a small tree or bush) or rarely in a tall tree such as a pine. **Clutch:** 1–3 eggs, usually 2. **Incubation:** 39–40 days by both sexes. **Nestling:** 50–53 days, fed mostly by female. Older chick often, but not always, kills younger sibling.

Origin of name: *Buteo* is Latin for a kind of raptor, while *rufofuscus* means 'dusky red', referring to the chest and tail.

Adult

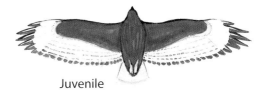

Juvenile

Geoff McIlleron

Adult

Albert Froneman

Adult

p. 38

p. 236

Ulrich Oberprieler

Pale adult

Mark Anderson

Juvenile

Ulrich Oberprieler

Juvenile

107

STEPPE BUZZARD
Buteo vulpinus

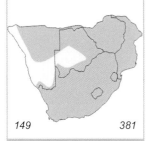

Measurements
Length: 45-50 cm
Wingspan: 102-128 cm
Weight: 453-1 000 g
Females are larger than males.

Distribution
Breeds in Eurasia. Migrates to Africa and southern Asia when not breeding.

149   381

Habitat
Favours open country, from fynbos to open woodland. May occur in denser vegetation.

Food
Mostly small rodents and large insects. Also small birds, reptiles and frogs.

Status
Common non-breeding summer visitor. Some birds may overwinter.

A: Bruinjakkalsvoël
F: Buse des steppes
G: Falkenbussard
P: Bútio-das-estepes

Field recognition: Medium. This common summer visitor may be confused with especially the resident Forest Buzzard, but also with the European Honey-Buzzard (a rare summer visitor), Long-legged Buzzard (a very rare vagrant) and juvenile Jackal and Augur Buzzards (both residents). The plumage varies from pale sandy brown to rufous brown to very dark brown. The upperparts are fairly uniform, but the barred tail is slightly rufous, and the head and rump often streaked. The underparts are extremely variable. The darkest individuals have completely dark chocolate-brown underparts. Most individuals, however, have pale underparts with a varying degree of darker markings and a characteristic, more or less distinct pale band across the lower chest. The upper chest may be mottled or blotched, whereas the belly is always barred, sometimes very heavily so that only indistinct pale bands are visible and sometimes so lightly that the darker bands are barely discernible. (The Forest Buzzard never has barred underparts.) The eyes are brown. The tail is barred, with a broad dark band at the tip. In flight the underwing coverts match the colour of the chest. The flight feathers are barred with a dark trailing edge. **Juv.** The juvenile is streaked, not barred, on the underparts. It also differs from the adult in that it has pale eyes and the band across the tip of the tail is the same width as the rest of the tail bands. It is virtually indistinguishable from the juvenile Forest Buzzard, although the streaks on the underparts are thinner.

Behaviour: One of Southern Africa's most common medium-sized brown raptors during the summer season. Usually seen perched on telephone posts or similar conspicuous perches, especially in open country. (The Forest Buzzard prefers forests and plantations.) Soars on wings held slightly forward. Solitary, but occurs in flocks at a good food source or on migration. Usually silent.

Feeding methods: Usually hunts by gliding down from a perch. May sometimes hover or walk around on the ground in search of prey.

Breeding: Breeds from eastern Europe to central Asia. Migrates to Southern and eastern Africa as well as southern Asia when not breeding.

Origin of name: The steppe is a flat grassy plain with few trees, especially in south-eastern Europe and Siberia. *Buteo* is Latin for a kind of raptor. *Vulpinus* means 'fox-like', referring to the colouration. The Steppe Buzzard used to be regarded as a subspecies of the Common Buzzard (*Buteo buteo*).

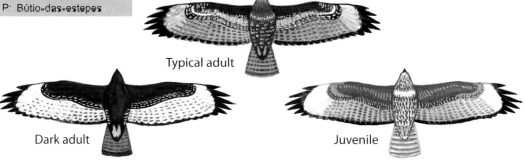

Typical adult

Dark adult

Juvenile

Niel Cillié

Adult

Niel Cillié

Adult

p. 38

p. 236

Fanie Hendriks

Juvenile

Heinrich van den Berg

Adult

Basil Boer

Dark adult

FOREST BUZZARD
Buteo trizonatus

Measurements
Length: 45-50 cm
Wingspan: 102-118 cm
Weight: ♂ ±570 g
♀ ±660 g
Females are larger
than males.

Distribution
Endemic to South Africa.

150   382

Habitat
Breeds in indigenous
forests and plantations of
exotic trees. Hunts mostly
in the mosaic of forest,
fynbos, grassland and
agricultural land.

Food
Mostly small rodents. Also
other small mammals and
birds, reptiles, frogs and
insects.

Status
Uncommon to locally
common resident and
local migrant.

A: Bosjakkalsvoël
F: Buse forestière
G: Waldbussard
P: Bútio-da-floresta

Field recognition: Medium. A small brown buzzard hard to distinguish from the Steppe Buzzard, although habitat and status are good pointers: the Forest Buzzard is an uncommon resident and local migrant inhabiting forests and plantations, whereas the Steppe Buzzard is a common summer visitor which occurs mostly in open country. As Steppe Buzzards sometimes overwinter and both species may occur outside their typical habitat, the following features of the Forest Buzzard should be noted. The underparts usually appear whiter than in the Steppe Buzzard as they show a similar, but broader pale band across the lower chest. The belly is blotched or streaked with tear-shaped markings, never barred. The adult Forest Buzzard thus resembles the juvenile Steppe Buzzard, except for the brown eyes and the broad band across the tip of the barred tail. The flight pattern resembles that of the Steppe Buzzard. **Juv.** The juvenile differs from the adult in that it is often even whiter on the underparts, the eyes are pale and it also lacks the wider band across the tail tip. It is basically indistinguishable from the juvenile Steppe Buzzard, although at close range the markings on the underparts are broader, more tear-shaped. Precise differentiation between the two is improbable in the field.

Behaviour: Usually seen when soaring over its forest habitat as the mottled plumage camouflages it well when perched quietly within the cover of a forest tree. Occurs singly or in pairs, not in flocks as Steppe Buzzards may. During the breeding season it calls often: a clear, drawn-out 'pee-ooo', repeated at intervals. (The Steppe Buzzard rarely calls.) It appears to be resident in the coastal forests of the southern part of its range. Non-breeding birds move northwards, especially during winter.

Feeding methods: Usually hunts from a perch within the canopy of a tree, dropping onto prey on the ground. It prefers to hunt in the mosaic of forest patches within various more open habitats, but may also hunt inside the forest.

Breeding: Season: August to November, peaking September to October. **Nest:** A fairly large platform of sticks built high up in the fork of a tree, often indigenous yellowwood or exotic pine trees. **Clutch:** 2 eggs. **Incubation:** Unrecorded, probably about 30 days. **Nestling:** About 50 days. Cared for by parents for another 80–130 days.

Origin of name: *Buteo* is Latin for a kind of raptor. *Trizonatus* refers to the three bands of patterning on the underparts. It used to be regarded as conspecific with the Mountain Buzzard (*Buteo oreophilus*) of eastern Africa.

Adult   Juvenile

Geoff McIlleron

Adult and chick on nest

Ulrich Oberprieler

Adult

Guy Palmer

Juvenile

Alan Knott-Craig

Adult

p. 38

p. 236

LONG-LEGGED BUZZARD
Buteo rufinus

Measurements
Length: 51-66 cm
Wingspan: 126-155 cm
Weight: ♂ 0,59-1,28 (1,04) kg
♀ 0,95-1,76 (1,31) kg

Distribution
Breeds in south-eastern
Europe, Asia and north
Africa. Migrates to north-
eastern Africa as well as
northern India when not
breeding.

151   383

Habitat
Savanna to semi-desert.

Food
Mostly small mammals.
Also reptiles, birds and
carrion.

Status
Rare non-breeding
summer vagrant. The
validity of most Southern
African records is
controversial.

A: Langbeenjakkalsvoël
F: Buse féroce
G: Adlerbussard
P: Bútio-mouro

Field recognition: Medium-large. An extremely rare summer vagrant easy to confuse with especially the Steppe Buzzard, but also the Forest Buzzard (an uncommon resident), European Honey-Buzzard (a rare summer visitor) and juvenile Jackal and Augur Buzzards (both residents). The distinguishing characteristics are the large size (like a small eagle), noticeably long legs when perched, plain pale rufous to almost white tail (except in the dark form) which contrasts with the darker rump and thighs, and the head and chest which are much paler than the rest of the body. The plumage is very variable, but three basic forms may be distinguished. The rare dark form is dark brown all over except for some rufous edges to the feathers of the head. The tail is barred with a broad dark band at the tip. The belly (always streaked, barred or mottled with brown to a varying degree) of the typical form varies from rufous to yellow-brown, whereas that of the pale form is almost white. The flight pattern also resembles that of the Steppe Buzzard, but the wings appear longer and more rectangular. Again the plain pale tail should be noted. **Juv.** The juveniles resemble the various adult morphs. It has pale yellow eyes, appears more mottled on the upperparts and the tail has numerous dark bars. It is extremely difficult to distinguish from the juvenile Steppe Buzzard except for the longer legs when perched. In flight it generally appears paler than the adult. The pale tail, although barred, remains characteristic.

Behaviour: A rather sluggish buzzard. Usually seen perched on a prominent post, tree, rock or on the ground in arid regions. Flies less often than smaller buzzards. The flight is slow and heavy when rising, but it soars easily. Rarely hovers while soaring into the wind, scanning the ground below. Usually silent. As this buzzard rarely occurs in Africa south of the equator, any possible sightings should be carefully authenticated.

Feeding methods: Hunts by perching prominently and scanning the ground for small prey. May also hunt on the ground or from soaring flight. Usually solitary, but may associate with Tawny or Steppe Eagles on occasions when rodent prey is abundant.

Breeding: Breeds in south-eastern Europe, Asia and Africa north of the Sahara. Non-breeding birds usually migrate into Africa to just south of the Sahara, or to northern India.

Origin of name: *Buteo* is Latin for a kind of raptor, while *rufinus* means 'reddish'.

Adult   Juvenile

C. Hans Gebuis (Aquila)

Jan Ševčík

Adult

Juvenile

p. 38

p. 236

Paul Bamford

Adult

Daniele Occhiato

Juvenile

113

EUROPEAN HONEY-BUZZARD
Pernis apivorus

Measurements
Length: 52-60 cm
Wingspan: 130-150 cm
Weight: ♂ 510-800 (684) g
♀ 625-1 050 (832) g

Distribution
Breeds in Europe and western Asia. Migrates to Africa when not breeding.

130   *346*

Habitat
Woodland and forest edge.

Food
Mainly the larvae and pupae of wasps. Also other insects and invertebrates, small vertebrates, birds' eggs and some vegetable matter such as berries.

Status
Uncommon but regular non-breeding summer visitor.

S: Eurasian Honey-Buzzard / Western Honey-Buzzard
A: Wespedief
F: Bondrée apivore
G: Wespenbussard
P: Bútio-vespeiro

Field recognition: Medium. Very variable and thus difficult to identify. Most easily confused with the Steppe Buzzard, but the more slender body and longer tail, bright eyes (orange in males and yellow in females) and especially the distinctly pigeon-like appearance of the head and bill are characteristic. Most diagnostic are the two broad dark bars at the base of the tail and its broad dark tip. The short legs are yellow and the cere grey. The upperparts are dark (usually grey-brown with a grey head in males and brown, including the head, in females). The colour of the underparts is extremely variable, but three basic forms may be recognised. The underparts of the most common form are barred brown and white. The pale form has white underparts, either plain or streaked and spotted to a varying degree, while the dark form has pale to dark brown unmarked underparts. The small, protruding head characterises the flight silhouette. The underwing is variable according to the colour form, but shows dark wrist patches. Again the pattern on the tail is diagnostic. Flies with deep, relaxed wing beats and holds the wings flat while soaring. **Juv.** As juveniles are as variable as adults, the pigeon-like head and bill remain a good field character. The eyes are brown, the cere and legs yellow and it has four evenly spaced but indistinct bars on the tail. The pale form has a white head with a dark eye patch.

Behaviour: Although large numbers of European Honey-Buzzards fly southwards from Europe at the end of the northern summer, it is considered uncommon to rare throughout Africa. This is probably because it is a solitary, secretive species which spends much time within the cover of trees.

Feeding methods: Various hunting techniques are employed. It snatches wasp nests from trees or from under the eaves of buildings, but may also hunt from a perch, catching insects either on the ground or in flight. It also walks around on the ground in search of prey and may even dig wasp nests out of the ground with its feet, sometimes to a depth of 40 cm. The dense feathers on the face and the thick leg scales protect it against stings.

Breeding: Breeds in Europe and western Asia. Migrates to Africa south of the Sahara when not breeding.

Origin of name: *Pernis* is a corruption of the Greek word *pternis*, 'bird of prey'. The Latin words *apis* and *vorare* mean 'bee' and 'to devour' respectively, i.e. a bee-eater.

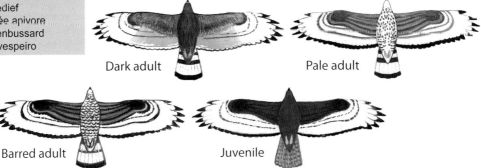

Dark adult   Pale adult

Barred adult   Juvenile

Dark female

Dark female

Pale female

Barred male

Barred male

Juvenile

p. 38

p. 236

115

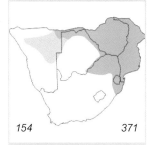

Measurements
Length: 35-37 cm
Wingspan: ±79 cm
Weight: ♂ 220-275 (246) g
♀ 248-374 (304) g

Distribution
Africa south of the Sahara.

154   371

Habitat
Woodland and savanna,
favouring mature
broadleaved woodland
when breeding, also
occurring in more arid
thornveld in winter.

Food
Mostly insects, also
lizards, small snakes,
rodents and other small
mammals, birds and frogs.

Status
Fairly common resident;
somewhat nomadic.

S: Lizard Hawk (probably a
    better name as it is not a
    typical buzzard)
A: Akkedisvalk
F: Buse unibande / Autour
    unibande
G: Sperberbussard /
    Kehlstreifbussard
P: Gavião-papa-lagartos

LIZARD BUZZARD
Kaupifalco monogrammicus

Field recognition: Medium-small. Mainly grey with black-and-white barring on the belly. The chest is grey. The eyes are dark red-brown. The cere and legs are red to orange-red. The vertical black streak on the centre of the throat distinguishes it from the similar Gabar Goshawk and the chanting goshawks. In flight the white rump and broad white tail bar (rarely two) are conspicuous. The flight pattern is undulating like that of a woodpecker. It is larger and bulkier than the Gabar Goshawk, which lacks the black streak on the throat, but has several pale bars on the tail in addition to the white rump. The chanting goshawks are larger and have a characteristic body shape. **Juv.** The juvenile resembles the adult very closely. It has a slight brown wash over its grey plumage with buff edges to the upperwing coverts. The colour of the legs and cere is slightly paler than the adult's. The eyes are brown.

Behaviour: Solitary. Usually seen perched in a tree, often quite conspicuously, while scanning the ground for prey. Regularly drops down from the perch, flies low over the ground and swoops up to a new vantage point. Rarely flies or soars above the tree canopy, except during courtship display. Most common in moist, broadleaved woodland such as miombo, but moves into more arid savanna during winter. Usually silent, except at the beginning of the breeding season when it utters a far-carrying clear and melodious whistle. Calls from a perch or in flight.

Feeding methods: Scans the ground intently from a perch and catches its prey after a short quick swoop. Unlike similar raptors it often hunts in long grass. Rarely pursues prey in flight.

Breeding: Season: Peaks from September to November. **Nest:** A small but compact platform of sticks built below the canopy in the main or an outer fork of a tree. Usually lined with *Usnea* lichens, but sometimes with dry grass or green leaves. **Clutch:** 1–3 eggs, usually 2. **Incubation:** 32–34 days, by female only. **Nestling:** 40 days, fed by female only at first. Dependent on parents for another 30–40 days.

Origin of name: Johan Jakob Kaup (1803–1873) was Director of the Natural History Museum in Darmstadt, Germany. He wrote extensively on birds, including a monograph on diurnal raptors. *Falco* is Latin for 'falcon'. *Monogrammicus* means 'with a single mark' and refers to the diagnostic stripe on the throat of this raptor.

Adult

Will Nichol

Adult on nest

Steve Garvie

Adult

Ulrich Oberprieler

Adult

Alan Knott-Craig

Adult

p. 39

p. 241

117

AFRICAN HARRIER-HAWK
Polyboroides typus

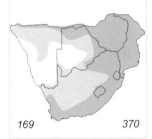

Measurements
Length: 55-66 cm
Wingspan: ±140 cm
Weight: 636-950 g
Females are larger than males

Distribution
Africa south of the Sahara.

169   370

Habitat
Mostly well-wooded areas such as forests, woodland, dense riverine vegetation, wooded kloofs and stands of tall exotic trees. Less often in open savanna and Karoo.

Food
Small mammals, small birds, eggs and nestlings, reptiles, frogs and insects. (In western Africa mostly Oil Palm fruit.)

Status
Locally common resident.

S: Gymnogene / Banded Harrier-Hawk
A: Kaalwangvalk
F: Gymnogène d'Afrique / Serpentaire gymnogène
G: Höhlenweihe / Schlangensperber
P: Secretário-pequeno

Field recognition: Medium. A very distinctive raptor which might be confused only with the chanting goshawks. The upperparts, head and chest are grey with some bold black spots on the wing coverts. (Females are less spotted than males.) The belly is finely barred black and white. The broad, white central band across the long tail is seen both when perched and in flight. The head is the most distinguishing feature: small and elongated with long floppy feathers on the back of the head and nape. The bare facial skin is usually yellow, but blushes pink or red in excitement. The legs are long and yellow. The flight is floppy and buoyant on broad wings. The underwing coverts are barred like the belly, while the rest of the wing is grey with a broad black trailing edge and tip. Again the broad white band on the tail is diagnostic. **Juv.** The juvenile varies from pale to dark brown. It could be confused with a variety of other medium-sized brown raptors. Its shape, however, is the same as the adult's with the characteristic small slim head, bare face and long feathers on the back of the head. Adult plumage is attained over two years.

Behaviour: Usually solitary. Unobtrusive while perched within the canopy of a large tree, but easily identified when soaring slowly overhead. Usually silent, but utters a plaintive whistling call during the courtship display.

Feeding methods: The ankle is 'double-jointed', allowing it to be flexed backwards and even slightly sideways. It can thus reach into various holes and crevices in trees or rock faces, or even into nests, to extract small prey. It usually hunts by clambering around or hanging underneath tree trunks with flapping wings. The small, elongated head is also an adaptation to pry into crevices. May also hunt by soaring, from a perch or on the ground.

Breeding: Season: June to March, peaking September to October. **Nest:** A fairly large stick platform lined with green leaves. Built in the canopy of a tree, in a bush on a rock ledge or on the cliff ledge itself. **Clutch:** 1–3 eggs, usually 2. **Incubation:** 35–36 days by both sexes, but mainly by female. **Nestling:** 44–45 days, fed by female. The older chick usually kills the younger sibling.

Origin of name: *Polyborus* is the genus name of the Crested Caracara, a Central and South American raptor, which the African Harrier-Hawk resembles superficially. The suffix *-oides* means 'like'. *Typus* is Latin for 'typical' (i.e. not the Madagascar Harrier-Hawk). The older name 'Gymnogene' refers to its bare cheeks.

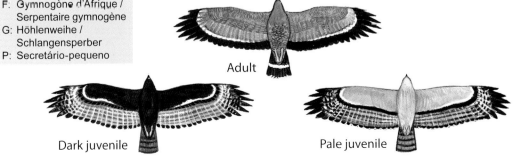

Adult

Dark juvenile

Pale juvenile

Niel Cillié

Adult

Niel Cillié

Adult blushing

Alan Knott-Craig

Adult hunting

Burger Cillié

Dark juvenile

p. 39

p. 241

Burger Cillié

Pale juvenile

Ulrich Oberprieler

Dark juvenile

119

Measurements
Length: 43-56 cm
Wingspan: ±101 cm
Weight: ♂ 646-695 g
♀ 841-852 g

Distribution
Africa south of the Sahara, south-western Morocco and southern Arabia.

163   372

Habitat
Favours well-developed woodland. Also savanna, but avoids arid areas and forests.

Food
Mostly lizards, small snakes, small ground-living mammals up to size of squirrel, and insects. Also birds up to size of guineafowl, and carrion.

Status
Fairly common resident.

A: Donkersingvalk
F: Autour-chanteur sombre / Autour sombre
G: Graubürzel-Singhabicht / Dunkler Grauflügelhabicht
P: Açor-cantor-escuro

DARK CHANTING GOSHAWK
Melierax metabates

Field recognition: Medium. Mainly grey with black-and-white barring on the belly. The chest is grey. The eyes are dark brown, the cere and legs red. Very like the Southern Pale Chanting Goshawk which occurs in the more arid western regions. Where the two species overlap, the Dark Chanting Goshawk is distinguished by its generally darker grey colour, its barred (not white) rump and in flight by the grey (not white) secondaries. The Gabar Goshawk is much smaller and has a white rump, whereas a black throat stripe, white rump and single white tail bar characterise the Lizard Buzzard. **Juv.** The juvenile is dark brown above with paler edges to the feathers. The chest is pale brown with darker brown streaks, while the belly is barred brown and white. The eyes are yellow, the cere and legs orange. Again the distribution and the finely barred (not white) rump distinguish it from the juvenile Southern Pale Chanting Goshawk. The juvenile Gabar Goshawk is much smaller.

Behaviour: Solitary or in pairs. Occurs in denser woodland and is more arboreal than the Southern Pale Chanting Goshawk and is thus less often seen. Perches for long periods while scanning the ground for prey. Usually silent but vocal during the breeding season, calling from a perch or on the wing. The call is similar to that of the Southern Pale Chanting Goshawk: an accelerated series of clear, melodious piping sounds. Other calls may be given at the nest.

Feeding methods: Opportunistic. Hunts mainly from a perch, gliding down to catch prey on the ground. Pursues prey on foot, but less often than the Southern Pale Chanting Goshawk. May catch birds in flight. Associates with Ratels (Honey Badgers) or Southern Ground-Hornbills, watching for disturbed prey.

Breeding: Season: July to November, peaking from September to October. **Nest:** A rather small but strong platform of sticks, often covered in spider web and sometimes cemented with mud. Built in the main fork of a tree within the canopy and lined with various soft materials. **Clutch:** 1–2 eggs, rarely 3. **Incubation:** Unrecorded, but probably similar to that of the Pale Chanting Goshawk. **Nestling:** ±50 days. Usually only 1 chick survives.

Origin of name: *Melierax* is derived from the Greek words *melos*, 'song', and *hierax*, 'hawk', referring to the melodious chanting calls of this group of goshawks. *Metabates* means 'changed' in Latin. This refers to the fact that this species is slightly different from the two pale chanting goshawks.

Adult   Juvenile

Adult

Pale juvenile

Adult

Sub-adult

p. 39

p. 241

Dark juvenile

Sub-adult

121

Measurements
Length: 46-63 cm
Wingspan: ±111 cm
Weight: ♂ 493-750 g
♀ 700 -1 250 g

Distribution
Southern Africa and southern Angola.

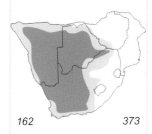

162   373

Habitat
Arid regions: thornveld, tree-lined watercourses and semi-desert, favouring Kalahari and Karoo vegetation types.

Food
Mostly lizards and insects. Also small mammals up to size of hare, birds up to size of korhaan, small snakes and carrion (road kills).

Status
Locally common resident.

S: Pale Chanting Goshawk
A: Bleeksingvalk
F: Autour-chanteur pale / Autour chanteur
G: Grosser Singhabicht / Grosser Grauflügelhabicht
P: Açor-cantor-pálido

SOUTHERN PALE CHANTING GOSHAWK
Melierax canorus

Field recognition: Medium. Mainly grey with black-and-white barring on the belly. The chest is grey. The eyes are dark brown, the cere and legs red. Very similar to the slightly smaller Dark Chanting Goshawk but occurs in the more arid western regions rather than in the eastern moister woodlands. Where the two species overlap, the Southern Pale Chanting Goshawk is distinguished by its generally paler grey colour, its white (not barred) rump and in flight by the white (not grey) secondaries which contrast strongly with the black wing tip. The much smaller Gabar Goshawk also has a white rump, but has pale bars on the tail. The Lizard Buzzard is characterised by its black throat stripe, white rump and single white tail bar. **Juv.** The juvenile is distinguished from the juvenile Dark Chanting Goshawk by its distribution and white (not barred) rump. The upperparts are dark brown with paler feather edges. The chest is pale brown with darker brown streaks, while the belly is barred brown and white. The eyes are yellow, the cere and legs orange. The juvenile Gabar Goshawk is much smaller.

Behaviour: Solitary or in pairs. Perches conspicuously, often on telephone poles, but is also regularly seen on the ground while pursuing prey. Silent outside the breeding season. The call is similar to that of the Dark Chanting Goshawk: a melodious, piping song uttered from a perch or in flight.

Feeding methods: Usually hunts from a perch and swoops down to catch prey on the ground. May catch birds in flight and regularly follows prey on foot. Follows small carnivores such as the Ratel, Black-backed Jackal and Slender Mongoose for prey they disturb. Sometimes hunts in small groups.

Breeding: Season: July to May, peaking October to November. May forgo breeding in drought years. **Nest:** A variable platform of sticks built in the main fork of a tree below the canopy or on a utility pole. The bowl is lined with dung, rags, mud, grass, skin or sheep's wool. **Clutch:** 1–2 eggs. **Incubation:** 35–38 days, mainly by female. **Nestling:** 7–8 weeks. Usually only 1 chick survives. Dependent on parents for at least 7 weeks after leaving the nest.

Origin of name: *Melierax* is derived from the Greek words *melos*, 'song', and *hierax*, 'hawk', referring to the melodious chanting calls of this group of goshawks. *Canorus* is Latin for 'melodious, singing'. This species used to be regarded as conspecific with the Eastern Chanting Goshawk (*Melierax poliopterus*) of eastern Africa.

Adult

Juvenile

Adult

Adult

Juvenile

Adults and chick on nest

p. 39

p. 241

Juvenile

Sub-adult

123

GABAR GOSHAWK
Melierax gabar

Measurements
Length: 28-36 cm
Wingspan: ±60 cm
Weight: ♂ 110-173 (142) g
♀ 180-221 (199) g

Distribution
Africa south of the Sahara and southern Arabia.

161   374

Habitat
Open woodland and savanna, preferring acacia-veld. Sometimes in closed woodland and even urban areas.

Food
Mostly small birds up to size of thrush, exceptionally up to size of small francolin. Also some small mammals, reptiles and insects.

Status
Locally common resident.

A: Witkruissperwer / Kleinsingvalk
F: Autour gabar
G: Gabarhabicht
P: Gavião-palrador

Field recognition: Small. Mainly grey with black-and-white barring on the belly. The chest is grey. The eyes are dark red-brown, the cere and legs red. The rump is white and the tail has pale grey bars. (Resembles the larger chanting goshawks which differ in body shape and habits. The Lizard Buzzard has a black throat stripe, white rump and single white tail bar.) Seen from underneath in flight, it has black-and-white barring on the flight feathers and tail. A rarer melanistic form lacks the white rump, but also shows barring on the flight feathers and tail. It resembles the rare melanistic Ovambo Sparrowhawk, but the cere is red and the legs red with black markings on the front. **Juv.** The juvenile is dark brown above with paler edges to the feathers. The underparts are pale brown with dark brown streaks on the chest and bars on the belly. The rump is white. The eyes are yellow, the cere and legs orange-red. (The similar juvenile Shikra lacks the white rump and has a blotched, not streaked, chest. The juvenile chanting goshawks are much larger.) The melanistic juvenile resembles the adult, but has orange-red legs.

Behaviour: Usually seen perched quietly within the canopy of a tree, or flying swiftly from one tree to the next. Rarely soars. Enters towns and becomes used to the presence of humans. Pairs probably remain together throughout the year. Usually silent except when breeding: 'kik-kik-kik-kik'.

Feeding methods: Hunts from a perch or on the wing, catching prey either on the ground or in flight. Often pursues prey into dense cover and may even follow it on foot. Robs nests of chicks and tears open weavers' nests.

Breeding: Season: August to March, peaking during September to November. **Nest:** A small stick nest built in a vertical fork in the upper branches of a tree, preferably an acacia. Lined with rags, earth and cobwebs. The nest is characteristically covered with the web of the colonial *Stegodyphus* spider, which is probably deliberately brought by the goshawk for the purpose of camouflage. **Clutch:** 2–4 eggs, usually 2–3. **Incubation:** 33–38 days by both sexes. **Nestling:** 30–35 days, fed mostly by female.

Origin of name: The Gabar Goshawk is closely related to the chanting goshawks. *Melierax* is derived from the Greek words *melos*, 'song', and *hierax*, 'hawk'. The name 'gabar' was given by François Levaillant (1753–1824) and is probably of Hottentot origin. The first syllable is correctly pronounced 'gar' as in 'garden', not 'gay'; the accent is on the second syllable.

Adult   Melanistic adult   Juvenile

Possible confusion: Lizard Buzzard p. 116, Dark Chanting Goshawk p. 120, Southern Pale Chanting Goshawk p. 122, Shikra p. 126

Richard du Toit

Adult

Chris van Rooyen

Juvenile

Albert Froneman

Adult

p. 39

p. 241

Niel Cillié

Melanistic adult

125

SHIKRA
Accipiter badius

Measurements
Length: 28-30 cm
Wingspan: ±58 cm
Weight: 75-158 g
Females are larger than males.

Distribution
Africa south of the Sahara, Middle East, southern and south-eastern Asia.

159   376

Habitat
Woodland and savanna. Stands of tall exotic trees in woodland regions.

Food
Feeds on a variety of small animals: lizards, small birds, mammals, snakes, frogs and insects.

Status
Common to scarce resident. Somewhat nomadic.

S: Little Banded Goshawk
A: Gebande Sperwer / Klein Gebande Sperwer
F: Épervier shikra
G: Schikrasperber / Schikra
P: Gavião-chicra

Field recognition: Small. The uniform dove-grey upperparts, without any white markings, distinguish it from similar goshawks and sparrowhawks, even in flight. (The central tail feathers are plain grey whereas the others are barred. The latter are only visible when the tail is spread.) The underparts, including the chest, are white with narrow grey bars in males and rufous bars in females. The bright red eye together with the yellow cere and orange-yellow legs are diagnostic. The body is more thickset and the legs shorter than in other goshawks. It may be confused with the male African Goshawk, which occurs in a different habitat, has yellow eyes, a grey cere and white eye-spots on the tail. **Juv.** The juvenile is dark brown above with paler edges to the feathers. The underparts are pale with rufous-brown blotches on the chest and bars on the belly. There is a dark line down the centre of the white throat. The cere, eyes and legs are yellow. It resembles the juvenile Gabar Goshawk which has brown streaks (not blotches) on the chest and a white rump.

Behaviour: Roosts in the same general area each night. Calls soon after dawn to advertise its position. It flies low, flapping and gliding until it swoops up to a new perch. May perch in the open. It is often seen as it is not only more vocal, even when not breeding, but also less shy than other hawks. The male calls 'kewick-kewick-kewick'. The female's call is a plaintive 'keeuu-keeuu'.

Feeding methods: A generalised, opportunistic hunter which takes a wide variety of small prey. Usually hunts from a perch within the leafy canopy of a tree. Frequently moves from one perch to the next. Most prey is caught on the ground after a forceful fast dive. Others may be snatched from foliage or tree trunks. Rarely pursues birds in flight, although quite capable of doing so.

Breeding: Season: August to December, sometimes even to April, but peaking in October. **Nest:** A smallish platform of twigs built in the main fork or on a horizontal branch of a tree and lined mainly with bark chips. **Clutch:** 1–4 eggs, usually 2–3. **Incubation:** 28–30 days, mostly by female. **Nestling:** ±30 days, fed by female only. Dependent on parents for another ±32 days.

Origin of name: *Accipiter* is Latin for 'hawk', while *badius* means 'reddish brown'. The name Shikra is derived from the Hindi word *shikari*, 'hunter'. (The scientific name of the Red-necked Falcon (*Falco chicquera*) is derived from the same word.)

Adult

Juvenile

Alan Knott-Craig

Female

Niel Cillié

Sub-adult

Alan Knott-Craig

Male

p. 39

p. 241

Albert Froneman

Juvenile

Alan Knott-Craig

Juvenile

127

OVAMBO SPARROWHAWK
Accipiter ovampensis

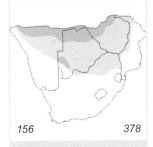

Measurements
Length: 31-40 cm
Wingspan: 65-70 cm
Weight: ♂ 105-190 (140) g
♀ 180-305 (260) g

Distribution
Africa south of the Sahara.

156   378

Habitat
Woodland and savanna, favouring a mosaic of tall woodland and open areas. Also stands of exotic trees.

Food
Small birds up to size of dove. Some insects.

Status
Rare to locally common resident. Range has expanded due to planting of tall exotic trees in grassland areas.

A: Ovambosperwer
F: Épervier de l'Ovampo
G: Ovambosperber
P: Gavião do Ovambo

Field recognition: Medium-small. Difficult to identify. The upperparts are plain grey, although there may be some faint white barring on the rump. The dull white underparts are completely barred grey, even on the chest and throat. The eyes are dark red, appearing dark in the field. The cere and legs are usually orange, but may be yellow-orange to orange-red. The unique pattern on the uppertail is diagnostic of all colour forms and age groups, but may be difficult to see: the dark uppertail has three broad pale bars, each with two white streaks in the centre (these are the white shafts of the two central tail-feathers). The head appears small with a large bill, while the wings seem longer than in similar hawks. The orange legs and cere and the uppertail pattern distinguish the very rare melanistic form from the melanistic Gabar Goshawk. **Juv.** Juveniles occur in two colour forms. The rufous form has a rufous head and rufous underparts, whereas those of the pale form are dull white. Both usually have some darker markings on the underparts, although those of the rufous form may be plain. Both are characterised by a prominent white eyebrow, a dark patch behind the eye, the unique tail pattern described above and the yellow-orange cere and legs. (These features also distinguish the rufous form from the adult and juvenile Rufous-chested Sparrowhawk.)

Behaviour: Most often seen during its agile, dashing but graceful flight. Regularly overlooked as it perches high within the cover of trees. Usually silent, except when breeding. The call is a sustained 'keep-keep-keep-keep'.

Feeding methods: It specialises in catching birds in flight, using a falcon-like hunting technique. It either perches high up on the edge of woodland, preferring to chase birds over open areas rather than through vegetation, or it stoops at prey from a high soaring flight. It thus has relatively long wings and short legs for a sparrowhawk.

Breeding: Season: August to January, peaking from August to November (earlier in the north than in the south). **Nest:** A platform of thin sticks lined with twigs, bark and leaves. Built high in a fork against the main trunk of a tall tree, usually on the edge of woodland or plantation. **Clutch:** 1–5 eggs, usually 3. **Incubation:** 33–39 days, mostly by female. **Nestling:** ±33 days, fed by female only on food brought by male. Usually 2 chicks survive out of a brood of 3. Dependent on parents for another ±30 days.

Origin of name: *Accipiter* is Latin for 'hawk', while *ovampensis* means 'of Owambo', a region in northern Namibia.

Adult   Melanistic   Rufous   Pale
               adult   juvenile   juvenile

Ron Hartley

Adult

Niel Cillié

Adult

Ulrich Oberprieler

Adult

p. 39

p. 241

Peter Steyn

Rufous juvenile

Steve Garvie

Pale juvenile

LITTLE SPARROWHAWK
Accipiter minullus

Measurements
Length: 23-28 cm
Wingspan: ±39 cm
Weight: 68-105 g
Females are larger than males.

Distribution
Southern Africa to the Congo River and Ethiopia.

157   377

Habitat
Prefers woodland and bushveld. In drier thornveld it occurs in the denser riverine thickets. Also gardens, forests and stands of exotic trees.

Food
Mainly small birds. Some insects, bats and lizards.

Status
Common to scarce resident. Range has expanded due to the planting of tall exotic trees.

S: African Little
   Sparrowhawk
A: Kleinsperwer
F: Épervier minule
G: Zwergsperber
P: Gavião-pequeno

Field recognition: Very small: the smallest sparrowhawk and the second smallest diurnal raptor in the region. (The smallest is the Pygmy Falcon.) The narrow white rump and two central white eye-spots, one above the other, on the tail are diagnostic. The upperparts are pure grey in males and grey-brown in females. The underparts are white with a rufous wash on the flanks. The barring is grey-brown in males, more rufous in females. The eyes are yellow-orange (males) to yellow (females), the cere and legs yellow. It is similar to the male African Goshawk which is larger, prefers a much denser habitat such as forests, has a grey cere and lacks the white rump. The yellow eye, white spots on the tail and the narrow white rump distinguish it from the larger Shikra. **Juv.** The juvenile is brown above. The rump appears brown as the rump feathers have white tips only. The tail has the same two white eye-spots as the adult. The underparts are dull white with prominent tear-shaped brown spots. The dark centre line on the white throat is either absent or faint. The eyes, cere and legs are yellow. Again it resembles the larger juvenile African Goshawk, which has a grey cere and a clear dark line on the centre of the throat, but lacks the white spots on the tail.

Behaviour: Mostly solitary. Hard to observe by day as it is a very small raptor which prefers to perch within the canopy of a tree. Quite active. Usually seen when it flies from one tree to the next. Rarely soars or flies in the open. Generally silent, except when breeding. Then the call is the easiest way to detect its presence. The female calls a rapid high-pitched 'kik-kik-kik-kik', while the male's call is a more mellow 'kew-kew-kew-kew'.

Feeding methods: A bold raptor. Despite being small it may catch birds the same size as itself. Hunts from a perch, often hiding near a water-hole to catch birds as they come down to drink. Very agile. Twists and turns when pursuing prey through foliage. Occasionally catches prey on the ground.

Breeding: Season: September to February (later in the south than in the north). **Nest:** A small platform of thick sticks, lined with thinner twigs and green leaves. Built high in a tree, usually in the main fork. **Clutch:** 1–4 eggs, usually 2. **Incubation:** 31–32 days, by both sexes. **Nestling:** 25–27 days, fed mostly by female. Usually only 1 chick survives, which becomes independent after about a month.

Origin of name: *Accipiter* (Latin) means 'hawk' and *minullus* 'very small'.

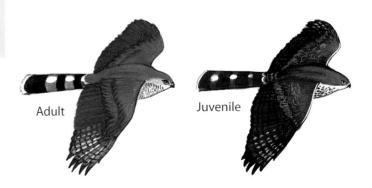

Adult   Juvenile

Niel Cillié

Female

Johann Knobel

Male

Chris van Rooyen

Juvenile

p. 39

p. 241

Lizeth Cillié

Male

Ulrich Oberprieler

Juvenile

AFRICAN GOSHAWK
Accipiter tachiro

Measurements
Length: 36-47 cm
Wingspan: ±70 cm
Weight: ♂ 168-230 (200) g
♀ 230-510 (350) g

Distribution
Southern Africa to the
Congo River and Ethiopia.

160   375

Habitat
Prefers dense vegetation
such as forests, mature
woodland, dense riverine
growth and thickets. Also
stands of tall exotic trees
and gardens.

Food
Mostly birds up to size
of turaco, and small
mammals. Also reptiles,
frogs, insects and some
invertebrates.

Status
Scarce to locally common
resident.

A: Afrikaanse Sperwer
F: Autour tachiro
G: Afrikanischer Habicht
P: Açor-africano

Field recognition: Medium-small. The typical hawk of forests and dense woodland. The female is not only much larger than the male, but also appears much browner. The upperparts are bluish-grey in the male, brown in the female. The white underparts are completely barred: rufous in the male and brown in the female. (Females may be lightly or heavily barred.) The male has two white eye-spots on the tail, one above the other, which are lacking in the female. The eyes are yellow but may appear dark. The legs are yellow. The cere is grey. It strongly resembles the much smaller Little Sparrowhawk which occurs in a wider variety of wooded habitats, has a yellow cere and a white rump. The Shikra is uniform grey above. The African Cuckoo-Hawk has a grey chest, short crest, long pointed wings and shorter legs. **Juv.** The juvenile is brown above with a white eyebrow. The underparts, which are usually white but may be pale brown, are boldly marked with brown teardrop-shaped spots. There is a dark streak down the centre of the throat. It has a grey cere and yellow legs. It differs from the juvenile Little Sparrowhawk in its larger size, grey (not yellow) cere, dark line on the throat and lack of white spots on the tail. The juvenile African Cuckoo-Hawk has a slight crest on the head, long wings, but shorter legs.

Behaviour: Unobtrusive. Not often seen in its densely wooded habitat. Most often observed during the early morning display when it circles above the forest canopy and calls its distinctive sharp and high-pitched 'krit-krit-krit-krit'. This happens throughout the year, but more frequently when breeding.

Feeding methods: Opportunistic, although catching mainly birds. Usually hunts from within cover, grasping prey in flight, on the ground or from foliage after a short, powerful dash. May also pursue prey above or below the forest canopy in fast flight. Makes use of cover to surprise prey.

Breeding: Season: September to April, peaking October to January (earlier in the south than in the north). **Nest:** A small platform of sticks built in a high fork or horizontal branch of a forest tree, usually well hidden among foliage. Lined with fine twigs, lichens and green leaves. **Clutch:** 2–3 eggs, rarely 1. **Incubation:** 35–37 days, by female only. **Nestling:** 32–35 days, fed by female. Dependent on parents for another 2 months.

Origin of name: *Accipiter* is Latin for 'hawk'. *Tachos* means 'swift' in Greek. (The Red-chested Goshawk (*Accipiter toussenelii*) of the central African rainforests is often considered a subspecies of the African Goshawk.)

Adult

Juvenile

Male

Male

Juvenile

Male

Female

p. 39

p. 241

133

Measurements
Length: 29-40 cm
Wingspan: ±72 cm
Weight: 180-210 g
Females are larger
than males.

Distribution
Scattered localities from
Southern Africa
to Ethiopia.

155   379

Habitat
Prefers a mosaic of forest
patches in montane
grassland and fynbos over
which it hunts. Also exotic
plantations.

Food
Mostly birds up to size
of dove. Some mice and
insects.

Status
Locally common to scarce
resident. Range has
expanded due to planting
of tall exotic trees in
grassland areas.

S: Red-breasted
    Sparrowhawk / Rufous-
    breasted Sparrowhawk /
    Rufous Sparrowhawk
A: Rooiborssperwer
F: Épervier menu
G: Rotbauchsperber
P: Gavião-ruivo

RUFOUS-CHESTED SPARROWHAWK
Accipiter rufiventris

Field recognition: Medium small. Adults are unmistakable. The upperparts are slate-grey, while the underparts, including the underwing coverts, are plain rufous. The eyes, cere and legs are yellow. The female is browner above, but deeper rufous below than the male. May be confused with the rufous juvenile of the Ovambo Sparrowhawk, which has a brown eye, white eyebrow and dark patch behind the eye, not the completely dark cap of the Rufous-chested Sparrowhawk. The distribution and habitat are also important to note. **Juv.** The juvenile is brown above with some paler markings. The underparts are somewhat variable, but are mostly rufous with fine dark streaks and faint white barring. There is an indistinct pale eyebrow. The eyes are pale greyish until the age of four months when they turn yellow. The cere and legs are yellow. It is very similar to the rufous juvenile Ovambo Sparrowhawk, which has a rufous head with a dark crown and ear patches, brown eyes and less mottled underparts. The characteristic uppertail pattern also distinguishes the Ovambo Sparrowhawk.

Behaviour: Solitary or in pairs. Not often seen as it is shy and unobtrusive, especially when not breeding. May perch in the open on the edge of a forest or plantation or may be seen hunting over open patches. Loses its shyness when exposed to the presence of people over time, for example, around farm houses. During courtship the male circles over its territory, calling a staccato, sharp 'kew-kew-kew-kew'.

Feeding methods: Usually hunts over open grassland and fynbos adjacent to patches of forest or stands of tall exotic trees. Looks for prey in a low coursing flight, then pursues it in a fast dash, either taking it in flight or forcing it to the ground or into cover. Regularly makes use of cover to surprise prey. Less often stoops from soaring flight or strikes from a perch. A swift, bold and aggressive hunter.

Breeding: Season: September to December. **Nest:** A platform of small sticks which is lined with moss, bark, grass or fine twigs. Built in the upper fork of a tall tree. **Clutch:** 2–4 eggs, usually 3. **Incubation:** 34–35 days, mostly by female. **Nestling:** 31–36 days, fed by female on food brought by male. Independent after ±2 months.

Origin of name: *Accipiter* is Latin for 'hawk', *rufus* means 'reddish' and *venter* 'abdomen or belly'.

Adult   Juvenile

134

Immature

Adult

Adult

Juvenile

Adult

p. 39

p. 241

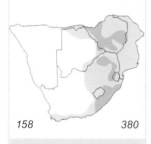

BLACK SPARROWHAWK
Accipiter melanoleucus

Measurements
Length: 46-58 cm
Wingspan: ±102 cm
Weight: ♂ 450-650 g
♀ 750-980 g

Distribution
Africa south of the Sahara.

158   380

Habitat
Mature woodland, dense riverine growth, forest and plantations of exotic trees.

Food
Mostly smaller birds, but up to size of guineafowl, specialising in doves. Also small mammals and insects.

Status
Scarce to locally common resident. Range has expanded due to planting of tall exotic trees in grassland areas.

S: Great Sparrowhawk / Black-and-white Sparrowhawk / Black Goshawk
A: Swartsperwer
F: Autour noir
G: Mohrenhabicht / Trauerhabicht
P: Açor-preto

Field recognition: Medium. Unmistakable. This is a large black-and-white sparrowhawk. The upperparts are black. (Although there is a pale patch on the nape, this is usually not visible.) The underparts, including the underwing coverts, are white with bold black barring on the flanks. The eye is deep wine-red, lightening to amber in old birds, but usually appears dark in the field. The cere and legs are yellow. A rare melanistic form is completely black except for a white patch on the throat. This patch as well as the large size and yellow cere and legs distinguish it from the melanistic Gabar Goshawk and Ovambo Sparrowhawk. **Juv.** Juveniles occur in two forms: one with rufous and the other with pale underparts. Both are dark brown above with some paler markings and both have brown streaks on the underparts. The eyes are grey-brown, the cere greenish-yellow and legs yellow. The pale form may be confused with the juvenile African Goshawk, but is distinguished by the narrow streaks (not bold blotches) on the underparts and the lack of a white eyebrow. The pale form juvenile may be confused with the adult African Hawk-Eagle and Ayres's Hawk-Eagle, while the rufous form juvenile resembles their juveniles.

Behaviour: Difficult to observe as it usually keeps to the dense cover of trees, seldom soaring above it or coming into the open. Unobtrusive, but adapts well to the presence of humans and can become quite bold. Mostly silent, except when breeding. The male calls a sharp musical 'kyip' and is answered by the female's deeper 'chep'. The two sexes may duet.

Feeding methods: A bold and powerful predator able to overtake a dove on the wing. Hunts mostly from a perch within cover, dashing out to catch prey mostly in flight, but sometimes on the ground. Sometimes pursues prey for considerable distances over open areas. May also make use of cover to surprise prey or stoop from high soaring flight.

Breeding: Season: May to February, peaking July to October (later in the south than in the north). **Nest:** A large stick platform built high in a tall tree, especially exotic eucalypts. Lined with green leaves. **Clutch:** 1–4 eggs, usually 3. **Incubation:** 36–38 days, by both sexes. **Nestling:** 37–47 days, fed mostly by female. Dependent on parents for another ±55 days.

Origin of name: *Accipiter* is Latin for 'hawk'. *Melanos* and *leukos* (Greek) mean 'black' and 'white' respectively.

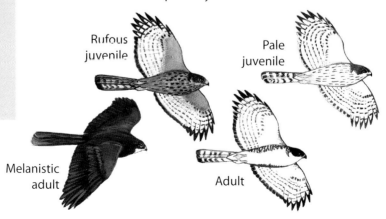

Rufous juvenile

Pale juvenile

Melanistic adult

Adult

Adult and chick on nest

Adult and chicks on nest

Melanistic adult

p. 39

p. 241

Pale juvenile

Rufous juvenile

137

Measurements
Length: 48-53 cm
Wingspan: ±100 cm
Weight: 383-574 g
Females are larger
than males.

Distribution
Endemic to Southern
Africa.

168   367

Habitat
Arid open areas such as
fynbos, grassland, Karoo,
semi-desert. Sometimes
marshes.

Food
Small birds and mammals
(especially vlei rats)
and large insects.
Occasionally reptiles,
frogs and carrion.

Status
Uncommon resident in
the south-western parts of
its distribution. Migrates
north and east after
breeding.

A: Witkruisvloivalk /
    Swartvleivalk /
    Witkruispaddavreter
F: Busard maure
G: Mohrenweihe
P: Tartaranhão-preto

BLACK HARRIER
Circus maurus

Field recognition: Medium. The black plumage makes this harrier unmistakable. The white rump is conspicuous in flight, as are the bars on the tail. (The tail is black with silvery grey bars above and boldly barred black and white below.) The underwing is boldly black and white: black coverts and white flight feathers with a black trailing edge to the wing. The eye, cere and legs are yellow. The sexes are alike. Some birds have a few white markings on the underparts. The white rump and barred tail distinguish it from the very rare melanistic Montagu's Harrier (which has not yet been seen in Southern Africa) and very dark brown female and juvenile Western Marsh-Harriers. **Juv.** The juvenile is dark brown above with buff markings on the wing coverts, cheeks and eyebrows, and white mottling on the nape. The underparts are buff with bold dark brown markings on the chest and flanks. In flight the broad white rump and boldly barred tail are characteristic. The underwing coverts are buff with dark brown markings, while the flight feathers are mainly white with some dark markings and a dark trailing edge. Unlike other juvenile harriers it has yellow eyes. May be confused with especially female and juvenile Pallid and Montagu's Harriers, which are less boldly marked below and on the tail.

Behaviour: A harrier of arid country. Breeds mostly in the fynbos region after winter rains. (There is a very small breeding population in north-western Namibia and birds have been recorded breeding as far north-east as the KwaZulu-Natal Drakensberg.) During autumn and winter non-breeding birds move to the north and east into Karoo, grassland and semi-desert habitats. Perches on the ground or on termite mounds. Silent, except when breeding.

Feeding methods: Hunts like a typical harrier by flying low over the ground and dropping onto prey. May hover with spread tail and slowly fanning wings. Occasionally hunts from a perch or pursues birds in flight.

Breeding: Season: July to December. **Nest:** An untidy pad of dry grass, sometimes on a base of stems, reeds and weeds, built well concealed in fynbos, wheat fields or marshes. Usually on the ground, but may be up to 50 cm above the ground in marshy areas. A few pairs may nest close together. **Clutch:** 3–4 eggs, sometimes 1–5. **Incubation:** ±34 days, by female only. **Nestling:** 36–41 days, fed by female. Dependent on parents for another 3 weeks.

Origin of name: *Kirkos* (Greek) means 'harrier', while *circus* (Latin) means 'circle', referring to the habit of harriers of flying to and fro. *Maurus* is the Greek word for 'black'.

Adult

Juvenile

138

Adult

Juvenile

Immature

p. 40

p. 250

Adult and chicks on nest

Measurements
Length: 48-56 cm
Wingspan: 115-130 cm
Weight: ♂ 405-667 (505) g
♀ 540-1 100 (728) g

Distribution
Breeds from Europe to central Asia and in north-western Africa. Migrates south when not breeding.

164   365

Habitat
Marshy and swampy regions, and adjacent moist grassland.

Food
Opportunistic: mostly smaller birds and mammals, especially rodents, frogs, reptiles, insects and carrion.

Status
Rare non-breeding summer visitor.

S: European Marsh-Harier / Eurasian Marsh-Harrier
A: Europese Vleivalk / Europese Paddavreter
F: Busard des roseaux
G: Europäische Rohrweihe
P: Tartaranhão-ruivo-dos-pauis

WESTERN MARSH-HARRIER
Circus aeruginosus

Field recognition: Medium. This rare visitor shares marshy habitats in Southern Africa with the resident African Marsh-Harrier in summer. The male resembles the latter species in that it is mostly brown with streaks on the chest, while the belly and leggings are rufous. It is characterised by its pale greyish head that contrasts with the rest of the body, the plain grey flight feathers and last row of upperwing coverts, and the plain grey tail. Seen from above in flight these features are diagnostic, together with the black wingtips. The underwing shows pale rufous coverts (almost white in very old males) and white flight feathers with a black tip and trailing edge to the wing. Both male and female have yellow eyes, cere and legs. **Female & Juv.** The female and juvenile are chocolate brown with a creamy white crown, nape, throat and 'shoulder'. (The head thus appears creamy with a darker mask through the eye.) The extent of the creamy patches varies between individuals and some may be completely dark brown. The juvenile differs from the female in that it is darker, has brown (not yellow) eyes and some darker streaks on the pale crown. The female and juvenile may be confused with the juvenile African Marsh-Harrier but are distinguished by the absence of both the pale chest band and any barring on the wings and tail.

Behaviour: Prefers the same wetlands as the African Marsh-Harrier, but occurs only patchily in the north and north-west. It is more common in years of good rain when especially females and juveniles migrate further south than their usual non-breeding grounds in western and central Africa. Their behaviour in Southern Africa is similar to the African Marsh-Harrier's. Usually silent.

Feeding methods: Similar to the African Marsh-Harrier: it quarters low over marshy vegetation, twists suddenly and drops down onto prey. Prefers to surprise prey on the ground or water, rather than catching it in flight.

Breeding: Breeds in Europe across Asia to Mongolia as well as in north-western Africa. Migrates to southern and western Europe, Africa south of the Sahara and southern Asia when not breeding.

Origin of name: *Kirkos* (Greek) means 'harrier', while *circus* (Latin) means 'circle', referring to the habit of harriers of flying to and fro. *Aeruginosus* is a Latin word meaning 'the colour of copper rust'. This probably refers to the male's general appearance.

Male

Female

140

Conrad Greaves (Aquila)

Male

Brendan Ryan

Markus Varesvuo

Juvenile

Male

p. 40

p. 250

Markus Varesvuo

Female

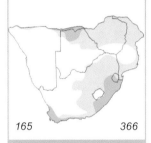

AFRICAN MARSH-HARRIER
Circus ranivorus

Measurements
Length: 44-50 cm
Wingspan: ±100 cm
Weight: 382-590 (518) g
Females are larger
than males.

Distribution
From Southern Africa
north to Sudan.

165   366

Habitat
Marshy and swampy
regions and adjacent
grassland. May hunt over
cultivated lands and open
savanna.

Food
Varied: mostly small
rodents and birds up to
size of Red-billed Teal.
Also birds' eggs, insects,
fish, frogs, reptiles and
carrion.

Status
Locally common resident.
Numbers are declining
due to habitat loss.

A: Afrikaanse Vleivalk /
    Afrikaanse Paddavreter
F: Busard grenouillard
G: Froschweihe /
    Afrikanische Rohrweihe
P: Tartaranhão-dos-
    pântanos

Field recognition: Medium-small. A brown harrier with a variable amount of pale streaking on the head, back, chest and flanks, and pale dappling on the 'shoulder' of the folded wing. The belly and leggings are rufous. Small white spots outline the owl-like facial disc typical of harriers. The eyes, cere and legs are yellow. The sexes are similar, but females are often darker on the upperparts and more rufous on the underparts than males, which are slightly greyer on the base of the flight feathers and the upper tail. In flight the boldly barred flight feathers and tail are characteristic of both sexes. In marshy habitat it may be confused with the male Western Marsh-Harrier, which is less streaky and has grey flight feathers and tail. Female and juvenile Montagu's and Pallid Harriers, which prefer open habitats away from water, have pale rumps. **Juv.** The juvenile is similar to the female and juvenile Western Marsh-Harrier in that it is chocolate brown with buff 'shoulders' on the folded wing and a variable amount of buff on the nape and throat. It is always distinguished by the pale chest band and the barred flight feathers and tail. The eyes are brown.

Behaviour: Solitary or in pairs. Prefers permanent marshes and vleis where it is often seen coursing low over the vegetation on wings held in a shallow V. Also soars high above the ground or rests on low perches. Juveniles wander widely and may arrive at isolated water bodies outside the normal range. Usually silent except when alarmed or at the nest.

Feeding methods: Hunts on the wing by slowly quartering 5–10 m above the ground. On hearing or seeing prey among the vegetation it checks suddenly and drops down with legs extended. Often catches birds in flight after surprising them by flying rapidly along a stream bed. May catch fish in shallow water. Is also attracted to carrion and the leftovers of other raptors' kills.

Breeding: Season: All months, but mainly January to July in the north-east and August to November in the south-west. **Nest:** A platform of sticks, reeds and weeds lined with dry grass. May be a scanty pad when built on dry ground, but becomes deeper in wetter situations. **Clutch:** 2–5 eggs, but up to 6. **Incubation:** 31–34 days, by female only. **Nestling:** 38–41 days, fed by female.

Origin of name: *Kirkos* (Greek) means 'harrier', while *circus* (Latin) means 'circle', referring to the habit of harriers of flying to and fro. *Ranus* is a 'frog' and *vorare* means 'to eat' in Latin. In spite of this name, small mammals and birds, rather than frogs, make up most of its diet.

Adult

Juvenile

Alan Knott-Craig

Adult

Heinrich van den Berg

Adult

p. 40

p. 250

Peter Pickford (SIL)

Juvenile

Warwick Tarboton

Adult and chicks on nest

MONTAGU'S HARRIER
Circus pygargus

Measurements
Length: 40-47 cm
Wingspan: 105-120 cm
Weight: ♂ 227-305 (261) g
♀ 310-445 (370) g

Distribution
Breeds in Europe, central Asia and north-western Africa. Migrates to southern Asia and Africa when not breeding.

166   369

Habitat
Mostly open grassland or marshy areas. Less commonly in arid scrub.

Food
Mostly large insects, small mammals and birds.

Status
Scarce to locally common non-breeding summer visitor.

A: Blouvleivalk /
   Bloupaddavreter
F: Busard cendré
G: Wiesenweihe
P: Tartaranhão-caçador

Field recognition: Medium-small. The male is similar to the male Pallid Harrier: mostly grey with a white belly. It is distinguished by the grey chest, the chestnut streaks on the belly and black bar on the upperwing. In flight it shows a large black wingtip; the underwing has two black bars over the secondaries and brown spots on the coverts. It may also be confused with Southern Pale and Dark Chanting Goshawks and the Black-shouldered Kite, especially in flight. In contrast to these birds, harriers do not perch high above the ground and have a typical flight pattern. A rare melanistic form, like a Black Harrier without a white rump, has not yet been seen in Southern Africa. **Female & Juv.** The brown female and juvenile are very similar to those of the Pallid Harrier and are probably not safely separated in the field. These are often collectively referred to as 'ringtails' as all have a narrow pale rump and distinctly barred tails. (The pale rump distinguishes them from the African and Western Marsh-Harriers.) Adults have yellow eyes, while those of the juvenile are dark. The juvenile is plain rufous brown below, while the female is streaked. At very close range they differ from the female and juvenile Pallid Harrier by a far less obvious pale collar behind the ear coverts, a narrower dark stripe at the back of the eye and a slightly broader pale eyebrow. The juvenile Montagu's Harrier is a darker, richer rufous than the juvenile Pallid Harrier.

Behaviour: Spends most of the day on the wing, flying gracefully and buoyantly 3–5 m above the ground, swerving and dropping onto prey. Sometimes perches on a low post or on the ground. Roosts communally on the ground, often with Pallid Harriers or even African Marsh-Harriers. Habits are similar to the Pallid Harrier's, but it prefers moister grassland. Usually silent.

Feeding methods: Hunts singly in typical harrier-fashion by quartering to and fro over open habitat, dropping onto prey. It is attracted to prey fleeing from grass fires, but abandons large burnt areas. Most prey is caught on the ground, but insects and sometimes small birds may be taken in flight.

Breeding: Breeds in Europe, central Asia and north-western Africa. A non-breeding visitor to the rest of Africa and southern Asia.

Origin of name: Col. George Montagu (1751–1815), a soldier and writer, collected numerous bird skins that were later given to the British Museum. *Kirkos* (Greek) means 'harrier', while *circus* (Latin: 'circle') refers to the flying habits of harriers. *Pygargus* is derived from the Greek *page*, 'rump', and *argos*, 'white', referring to the white rump of females and immatures.

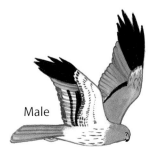

Male

Female

Possible confusion: Pallid Harrier p. 146. Dark Chanting Goshawk p. 120, Southern Pale Chanting Goshawk p.122, Black-shouldered Kite p. 148, African Marsh-Harrier p. 142

Male

Male

Sub-adult male

Female

p. 40

p. 250

Juvenile

Sub-adult female

Measurements
Length: 40-48 cm
Wingspan: 95-120 cm
Weight: ♂ 235-416 (312) g
♀ 255-454 (404) g

Distribution
Breeds from eastern
Europe to central Asia.
Migrates to southern
Asia and Africa when not
breeding.

167   *368*

Habitat
Open grassland. May
occur in open savanna
and agricultural lands.

Food
Especially large insects,
but in addition small
mammals, small birds,
lizards and frogs.

Status
Locally common to rare
non-breeding summer
visitor.

A: Witborsvleivalk /
    Witborspaddavreter
F: Busard pâle
G: Steppenweihe
P: Tartaranhão-pálido

PALLID HARRIER
Circus macrourus

Field recognition: Medium-small. The male is pale grey above and whitish below. It is distinguished from the male Montagu's Harrier in lacking the grey chest, chestnut streaks on the white belly and black bar on the upperwing. In flight it shows a much smaller black patch on the wingtip as only four primaries are black. The rest of the underwing is white. Generally the male Pallid Harrier appears much paler, almost gull-like, compared to the male Montagu's Harrier. Both may be confused with the two chanting goshawks and the Black-shouldered Kite, especially in flight, but they have the typical flight pattern of harriers and seldom sit on conspicuous high perches. **Female & Juv.** The brown female and juvenile are virtually indistinguishable in the field from those of Montagu's Harrier. The tails are distinctly barred, while the narrow pale rump (hence the collective name 'ringtails') distinguishes them from the similar African and Western Marsh-Harriers. The female differs from the juvenile in having yellow (not dark) eyes and streaked underparts. At very close range both female and juvenile may be distinguished from those of Montagu's Harrier by a more obvious pale collar behind the ear coverts, a broader dark brown band at the back of the eye and a narrower pale eyebrow. The underparts of the juvenile Pallid Harrier are less rufous than those of the juvenile Montagu's Harrier.

Behaviour: Solitary by day. The longer wings and tail indicate that it spends even more time on the wing than other harriers, flying low over the ground and quartering to and fro while scanning the ground for prey. Rarely soars. Lands for short periods on the ground, rather than on a low post as Montagu's Harrier may do. Roosts singly or communally on the ground, often with Montagu's Harrier. Its habits resemble those of the Montagu's Harrier, but it prefers more arid grassland and even open savanna. Usually silent.

Feeding methods: Hunts like other harriers by flying to and fro over open areas. It twists suddenly to drop onto prey on the ground or on low vegetation. Is attracted to grass fires to catch insects in flight.

Breeding: Breeds from eastern Europe to central Asia. Migrates to Africa and southern Asia as a non-breeding visitor.

Origin of name: *Kirkos* (Greek) means 'harrier', while *circus* (Latin) means 'circle', referring to the flying habits of harriers. *Macrourus* is derived from the Latin *macro*, 'large', and *urus*, 'tail', referring to the tail that is longer than in other harrier species.

Male

Female

Male

Male

Female

Juvenile

p. 40

p. 250

Immature

Female

147

BLACK-SHOULDERED KITE
Elanus caeruleus

Field recognition: Small. Easy to identify. Upperparts are mostly grey, the underparts are white and there is a diagnostic black patch on the 'shoulder' (which is actually the wrist). The eye is red, while the cere and legs are yellow. The long, pointed wings project beyond the tip of the tail. In flight the dark patch from the base of the wing to the wrist is conspicuous from above. From below it is mainly white except for the black wingtips. It resembles the male Pallid Harrier, but is smaller with a shorter tail. It also perches or hovers regularly rather than flying low over open country like a harrier. **Juv.** The juvenile is similar to the adult. The upperparts are brownish with pale edges to the feathers, giving a scaled appearance. The underparts are washed rufous with fine brown streaks on the chest. The 'shoulder patch' is dark with white markings. The eye is pale brown, gradually changing to orange and then to red in the adult bird. The time it takes for a juvenile to moult into the adult plumage varies roughly from 9–15 months, depending on the season when it leaves the nest, as moulting takes place only in summer.

Behaviour: Breeding birds occur in pairs. Non-breeding birds roost communally at night, usually in groups of 10–20, rarely over 100 individuals. Flies to hunting territories, each occupied by a single bird, after dawn and often returns only after dusk. Pumps the tail up and down when excited. Often nomadic, congregating and breeding where rodents are abundant. Calls softly.

Feeding methods: Perches conspicuously for long periods while scanning the ground for prey, mostly mice. Hovers regularly with flapping wings and spread tail, especially at dusk. Then drops down in stages, with the wings held high above the back and the legs extended, to suddenly plunge onto prey.

Breeding: Season: Throughout the year depending on the availability of rodent prey, but peaking in spring in the south-west and both in spring and autumn in the north-east. **Nest:** A shallow platform of sticks lined with grass. Built in the top of a tree canopy or sometimes on telephone poles. Always accessible from above. **Clutch:** 2–6 eggs, usually 3–4. **Incubation:** 30–33 days, mostly by female. **Nestling:** 30–35 days, fed by female only on food brought by male. Fledgling cared for by male only for another 80–90 days, while female may attempt breeding with another male if prey is abundant.

Origin of name: *Elanus* is a Greek word for 'kite', while *caeruleus* is Latin for 'blue', referring to the overall bluish-grey appearance.

Measurements
Length: ±30 cm
Wingspan: ±84 cm
Weight: ♂ 197-277 (236) g
♀ 219-343 (257) g

Distribution
Africa, Madagascar, Iberia and tropical Asia.

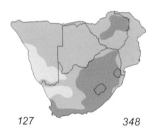

127   348

Habitat
Varied: from desert to open woodland. Most common in grassland and fynbos, especially where these form a mosaic with agricultural lands.

Food
Mostly small rodents. Also shrews, small birds, reptiles and insects.

Status
Common to very common resident. Nomadic.

S: Common Black-shouldered Kite / Black-winged Kite
A: Blouvalk
F: Élanion blanc
G: Gleitaar
P: Peneiroiro-cinzento

Adult

Juvenile

Possible confusion: Male Montagu's Harrier p. 144, male Pallid Harier p. 146

Niel Cillié

Adult

Niel Cillié

Adult

Trevor Hardaker

Immature

Burger Cillié

Juvenile

Albert Froneman

Adult displaying

Burger Cillié

Juvenile

p. 41

p. 254

AFRICAN CUCKOO-HAWK
Aviceda cuculoides

Measurements
Length: ±40 cm
Wingspan: ±90 cm
Weight: 220-296 g
Females are larger than males.

Distribution
Africa south of the Sahara.

128   345

Habitat
Prefers densely wooded areas such as forests, mature woodland, dense riverine growth and stands of tall exotic trees.

Food
Mostly large insects, especially grasshoppers. Also lizards, chameleons, small snakes, small mammals and rarely birds.

Status
Uncommon resident. Nomadic.

S: African Cuckoo-Falcon / African Baza
A: Koekoekvalk
F: Baza coucou
G: Kuckucksweih
P: Falcão-cuco

Field recognition: Medium-small. A dark grey raptor with broad rufous bars across the white (male) or buff (female) belly, thus resembling a large cuckoo. On the back of the head there is a small pointed crest with a pale centre. The rufous patch below the crest is diagnostic when seen from behind. It has short yellow legs. The wings are long and pointed, nearly reaching to the tip of the tail when perched. They are often held slightly drooped, thus exposing the tail and rump. The body shape distinguishes it from the similar African Goshawk, which also lacks the grey chest and short crest. In flight the long pointed wings are characteristic. The rufous bars of the belly extend onto the underwing coverts. The tail is dark grey above and silvery below with three broad dark bars. **Juv.** The juvenile is brown above with pale edges to the feathers. It has white streaks on the eyebrow, forehead and back of the head. The underparts are whitish with large dark brown blotches. In flight the underwing is mainly pale buff with some darker blotches on the coverts and barring on the flight feathers. The pale brown tail has dark brown bars. It resembles the juvenile African Goshawk or even the much smaller juvenile Little Sparrowhawk, but has the same distinctive body shape as the adult.

Behaviour: Solitary. Easily overlooked as it is secretive and retiring, perching within a leafy tree canopy. The flight is graceful and kite-like. Usually silent, but noisy during courtship, uttering loud whistling calls.

Feeding methods: Hunts mostly from a perch within the canopy of a tree. Swoops down slowly to take prey on the ground. May follow insects on the ground by hopping clumsily. Tree-living prey such as chameleons are snatched from branches. May pursue aerial prey in flight.

Breeding: Season: September to May, peaking in the rainy season. **Nest:** An untidy and flimsy platform of leafy branches resembling a pile of debris. Built high in the canopy of a leafy tree such as an exotic eucalypt. **Clutch:** 1–2, rarely 3, eggs. **Incubation:** 32–33 days, by female only or by both sexes. **Nestling:** 28–36 days, fed by both parents.

Origin of name: The name *Aviceda* is a misnomer (*avis* is Latin for 'bird', while *caedere* means 'to eat'), as all cuckoo-hawks and the related bazas are mainly insectivorous. *Cuculoides* refers to its cuckoo-like appearance.

Adult

Juvenile

Possible confusion: African Goshawk p. 132, Little Sparrowhawk p. 130

Peter Steyn (Photo Access)

Juvenile

Albert Froneman

Adult

Albert Froneman

Adult

HPH Photography (Photo Access)

Adult

Warwick Tarboton

Adult on nest

Ulrich Oberprieler

Juvenile

p. 41

p. 254

151

BLACK KITE

Milvus migrans migrans and *M. m. lineatus*

Measurements
Length: 51-60 cm
Wingspan: 160-180 cm
Weight: ♂ 450-850 (754) g
♀ 750-1 076 (857) g

Distribution
Breeds in north-western
Africa, Europe and
Asia. Migrates to Africa,
southern and south-
eastern Asia
after breeding.

126a   349

Habitat
Prefers open woodland
and savanna, but may
occur from forest edge to
semi-desert.

Food
Very varied: mostly
insects, also small
mammals, birds, reptiles,
frogs and carrion.

Status
Locally common non-
breeding summer visitor.

A: Swartwou
F: Milan noir
G: Schwarzmilan
P: Milhafre-preto

Field recognition: Medium. The bare yellow legs and long forked tail distinguish it from all similar raptors, except the Yellow-billed Kite. It appears uniformly dark brown from afar, but the greyish or whitish head distinguishes it from its juvenile as well as from the adult and juvenile Yellow-billed Kite. The bill is black with a yellow cere, not completely yellow as in the adult Yellow-billed Kite. At close range the rufous-brown belly and dark streaks on the chest may be seen. The flight pattern is distinctive, resembling only that of the Yellow-billed Kite. The wings are markedly angled at the wrist joint, the flight is light and buoyant. The tail is continuously twisted while steering. The tip of the closed tail is less deeply forked than that of the Yellow-billed Kite and is nearly straight when spread, although this is not a good field character. **Juv.** The juvenile resembles the adult, but the head is the same brown colour as the rest of the body. The feathers on the upperparts have pale edges, whereas the head and underparts are streaked whitish. Overall it appears paler and duller than the adult with a less deeply forked tail. It is extremely difficult to distinguish from the juvenile Yellow-billed Kite, but is more streaked on the head and underparts.

Behaviour: Although they are less common than Yellow-billed Kites, Black Kites usually occur in large flocks, sometimes numbering hundreds of birds and including other migrant raptors such as Steppe Eagles, Lesser Kestrels or Yellow-billed Kites. These flocks follow rain belts in search of flying termites. Roost communally. Usually silent.

Feeding methods: Although as opportunistic and versatile in its feeding habits as the Yellow-billed Kite, the Black Kite's diet consists mostly of insects, especially termite alates. These are caught with the feet and eaten in flight, but may also be picked up from the ground. (See the Yellow-billed Kite for further details.)

Breeding: Two subspecies visit Southern Africa. *M. m. migrans* breeds in north-western Africa and eastern Europe to central Asia. It migrates to Africa south of the Sahara. The slightly larger subspecies *M. m. lineatus* is far less common in Southern Africa as it breeds in eastern Asia and usually migrates to southern and south-eastern Asia.

Origin of name: *Milvus* is the Latin name for 'kite', while *migrans* means 'migrating', and *lineatus* 'striped'. (The Yellow-billed Kite is usually considered to be a subspecies of the Black Kite.)

Adult   Juvenile

Possible confusion: Yellow-billed Kite p. 154

Albert Froneman

Adult

Dave Richards

Adult

Albert Froneman

Juvenile

Burger Cillié

Juvenile

p. 41

p. 254

Measurements
Length: 51-60 cm
Wingspan: 133-140 cm
Weight: ♂ 567-760 (637) g
♀ 617-750 (696) g

Distribution
Africa and Arabia.

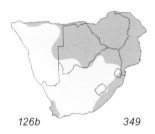

126b   349

Habitat
Occurs from desert to forest edge, but prefers woodlands, especially those with dense rural human habitation.

Food
Very varied: small mammals, birds, reptiles, frogs, carrion and various invertebrates.

Status
Common to very common breeding summer resident and non-breeding summer visitor.

A: Geelbekwou
F: Milan d'Afrique /
   Milan à bec jaune
G: Schmarotzermilan
P: Milhafre-de-bico-
   amarelo

YELLOW-BILLED KITE
Milvus migrans parasitus

Field recognition: Medium. Yellow-billed and Black Kites are the only raptors in Southern Africa with long forked tails. The adult Yellow-billed Kite appears uniform brown at a distance, lacking the distinctive greyish head of the adult Black Kite. The bill is completely yellow, not black with a yellow cere as in its juvenile, or the adult and juvenile Black Kite. It appears browner than the Black Kite with a more deeply forked tail, although this feature is only apparent when the tail is held closed. The flight pattern resembles only that of the Black Kite. The wings are markedly angled at the wrist joint, while the flight is leisurely and buoyant. The tail is continuously opened, closed and twisted while steering. **Juv.** The juvenile resembles the adult, but the bill is black with a yellow cere. The brown (not greyish) head and pale streaks on the head and underparts distinguish it from the adult Black Kite, with which it is often confused. It is distinguished from the juvenile Black Kite only with great difficulty, although the latter appears more streaked.

Behaviour: Inconspicuous while breeding during spring and early summer. Non-breeding birds gather in large flocks late in the season. May give a shrill squeal. Much more common than the Black Kite.

Feeding methods: Extremely versatile and opportunistic: feeds on a large variety of small animals, carrion and scraps. Spends long periods in the air, suddenly dropping and diving to catch prey on the ground or in flight. The agile and manoeuvrable flight allows it to take fish from the water's surface, catch flying insects, pick up prey between moving vehicles, rob other birds of their prey and even steal food from a picnic table.

Breeding: Not all Yellow-billed Kites migrating to Southern Africa breed here. **Season:** August to December, peaking from September to October in most of the region, but slightly later in the south-west. **Nest:** A substantial platform of sticks, lined with soft material such as wool, dung, skin and rags. Built in the main fork or on a lateral branch within the canopy of a tree. **Clutch:** 1–4, usually 2–3 eggs. **Incubation:** 31–38 days, by both sexes but mainly by female. **Nestling:** 42–45 days, fed by the female only. Becomes independent after a further 5–7 weeks.

Origin of name: *Milvus* is the Latin name for 'kite'. *Migrans* means 'migrating'. *Parasitus* probably refers to the kite's opportunistic feeding methods and the habit of pirating food from other raptors, thus parasitising on them. The Yellow-billed Kite is sometimes considered to be a separate species, i.e. not just a subspecies of the Black Kite.

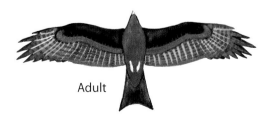

Adult

Juvenile

Fanie Hendriks

Adult

Albert Froneman

Juvenile

Niel Cillié

Juvenile

Niel Cillié

Adult in flight

Burger Cillié

Adult

Albert Froneman

Adult

p. 41

p. 254

BAT HAWK
Macheiramphus alcinus

Field recognition: Medium-small. A characteristic raptor if a clear view can be obtained. The plumage is mostly dark brown, appearing black at a distance. There is a varying amount of white on the throat, with a dark line down its centre. The slim and slightly crested head, small slender bill, large yellow eyes, upright falcon-like posture and long wings reaching almost to the tip of the tail are distinctive. The white line above and below the eye, two white patches on the nape, variable white patches on the belly and the bluish-white legs may not always be clearly visible. In flight it resembles a large falcon. As it flies mostly at dusk when colours are difficult to discern, the body shape and flight pattern should be noted. The wings are long and pointed with a broad base and a characteristic bend at the wrist. The tail is relatively short with a square tip. It flies in a leisurely and kite-like manner with slow wing beats, but pursues prey in fast twisting flight. **Juv.** The juvenile resembles the adult, but the belly, throat and upper chest are mostly white, leaving a brown band across the lower chest.

Behaviour: Spends most of the day perched in a leafy tree, returning to the same perch almost daily and hunting over the same open areas in the evening. Usually silent, but noisy when breeding: a high-pitched 'kwik-kwik-kwik'.

Feeding methods: Hunts over open areas when bats emerge at dusk. It rarely hunts at dawn, but may be active on moonlit nights. Pursues a bat in swift flight, catches it in the feet and swallows it whole while flying. Only larger prey may be taken to a perch. Selects small insectivorous bats, usually 20–30 g but up to 75 g in weight. Usually catches its daily food requirements within 20–30 minutes. May catch birds such as swifts and swallows and rarely larger flying insects. The flight feathers have soft edges like those of an owl to ensure silent flight. The large gape is an adaptation to swallow prey whole.

Breeding: Season: May to January, peaking September to November. **Nest:** A fairly large platform of sticks, which are broken off with the feet in flight. Built on an outer lateral branch of large trees (such as eucalypts or Baobabs) with pale bark to increase visibility at night. **Clutch:** 1 egg, rarely 2. **Incubation:** 51–53 days, by both sexes. **Nestling:** 67 days, fed by both sexes.

Origin of name: *Macheiramphus* refers to this bird's bill; derived from the Greek words *macheira*, 'hooked dagger', and *ramphos*, 'bill'. *Alcinus* is probably derived from *alce*, 'elk', and refers to the overall colour.

Measurements
Length: ±45 cm
Wingspan: ±110 cm
Weight: 600-650 g
Females are larger than males.

Distribution
Africa south of the Sahara, Madagascar and south-eastern Asia.

129   347

Habitat
Mostly moist woodland and tall riverine growth. Also uses plantations of exotic trees. Prefers pale-barked trees.

Food
Mostly small bats. Also small birds, especially swifts and swallows, and rarely insects.

Status
Rare resident. Somewhat nomadic.

S: Bat Kite /
    Bat-eating Hawk
A: Vlermuisvalk
F: Milan des chauves-
    souris
G: Fledermausaar
P: Gavião-morcegueiro

Adult   Juvenile

Ron Hartley

Adult

Ron Hartley

Adult and chick on nest

Warwick Tarboton

Juvenile

Johann Grobbelaar

Adult

p. 41

p. 254

PEREGRINE FALCON
Falco peregrinus

Measurements
Length: 34-43 cm
Wingspan: 80-117 cm
Weight: 2 subspecies:
F. p. minor ♂ ±500 g
♀ 610-750 g
F. p. calidus ♂ 678-740 g
♀ 825-1 300 g

Distribution
Worldwide, except
Antarctica.

171　　　　　　412

Habitat
Prefers cliffs, mountains
and gorges, but may hunt
over adjacent habitats.

Food
Mostly birds, especially
doves, caught in flight.
Rarely bats and termite
alates.

Status
Scarce resident and rare
non-breeding summer
visitor.

A: Swerfvalk
F: Faucon pèlerin
G. Wanderfalke
P: Falcão-peregrino

Field recognition: Medium-small. A powerfully built falcon. The upperparts are dark slate grey. The dark cap on the head with the broad moustachial stripes gives it the diagnostic appearance of a 'hangman's hood'. The underparts are pale and variously barred and spotted on the lower chest and belly. The eye-ring, cere and legs are yellow. At rest it appears broad-shouldered with long wings that nearly reach the tip of the tail. Seen in flight from below it appears dark as both the underwing coverts and the flight feathers are barred. The tail is often held closed. The resident race *F. p. minor* is not only smaller than the visitor *F. p. calidus*, but is also washed pale rufous below whereas the visitor has white underparts. These distinctions, however, are difficult to see in the field. It may be confused with the slightly larger Lanner Falcon, which has a rufous crown and plain underparts. In flight the Peregrine Falcon appears darker with shorter wings and tail, but has a more dynamic flight action. **Juv.** The juvenile has dark brown upperparts with paler edges to the feathers. The underparts vary from buff to white, always with heavy dark streaks. Again the 'hangman's hood' distinguishes it from similar juvenile falcons.

Behaviour: Two subspecies occur in Southern Africa. *F. p. minor* is smaller and a breeding resident, whereas the larger *F. p. calidus* is a non-breeding summer visitor from northern Eurasia. Neither is common, as the Peregrine Falcon is specialised in its habitat requirements and prey preference. Usually solitary or in pairs. Not often seen as it spends long periods perched on a cliff. Bathes and drinks regularly.

Feeding methods: Specialises in catching birds on the wing. Sometimes pursues prey in level flight, but usually stoops at prey, either from a high perch or from soaring flight. Prey is either killed on impact or by biting the back of the neck. This hunting method is one of the most spectacular among raptors.

Breeding: Only *F. p. minor* breeds in Southern Africa. *F. p. calidus* breeds in northern Eurasia. **Season:** August to December (later in the south than in the north). **Nest:** A scrape in the soil on a sheltered ledge of a high cliff, often overlooking water. Sometimes uses the stick platform of another cliff-nesting bird. **Clutch:** 1–4 eggs, usually 3. **Incubation:** 29–36 days, by both sexes. **Nestling:** 35–46 days, fed by female only at first and later by both parents. Dependent on parents for another 8 weeks.

Origin of name: *Falco* is Latin for 'falcon'. *Peregrinus* (Latin: 'wanderer') refers to the migratory habits of some of the subspecies.

Adult

Juvenile

Adult (*F. p. calidus*)

Juvenile

Adult (*F. p. minor*)

Juvenile

Adult (*F. p. calidus*)

Adult (*F. p. minor*)

p. 42

p. 257

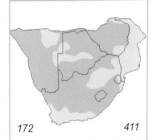

LANNER FALCON
Falco biarmicus

Measurements
Length: 35-48 cm
Wingspan: 95-115 cm
Weight: ♂ ±430-600 g
♀ 600-910 g

Distribution
Africa, the Middle East
and southern Europe.

172   411

Habitat
Varied: from woodland
to deserts, but avoids
forests. Prefers open
habitats, especially in
mountainous country. Also
in cities.

Food
Mostly small to medium
birds, but up to size of
guineafowl. Also small
mammals, reptiles and
insects.

Status
Fairly common resident.

A: Edelvalk
F: Faucon lanier
G: Lannerfalke
P: Falcão-alfaneque

Field recognition: Medium-small. The rufous crown of this large falcon is diagnostic. The upperparts are bluish-grey, while the plain pinkish-buff to whitish underparts distinguish it from similar falcons. The moustachial stripe is well developed. The eye-ring, cere and legs are yellow. In flight the underwing coverts are the same colour as the underparts, while the flight feathers and tail are barred. The tail is usually spread while flying. This falcon may be confused with the slightly smaller Peregrine Falcon, which has a diagnostic 'hangman's hood', is darker above and is spotted or barred below. In flight the Peregrine also appears stockier with shorter wings and tail and a more dynamic flight action. The underwing is darker than that of the Lanner Falcon. **Juv.** The juvenile is also identified by its rufous crown, although it is paler than that of the adult and may sometimes be nearly completely buff with only small rufous blotches. The rest of the head pattern is similar to that of the adult. It is brown above, with buff feather edges. The underparts are buff with heavy streaks. The eye-ring and cere are greenish-white at first, but turn yellow after 3–4 months. The legs are yellow. The rufous crown and thinner moustachial stripes distinguish it from the juvenile Peregrine Falcon.

Behaviour: Usually solitary or in pairs, but flocks may temporarily congregate at an abundant food supply, such as a waterhole or flock of Red-billed Queleas. Often seen on a prominent perch. Much more common than the similar Peregrine Falcon and may even occur in larger cities.

Feeding methods: A versatile hunter. May employ the spectacular stoop typical of the Peregrine Falcon to catch birds in flight, but also chases them in level pursuit. May hawk insects in flight or pounce from a perch onto ground-living prey. May even raid birds' nests, pirate prey from other raptors, feed on carrion or accompany hunters to steal their quarry. Pairs may sometimes hunt together, the one flushing prey while the other catches it.

Breeding: Season: June to December, peaking July to August (later in the south than in the north). **Nest:** Most often uses old nests of crows, herons or other raptors in a tree, on a cliff or on a power pylon. Also a scrape on a ledge of a cliff or tall building. **Clutch:** 1–5 eggs, usually 3–4. **Incubation:** 30–32 days, by both sexes. **Nestling:** 38-47 days, fed mostly by female.

Origin of name: *Falco* is Latin for 'falcon'. *Biarmicus* means 'two armed' and is a reference to the tip of the bill and the notch behind it. This feature, however, is typical of all falcons and is used to kill prey.

Adult

Juvenile

Christo Joubert

Immature

Heinrich van den Berg (Gallo Images)

Adult

Geoff McIlleron

Juvenile

Geoff McIlleron

Adult

Albert Froneman

Adult

Johann Knobel

Juvenile

p. 42

p. 257

161

Measurements
Length: 25-30 cm
Wingspan: ±70 cm
Weight: ♂ 212-233 (217) g
♀ 297-346 (320) g

Distribution
Two populations: one in the north-eastern parts of Southern Africa to Zambia and Malawi, and another in eastern Africa, from Tanzania to Ethiopia.

176   413

Habitat
High cliffs and gorges where it breeds. Immatures and hunting adults may occur over adjacent woodland.

Food
Mostly small birds, but up to size of turaco. Also insects.

Status
Rare resident.

A: Taitavalk
F: Faucon taita
G: Kurzschwanzfalke / Taitafalke
P: Falcão de Taita

TAITA FALCON
Falco fasciinucha

Field recognition: Small. A stockily built falcon with a short tail. The upperparts are slate grey with two distinct rufous patches on the nape and a bold moustachial stripe. The underparts are rufous with a white throat and cheeks. The fine black streaks on the underparts are rarely seen in the field. The eye-ring, cere and legs are yellow. Seen from below in flight it appears mostly rufous with a white throat and some barring on the flight feathers. From above the rufous nape patches and the slightly paler rump distinguish it from the larger Peregrine Falcon which occurs in the same habitat. May also be confused with the African Hobby which is more slenderly built, and lacks the rufous patches on the nape and the white throat. Its habits also differ from those of the Taita Falcon. **Juv.** The juvenile resembles the adult, but is browner above with buff edges to the feathers. It is more heavily streaked below with black spots on the flanks. The nape patches are paler than those of the adult, it has some cinnamon wash on the middle of the crown and the rump is as dark as the back.

Behaviour: Although this rare falcon also occurs elsewhere in Zimbabwe and even in South Africa, it is most common in the Batoka Gorge system below Victoria Falls. A highly visible pair breeds close to the JG Strijdom Tunnel in South Africa's Limpopo Province. Even here it is difficult to spot as it perches for hours on a cliff face or small tree. Immatures may forage further away. Flies with quick shallow wing beats, resembling a parrot. The call is a high-pitched screaming, similar to but weaker than that of the Peregrine Falcon.

Feeding methods: Typical breathtaking hunting technique of a true falcon. Specialises in taking small birds, often swifts or swallows, on the wing. It soars high above prey, and then accelerates down with rapidly beating wings. The wings are folded back as it plunges downwards, grabbing its prey in flight. Sometimes it overshoots its prey and then swoops upwards to grab it from below. The prey is carried back to a cliff where it is eaten.

Breeding: Season: July to October. **Nest:** A scrape or an old stick nest at the back of a shaded hole high on a cliff. **Clutch:** 3–4 eggs. **Incubation:** ±34 days, mainly by female. **Nestling:** 30–35 days. Dependent on parents for at least 3 weeks after leaving the nest.

Origin of name: Taita is a place in Kenya where this bird was originally collected. *Falco* is Latin for 'falcon'. *Fasciinucha* is derived from the Latin words *fascia*, 'banded', and *nucha*, 'nape' and refers to the diagnostic nape patches.

Adult

Juvenile

Peter Ginn

Juvenile

Geoff McIlleron

Juvenile

Ron Hartley

Adult

p. 42

p. 257

163

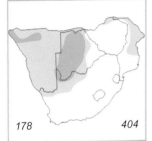

Measurements
Length: 30-36 cm
Wingspan: ±69 cm
Weight: ♂ 139-176 (163) g
♀ 225-305 (251) g

Distribution
Africa south of the Sahara,
and India.

178   404

Habitat
Prefers palm savanna
and floodplains. Also
around waterholes in
arid habitats, such as
thornveld, semi-desert
and desert.

Food
Mostly small birds caught
in flight. Sometimes small
mammals, including bats,
lizards and insects.

Status
Uncommon to rare
resident.

S: Red-headed Merlin /
   Red-headed Falcon /
   Turumti
A: Rooinekvalk
F: Faucon chicquera
G: Rothalsfalke
P: Falcão-de-nuca-
   vermelha

RED-NECKED FALCON
Falco chicquera

Field recognition: Small. Unmistakable. The chestnut crown and nape are diagnostic. The upperparts are pale blue-grey with fine black bars. The lower chest and belly are white with conspicuous black bars. The upper chest is washed rufous and the throat is white. The eyebrow and moustachial stripe are dark brown. The eye-ring, cere and legs are yellow. Seen from below in flight it appears white with black barring on the underwing. The tail has a conspicuous broad black band near its tip, which may be seen from above or below. **Juv.** The juvenile appears browner than the adult and resembles the female Red-footed Falcon. The cap and nape are brown, not chestnut. The upperparts are darker grey than those of the adult with some paler edges to the feathers on the back and upperwing coverts. The upperparts are dull rufous with very fine, barely visible streaks on the upper chest and barring on the lower chest coverts. The broad dark band near the tip of the tail remains diagnostic.

Behaviour: In northern Namibia and Botswana as well as in Mozambique it prefers open moist grassland with palms. In the Kalahari and Namib it usually occurs near tree-lined watercourses. Easily overlooked as it perches inside the canopy of a tree. Occurs singly or in pairs. Usually silent.

Feeding methods: Employs a sparrowhawk-like perch-and-chase hunting method. Perches unobtrusively within the canopy of a tree or on a low perch, often near a waterhole. If suitable prey comes within striking range, it launches itself on a high-speed chase, sometimes over hundreds of metres. It is a strong flyer with a remarkable rate of acceleration, which enables it to overtake even such fast-flying birds as doves. Rarely stoops at prey from soaring flights. Pairs may hunt together.

Breeding: Season: July to December with a peak from August to September. **Nest:** Breeds high up in palm trees in cavities at the base of the fronds, or in the old nests of crows or other raptors built in trees. **Clutch:** 2–4, usually 3, eggs. **Incubation:** 32–35 days, mostly by female. **Nestling:** 34–37 days, fed by female on food brought by male.

Origin of name: *Falco* is Latin for 'falcon'. *Chicquera* is derived from the Hindu word *shikari*, meaning 'hunter'. (The Red-necked Falcon was first described from a specimen collected in India. The Shikra's name has the same origin.)

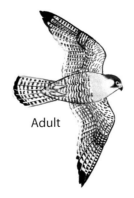

Adult

Juvenile

Niel Cillié

Adult

Clem Haagner

Juvenile

Burger Cillié

Juvenile

Chris van Rooyen

Adult

p. 42

p. 257

EURASIAN HOBBY
Falco subbuteo

Measurements
Length: 28-36 cm
Wingspan: 82-92 cm
Weight: ♂ 131-222 (180) g
♀ 141-325 (225 g)

Distribution
Breeds in Europe and Asia. Migrates to Africa and southern Asia after breeding.

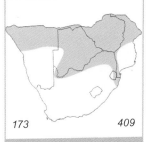

173   409

Habitat
Broadleaved woodland and savanna, often near open water.

Food
Mostly flying insects, such as termites, caught on the wing. Also small birds, such as swifts and swallows, and bats.

Status
Uncommon non-breeding summer visitor.

S: Eurasian / European
   Hobby Falcon
A: Europese Boomvalk
F: Faucon hobereau
G: Europäischer Baumfalke
P: Ógea-europeia

Field recognition: Small. A slender falcon with long wings which extend to the tip of the tail. The upperparts, including the cap and moustachial stripe, are slaty black. The throat, cheeks and patches on the nape connected to the cheeks are white. The rest of the underparts are buff, heavily streaked with black, but deep rufous on the lower belly and leggings. The eye-ring, cere and legs are yellow. The underwing is heavily streaked and barred. The tail is barred. Seen from below in flight it thus gives the impression of a dark, slender falcon with pale, heavily streaked underparts except for the rufous lower belly. It is larger, darker and more heavily streaked on the underparts than the female Amur Falcon, which has orange-red eye-rings, cere and legs. **Juv.** The juvenile is brown above with pale edges to the feathers. The underparts are completely buff and heavily streaked with dark brown. It thus resembles the juvenile Peregrine and Lanner Falcons, but is much slimmer with a swift-like silhouette in flight. It is more difficult to distinguish from the juvenile pale form of Eleonora's Falcon, which is larger with more contrasting underwing coverts, or the juvenile Sooty Falcon, which is slatier above, more heavily streaked below but with a less defined facial pattern. Such differences, however, are hard to see in the field.

Behaviour: Most common in the northern and north-eastern parts of Southern Africa, although vagrants may be recorded elsewhere. Spends most of the day perched unobtrusively. Follows rainstorms to hunt flying termites. May occur in flocks and mixes with other gregarious falcons or kestrels.

Feeding methods: Hunts mostly on the wing, very rarely catching prey on the ground. Follows thunderstorms to utilise its main food in Africa, namely flying termites. These are caught and eaten on the wing. Also catches small birds, such as swallows and swifts, in fast and agile flight. Hunts mostly at dawn or dusk.

Breeding: Breeds in Europe and northern Asia. Uses old tree nests of other birds - hence the Afrikaans and German names. Migrates to central and southern Africa as well as southern Asia when not breeding.

Origin of name: The name 'hobby' is said to come from the Old French *hober*, 'to move', referring to the hobby's swift flight. *Falco* is Latin for 'falcon'. The prefix *sub-* means 'less than' or 'smaller', while *buteo* is the Latin name for 'buzzard'. This falcon is thus smaller than a buzzard.

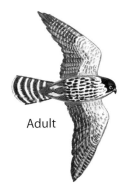

Adult

Juvenile

Ulrich Oberprieler

Adult

Stoeckle Tanguy (BIOS)

Juvenile

Markus Varesvuo

Adult

Jiří Bohdal

Juvenile

Juan M. Simon (Aquila)

Adult

p. 42

p. 257

Measurements
Length: 28-30 cm
Wingspan: ±90 cm
Weight: ♂ 150-178 (166) g
♀ 186-224 (200) g

Distribution
Tropical Africa.

174 *410*

Habitat
Palm savanna, moist
broadleaved woodland
and adjoining open
country.

Food
Mostly flying insects when
not breeding. Otherwise
mostly small birds, up to
size of dove.

Status
Rare breeding summer
resident to the north of
Southern Africa. Vagrants
may occur elsewhere.

S: African Hobby Falcon
A: Afrikaanse Boomvalk
F: Faucon de Cuvier
G: Afrikanischer Baumfalke
P: Ógea-africana

AFRICAN HOBBY
Falco cuvierii

Field recognition: Small. A slenderly built falcon with long slender wings that reach to the tip of the tail. The upperparts, including the cap and prominent moustachial stripes, are slaty black. The underparts are completely rufous, finely streaked with black, but appear plain at a distance. The eye-ring, cere and legs are yellow. In flight the underwing coverts are rufous. The flight feathers and tail are barred with buff. Seen from below in flight it thus has a mainly rufous appearance. It resembles the female Red-footed Falcon, which has grey upperparts with darker mottling and orange-red eye-ring, cere and legs. Red-footed Falcons also occur in flocks and often hover. It might also be confused with the more stoutly built Taita Falcon, which has a white throat and two rufous patches on the nape, plus a different behaviour. **Juv.** The juvenile resembles the adult. The dark feathers on the upperparts are slightly edged rufous. Most distinctive is that the rufous underparts are clearly streaked. The head and throat are often paler than the adult's. The adult Eurasian Hobby has a similar body shape, but the rufous colour of the underparts is confined to the lower belly and leggings.

Behaviour: Most common in moist woodlands of north-western Zimbabwe and north-eastern Namibia. Probably often overlooked as it perches quietly in a tree for most of the day and hunts mainly at twilight when it is difficult to identify. Adults are very aggressive at the nest.

Feeding methods: Like other hobbies it hunts mostly at dawn and dusk, when it may be seen flying swiftly and dextrously close to the ground or just over the treetops. Probably catches and eats most of its insect prey in flight. May also hunt from a perch. During the breeding season it preys on small birds that are fed to the nestlings.

Breeding: Season: September to December. **Nest:** Uses the old nests of crows or other raptors built in tall trees. May sometimes eject the rightful owners to take over a nest. **Clutch:** 2–4 eggs, usually 3. **Incubation:** Probably ±30 days, by female only. **Nestling:** Around 30 days, fed by female on birds caught by male.

Origin of name: The name 'hobby' is probably derived from the Old French *hober*, 'to move'. This refers to the swift flight characteristic of hobby falcons. *Falco* is the Latin word for 'falcon'. Frédéric Cuvier (1773–1838) was a leading French zoologist and author.

Adult

Juvenile

Peter Steyn (Photo Access)

Adult

Peter Steyn (Ardea)

Juvenile

Wiegert de Leeuw

Juvenile

Sue Robinson

Adult

p. 42

p. 257

169

Measurements
Length: 36-42 cm
Wingspan: 110-130 cm
Weight: ♂ ±350 g
♀ 340-450 (388) g

Distribution
Breeds on Mediterranean islands and along the north-western coast of Africa. Migrates mainly to Madagascar after breeding.

177   *407*

Habitat
Broadleaved woodland and adjoining grassland.

Food
Mostly insects when not breeding. Small migratory birds at breeding colonies.

Status
Rare non-breeding summer vagrant.

A. Eleonora-valk
F: Faucon d'Éléonore
G: Eleonorenfalke
P: Falcão-da-rainha

ELEONORA'S FALCON
Falco eleonorae

Field recognition: Medium-small. A large but slenderly built falcon with long wings which extend beyond the tail tip when the bird is perched. The upperparts are dark sooty brown. The moustachial stripe is well developed. In the typical form the underparts are pale to dark rufous with dark streaks, except for the throat and cheeks, which are white. The eye-ring and cere are yellowish in the male and bluish in the female and juvenile. The legs are dull yellow. In flight the dark brown underwing coverts contrast with the dark grey flight feathers. (It may be confused with the Eurasian Hobby, which is much smaller, has a rufous lower belly and leggings only, and a paler barred underwing in flight.) The dark form makes up about 25% of the total population. The plumage is completely dark sooty brown all over, or in very rare cases even black. It is difficult to distinguish from the Sooty Falcon, but is larger and darker and the tail is longer and rounded, not wedge-shaped.
Juv. The juvenile is similar to the adult. The dark feathers on the upperparts have rufous edges. The underparts, including the throat and cheeks, are pale rufous. In flight from below the underwing coverts are barred rufous and the flight feathers are almost plain and dark. It may be confused with the juvenile Peregrine Falcon because of its large size, but the underparts are pale rufous and the underwing appears dark.

Behaviour: A rare vagrant to Southern Africa, mostly to the east. May be more common than reported as it is easily mistaken for other medium to large falcons. Perches quietly during the day and hunts at dusk and dawn. The slender body with long slender wings and tail make it a fast flyer. The wing beats are shallow when flying casually, but deep and driving when hunting.

Feeding methods: Hunts mostly early morning or late afternoon and early evening. Catches and eats insects in flight.

Breeding: Breeds in dense colonies on rocky islands, mainly off the coast of Greece but also on other islands in the Mediterranean, and on rocky coasts of north-western Africa and the Canary Islands. Migrates mainly to Madagascar when not breeding. Breeds from mid-July to August so that the rearing of young coincides with the southwards migration of small birds.

Origin of name: *Falco* is Latin for 'falcon'. Eleonora d'Arborea (c. 1350–1404) was a national heroine and warrior princess of Sardinia, who passed legislation protecting birds of prey. This may, however, have been simply a way in which to protect the use of falcons for the nobility.

Typical adult

Dark adult

Juvenile

Gabriele Grilli

Males

Gabriele Grilli

Male

Guy Robrecht (Ardea)

Female

Gabriele Grilli

Dark male

Peter Pickford (SIL)

Juvenile

p. 42

p. 257

171

SOOTY FALCON
Falco concolor

Measurements
Length: 32-36 cm
Wingspan: 71-110 cm
Weight: ±210 g
Females are slightly larger
than males.

Distribution
Breeds in north-eastern
Africa and the Middle
East. Migrates to south-
eastern Africa and
Madagascar when not
breeding.

175   408

Habitat
Well-wooded areas,
usually near water.

Food
Mostly small birds, also
insects and bats.

Status
Rare non-breeding
summer visitor and
vagrant.

A: Roetvalk / Woestynvalk
F: Faucon concolore
G: Schieferfalke / Blaufalke
P: Falcão-sombrio

Field recognition: Small. A slenderly built, uniform grey falcon with a yellow eye-ring, cere and legs. Most individuals are pale grey, but some may be darker. A dark moustachial stripe may be seen at close range. The wings are long and slender, reaching the tip of the tail when the bird is perched. In flight the long pointed wings and the wedge-shaped tail, both without bars, are characteristic. The wingtips are darker and the rump paler than the rest of the upperparts. May be confused with the Grey Kestrel, which occurs in far northern Namibia only and is more stockily built, with a heavier bill and shorter wings, which do not reach the tip of the tail. The dark form of the rare Eleonora's Falcon is larger and darker with a more rounded tail. Dickinson's Kestrel is distinguished by its pale grey head, while the pale rump and barred tail may be seen in flight. The male Red-footed and Amur Falcons have red eye-rings, ceres and legs, and rufous lower bellies and leggings. **Juv.** The juvenile is grey above with buff feather edges. The underparts are buff with poorly defined grey blotches. The head has the typical dark cap and broad moustachial stripe of a falcon. The eye-ring, cere and legs are yellow. In flight from below the underwing coverts are mottled grey and buff, whereas the flight feathers and tail are barred. It is very difficult to distinguish from the juvenile Eleonora's Falcon and juvenile Eurasian Hobby except by its size and the more diffuse markings on the underparts.

Behaviour: Occurs mostly in coastal KwaZulu-Natal and Mozambique, but is more and more frequently recorded elsewhere in Southern Africa. Spends most of the day quietly roosting within the foliage of a large tree. Hunts mainly at dusk, flying rapidly with shallow wing beats interspersed with glides. Breeds late in the season in the northern hemisphere in order to catch small birds migrating south. Thus arrives later than other migratory raptors in Southern Africa.

Feeding methods: Hunts mainly at dusk, but also at dawn. An extremely fast and agile hunter that takes most of its prey in flight. Attacks on the wing, but also from a perch in a large tree.

Breeding: Breeds solitarily or in loose colonies in the desert regions of northern Africa and the Middle East. Migrates mainly via eastern Africa to Madagascar but also to south-eastern Africa when not breeding.

Origin of name: *Falco* is Latin for 'falcon'. *Concolor* (Latin) means 'the same colour', referring to the falcon's uniform grey plumage.

Adult

Juvenile

John Calryon (Aquila)

Sub-adult

Xavier Eichaker (BIOS)

Adult

H&J Eriksen (BBC)

Juvenile

Sergio Bianchi

Adult

p. 42

p. 257

173

GREY KESTREL
Falco ardosiaceus

Measurements
Length: 30-33 cm
Wingspan: ±70 cm
Weight: ♂ 215-232 g
♀ 195-300 (248) g

Distribution
Tropical Africa.

184   402

Habitat
Palm savanna, trees along watercourses and artificially cleared areas in adjacent dry woodland.

Food
Varied: insects, lizards, frogs, worms, small mammals and small birds. Occasionally Oil Palm fruit.

Status
Rare and localised resident. Occurs in Southern Africa at the edge of its range.

A: Donkergrysvalk
F: Faucon ardoisé
G: Graufalke
P: Falcão-cinzento

Field recognition: Small. A stockily built, uniform grey-coloured kestrel whose African distribution just reaches into far northern Namibia. The prominent eye-ring, cere and legs are yellow. The head appears heavy with a large bill. In flight the faint bars on the flight feathers and tail may be seen at close range from below. It may be confused with the Sooty Falcon, although the two species have different habits and their distributions probably do not overlap. Compared to the Sooty Falcon, the Grey Kestrel is stockily built, the tips of the short broad wings do not reach the tip of the tail and the darker moustachial stripe is absent. In flight the Sooty Falcon has plain grey underwings and appears slender with longer, more pointed wings. Dickinson's Kestrel is easily distinguished from the Grey Kestrel by its pale grey head, while the pale rump and barred tail may be seen in flight. The yellow eye-ring, cere and legs distinguish the Grey Kestrel from the male Red-footed and Amur Falcons. **Juv.** The juvenile closely resembles the adult, but has a brown wash to the plumage, especially on the head and underparts. The facial skin is greenish at first, but soon turns yellow.

Behaviour: A small resident breeding population of ±40 pairs occurs in far northern Namibia, where they are most common in the Cuvelai drainage system, adjacent woodland and around Ruacana. Prefers open patches where it may be seen on a prominent perch. Solitary or in pairs. Usually silent.

Feeding methods: Hunts mostly from a prominent high perch, from where it is able to scan the ground below. Glides down diagonally to catch prey on the ground on in low foliage. May also surprise prey in a swift low flight over open grassland or recently burnt areas. Sometimes pursues birds on the wing or hawks insects in flight. Rarely hovers. Is not attracted to veld fires like Dickinson's Kestrel.

Breeding: Breeding has rarely been recorded in Southern Africa, although it probably breeds regularly. **Season:** Probably August to September. **Nest:** Usually breeds in Hamerkop nests in the rest of its range. May use old nests or evict the rightful occupants. In Southern Africa probably uses tree cavities, especially in palm trees, as Hamerkops are rare in far northern Namibia. **Clutch:** 3–5 eggs. **Incubation:** Unrecorded, probably ±30 days, mainly by female. **Nestling:** About 30 days, fed by female.

Origin of name: *Falco* is Latin for 'falcon'. *Ardosiaceus* (a Latinised word from the French ardoisé) refers to this kestrel's slaty-grey colour.

Adult

Sue Robinson

Adult

Dave Richards

Adult

Steve Garvie

Adult

Ron Eggert

Juvenile

p. 42

p. 257

175

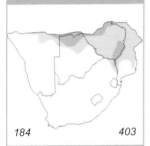

Measurements
Length: 28-30 cm
Wingspan: ±70 cm
Weight: ♂ 169-207 g
♀ 207-235 g

Distribution
Southern tropical Africa.

184   403

Habitat
Usually associated with palms and Baobab trees in tropical savanna woodlands and swampy floodplains.

Food
Mostly insects when not breeding. Otherwise varied: small birds, bats, rodents, lizards, frogs and even crabs.

Status
Uncommon to rare resident. Moves about locally when not breeding.

S: White-rumped Kestrel
A: Dickinson-grysvalk / Dickinson-valk
F: Faucon de Dickinson
G: Schwarzrückenfalke
P: Falcão de Dickinson

DICKINSON'S KESTREL
Falco dickinsoni

Field recognition: Small. Unmistakable. A primarily grey, stockily built kestrel with a squarish head. The pale grey head and, in flight, the pale grey rump and boldly barred tail are diagnostic, distinguishing it from the uniform-coloured Grey Kestrel and Sooty Falcon. The chest and belly are slightly paler grey than the back. The yellow eye-ring, cere and legs distinguish it from the male Red-footed and Amur Falcons. Individuals vary in the intensity of the grey coloration. Some may have almost white heads and much paler underparts than others. **Juv.** The juvenile is very similar to the adult. It is generally slightly browner and the pale head contrasts less with the rest of the body. The upperwing coverts are marked with some brown streaks and there may be some faint white barring on the flanks. The eye-ring, cere and legs are dull yellow. As adults vary in colour, the juvenile may be difficult to distinguish.

Behaviour: Usually solitary or in pairs. Mostly seen while scanning the ground from a prominent perch. Sits very upright. Usually silent, except when breeding. The call is a high-pitched 'kee-kee-kee'.

Feeding methods: Most hunting is done from a prominent perch such as a dead tree stump. Prey is caught on the ground after a slanting swoop. Occasionally hovers to scan the ground below. Rarely pursues birds in a fast aerial chase or hawks insects in flight. Is attracted to veld or cane field fires where it catches small prey fleeing from or disorientated by the smoke. May also watch for prey when fields are being ploughed. Caches prey on a favourite perch to be collected later.

Breeding: Season: September to January, peaking September to November. **Nest:** Breeds in the hollow tops of *Hyphaene* palms where the top has broken off, or in cavities in large trees such as Baobabs, less often inside Hamerkop nests. **Clutch:** 1–5 eggs, usually 3–4. **Incubation:** Unrecorded, probably ±30 days, mainly by female. **Nestling:** 33–35 days, fed at first by female only. May feed nestlings on food cached previously.

Origin of name: *Falco* is Latin for 'falcon'. Dr John Dickinson (1832–1863) was a medical doctor and later a missionary who joined Dr David Livingstone's Shire River expedition in 1861. He found the first specimen of this kestrel, but died of blackwater fever at the early age of 31 at the Mikorongo mission station on the Shire.

Adult

Possible confusion: Sooty Falcon p. 172, Grey Kestrel p. 174, male Red-footed Falcon p. 178, male Amur Falcon p. 180

Brendan Ryan

Adult

Daryl Balfour (Gallo Images)

Adult

Bruce Ward-Smith

Juvenile

Burger Cillié

Adult

p. 42

p. 257

177

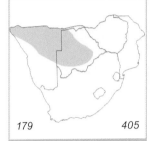

Measurements
Length: 28-31 cm
Wingspan: 66-78 cm
Weight: ♂ 115-190 (154) g
♀ 130-197 (170) g

Distribution
Breeds from eastern
Europe to central Asia.
Migrates to Southern
Africa when not breeding.

179   405

Habitat
Semi-arid savanna and
open grassland.

Food
Insects, mostly
flying termites and
grasshoppers.

Status
Non-breeding summer
visitor. Common in
northern Namibia and
north-western Botswana.
Elsewhere uncommon to
rare.

S: Western Red-footed
    Falcon / Western Red-
    footed Kestrel
A: Westelike Rooipootvalk
F: Faucon kobez
G: Rotfussfalke
P: Falcão-de-pés-
    vermelhos-ocidental

RED-FOOTED FALCON
Falco vespertinus

Field recognition: Small. Similar to the Amur Falcon. Both sexes are characterised by the red to orange cere, eye-ring and legs as well as by the rufous lower belly and leggings. The rest of the male's plumage is plain grey, including the underwing, which may be seen in flight. (The similar male Amur Falcon has white underwing coverts.) The female is grey above with black barring. The head and underparts are pale rufous with faint streaks. She has a dark mask through the eye and a dark moustachial stripe. The throat and cheeks are whitish. In flight from below the pale rufous underwing coverts and the boldly barred flight feathers and tail are distinctive. She may be confused with the female Lesser Kestrel, which is brown above and more clearly streaked below. (Also see the African Hobby.) **Juv.** The juvenile resembles the female. It is browner above with buff markings. The rufous but clearly streaked underparts, pale cheeks with a narrow white collar on the back of the neck and dark moustachial stripe are diagnostic. The crown is pale brown. It is very difficult to distinguish from similar juvenile falcons and kestrels, especially the juvenile Eurasian Hobby. The presence of adults in a mixed flock is a valuable identification pointer.

Behaviour: Migrates via the Middle East and eastern Europe to Southern Africa. Highly gregarious. Large flocks roost in large trees at night, often eucalypts growing in towns. May mix with Lesser Kestrels and even Amur Falcons, but prefers semi-arid savanna. Mostly silent, but very noisy at the roost: a continuous high-pitched 'kiwee-kiwee'.

Feeding methods: Usually hunts on the wing. Graceful and buoyant in flight, resembling a small hobby. Insects may be caught in the air or picked up from the ground without alighting. Although it hovers regularly to scan the ground below, it does so less often than the kestrels. May also hunt from a prominent perch such as a utility pole or dead tree.

Breeding: Breeds solitarily or colonially from eastern Europe to centrala Asia. Migrates mainly to south-western Africa when not breeding.

Origin of name: *Falco* is Latin for 'falcon'. *Vespertinus* (Latin) means 'in the evening'. It is here used in the context of where the sun is setting, i.e. to the west of where the Amur Falcon occurs in its breeding distribution. It was also known as the Western Red-footed Kestrel, as it has a mixture of kestrel and falcon-like characteristics.

Male

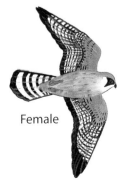

Female

Clem Haagner

Male

Clem Haagner

Male

Clem Haagner

Female

Richard du Toit

Juvenile

Niel Cillié

Female

p. 42

p. 257

179

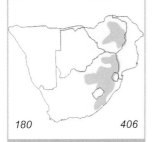

Measurements
Length: 28-30 cm
Wingspan: 58-70 cm
Weight: ♂ 97-155 (136) g
♀ 111-188 (148) g

Distribution
Breeds in eastern Asia. Migrates via India to Southern Africa, where it is more common in the eastern parts.

180   406

Habitat
Mostly open grassland, but also lightly wooded areas.

Food
Insects, mostly flying termites and grasshoppers.

Status
Common non-breeding summer visitor, but numbers are declining.

S: Eastern Red-footed Falcon / Eastern Red-footed Kestrel / Manchurian Red-footed Falcon
A: Oostelike Rooipootvalk
F: Faucon de l'Amour
G: Amur-Rotfussfalke
P: Falcão-de-pés-vermelhos-oriental

AMUR FALCON
Falco amurensis

Field recognition: Small. May be confused with the Red-footed Falcon. Both sexes are characterised by the red to orange cere, eye-ring and legs. The lower belly and leggings are rufous, darker in males than in females. The male is mostly plain grey, and can be distinguished in flight from the smaller male Red-footed Falcon by the white underwing coverts. The female is grey above with faint black barring, white below with distinct barring and blotching. The throat and cheeks are white, the moustachial stripes fairly prominent. (The female Red-footed Falcon is similar, but has a pale rufous head and underparts.) May also be confused with the Eurasian Hobby, which is heavily streaked on the chest and belly, and has a more chestnut lower belly. Its cere, eye-ring and legs are yellow. **Juv.** The juvenile resembles the female, but is less rufous on the lower belly and thighs, more heavily marked on the chest and upper belly, and browner above with buff feather edges.

Behaviour: Performs the most extraordinary migration of any raptor occurring in Africa: from its breeding grounds in eastern Asia via India across the Indian Ocean (over 3 000 km of open ocean) to eastern Africa and on to Southern Africa, where it spends the southern summer. Fat migrating birds are considered good eating by some African communities. Gregarious at all times, often perching on telephone wires. Thousands of birds roost communally in large trees, often eucalypts growing in towns. Here the species may associate with the Lesser Kestrel and even the Red-footed Falcon, but prefers a more eastern, moister habitat. The flight is fast, resembling that of a hobby or large swift. Mostly silent, but very noisy at the roost: a continuous high-pitched 'kiwee-kiwee'.

Feeding methods: All birds leave the communal roost within a very short period around sunrise. Hunts on the wing and hovers frequently. Flying insects such as termites are snatched and eaten in flight. Grasshoppers and similar insects are caught on the ground without alighting.

Breeding: Breeds in eastern Siberia, Mongolia, northern China and Korea. Uses the tree nests of mostly ravens and magpies. May breed in loose colonies.

Origin of name: *Falco* is Latin for 'falcon'. This falcon breeds in the region of the Amur River in eastern Asia. As it has a mixture of kestrel and falcon-like characteristics, it is also known as the Eastern Red-footed Kestrel.

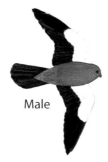

Male

Female

Fanie Hendriks

Female

Ulrich Oberprieler

Male

Mark Anderson

Sub-adult male

Chris van Rooyen

Female

Clive Johnstone

Juvenile

p. 42

p. 257

Measurements
Length: 26-33 cm
Wingspan: 58-74 cm
Weight: ♂ 90-172 g
♀ 138-208 g

Distribution
Breeds from southern Europe and northern Africa to central Asia and China. Migrates to Africa and irregularly to India when not breeding.

183   *399*

Habitat
Prefers semi-arid grasslands and Karoo.

Food
Mostly insects. Rarely small birds, lizards and rodents.

Status
Locally common non-breeding summer visitor, but numbers are declining.

A: Kleinrooivalk
F: Faucon crécerellette
G: Rötelfalke
P: Peneireiro-das-torres

LESSER KESTREL
Falco naumanni

Field recognition: Small. The slender graceful body shape of both sexes and their gregarious behaviour are good identification pointers. Males are handsomely coloured. The plain grey head and wing-bar, plain rufous back and the buff-coloured and slightly streaked underparts, which contrast with the darker upperparts, distinguish it from the Rock Kestrel, which has a streaked grey head, spotted back, rufous underparts and lacks the grey wing-bar. The tail is uniform grey except for the broad black bar just beyond its white tip. In flight the underwing is white, unmarked or faintly spotted. The female is pale rufous above with dark barring on the back, upperwing coverts and tail, and a streaky head. The underparts are buff with darker streaks. There is a small moustachial stripe below the eye. The buff-coloured and spotted underwing may be seen in flight. (The Rock Kestrel is not as slender, is deeper rufous, has spotted underparts and barred underwings. The Greater Kestrel is larger and more robust, lacks the moustachial stripe and pale underparts and, in the adult, has pale eyes and a grey, barred tail.) Both sexes have dark eyes, yellow eye-rings, cere and legs, and white claws. The latter are characteristic at very close range. **Juv.** The juvenile is almost identical to the female, but paler and duller with a less distinct moustachial stripe.

Behaviour: Unlike Rock and Greater Kestrels, this is a highly gregarious species. Hundreds or thousands of individuals congregate in the evenings to roost in large trees, often eucalypts growing in towns. Although preferring the grasslands of the highveld and parts of the Karoo, it may mix with Amur or even Red-footed Falcons. Mostly silent, but very noisy at the roost.

Feeding methods: Gregarious even when hunting. Feeds mostly on insects that are taken in a graceful stoop on the ground or are caught in flight. Typically swings into the wind to hang 5–10 m above the ground, or hovers briefly. May also hunt from a perch such as a utility pole, or even on the ground. Attracted to grass fires to catch fleeing insects.

Breeding: Breeds colonially on either natural or man-made sites, such as ledges on rock faces or buildings, in northern Africa and Eurasia. Migrates to Africa and sometimes India when not breeding.

Origin of name: *Falco* is Latin for 'falcon'. Johann Friedrich Naumann (1780–1857), a German zoologist and artist, is regarded as the father of scientific ornithology in Europe. His artwork is still regarded as among the best of European bird illustrations. (Used to be known as Naumann's Kestrel.)

Male

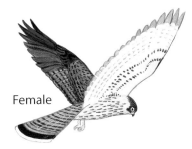

Female

Mark Anderson

Male

Warwick Tarboton

Male

Bruce Ward-Smith

Male

Niel Cillié

Female

Trevor Hardaker

Juvenile

p. 42

p. 257

183

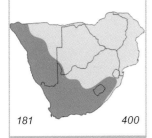

Measurements
Length: 30-33 cm
Wingspan: ±70-80 cm
Weight: ♂ 113-230 (180) g
♀ 170-271 (223) g

Distribution
Confined to the southern half of Africa.

181   400

Habitat
Variable, from desert to forest edge. Prefers montane grassland, Karoo and fynbos, especially with rocky outcrops for breeding.

Food
Mostly small mammals. Also small birds, lizards, snakes and insects.

Status
Common resident. Moves about locally.

A: Kransvalk / Rooivalk
F: Faucon des rochers
G: Felsenfalke
P: Peneireiro-das-rochas

ROCK KESTREL
Falco rupicolus

Field recognition: Small. A rufous kestrel, which may be confused with especially the male Lesser Kestrel. The grey head is streaked, the upperparts are spotted (without a grey wing-bar) and the streaked underparts are the same shade of rufous as the upperparts, unlike the male Lesser kestrel whose head is plain grey, the back plain rufous with a grey wing-bar and whose pale underparts contrast strongly with the darker rufous upperparts. In flight the underwing is white and appears barred on the flight feathers. (The Greater Kestrel is larger and more robust, lacks the grey head and, in the adult, has pale eyes, barred upperparts and flanks and a grey, distinctly barred tail.) The eyes are dark. The eye-ring, cere and legs are yellow. The female is slightly duller than the male and has a grey tail with narrow dark bars, whereas that of the male is uniform grey except for the broad black bar just beyond its white tip. **Juv.** The juvenile resembles the female, but the streaked head and barred tail are rufous like the rest of the plumage. It is similar to the female and juvenile Lesser Kestrel, which may be distinguished by their paler underparts, more slender bodies with longer tails and wings and, at close range, white claws.

Behaviour: Solitary or in pairs, not gregarious like the Lesser Kestrel. Usually, but not always, found in the vicinity of rocky outcrops where it breeds. May occur in towns. Often seen on prominent perches such as telephone poles. Hovers frequently. Usually silent except when breeding.

Feeding methods: Hovers frequently on fanning wings or hangs quietly in strong wind scanning the ground below for prey. Drops down by holding the wings above the back and parachuting in stages. May also hunt from a perch. Rarely pursues birds in stooping flight.

Breeding: Season: August to January, peaking September to December. **Nest:** Usually breeds on a ledge or in a hollow in a cliff, or in quarries, dongas, bridges or buildings. Also on nests of cliff-nesting birds, rarely in trees. **Clutch:** 1–6 eggs, usually 4. **Incubation:** 26–32 days, mostly by female. **Nestling:** 30–36 days, fed by both parents. Independent after another month.

Origin of name: *Falco* is Latin for 'falcon'. *Rupicolus* is derived from the Latin words *rupes*, 'rock' and *incolare*, 'to inhabit', i.e. a rock-dweller. The Rock Kestrel used to be regarded as a subspecies of the Common Kestrel *Falco tinnunculus*.

Male

Juvenile

Chris van Rooyen

Male

Basil Boer

Female

Alan Knott-Craig

Juvenile

Fanie Hendriks

Adult

p. 42

p. 257

185

Measurements
Length: 33-36 cm
Wingspan: ±84 cm
Weight: ♂ 209-285 (260) g
♀ 240-299 (274) g

Distribution
Discontinuous from
Southern Africa to
Somalia.

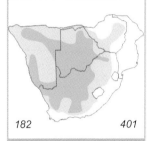

182   401

Habitat
Prefers arid, open
country, such as savanna
and grassland. Also
agricultural lands and
clearings in woodlands.

Food
Mostly insects and other
arthropods. Also small
mammals, reptiles and
birds.

Status
Fairly common resident.
Moves about locally,
especially in the west.

S: White-eyed Kestrel
A: Grootrooivalk
F: Crécerelle aux yeux
    blancs / Faucon aux
    yeux blancs
G: Steppenfalke
P: Peneireiro-grande

GREATER KESTREL
Falco rupicoloides

Field recognition: Medium-small. Large for a kestrel. The colour varies from light tawny to rufous. It lacks the grey head of the Rock Kestrel and male Lesser Kestrel. The upperparts are coarsely barred and the underparts streaked, with distinct barring on the flanks. The pale cream eye is diagnostic and can be seen from quite a distance. (This is the only kestrel in the world whose adult has a pale eye – hence the alternative name White-eyed Kestrel.) The eye-ring, cere and legs are yellow. In flight the underwing is mostly white. The tail is grey with darker bars. (Male Lesser and Rock Kestrels have plain grey tails with a darker band close to the tip. The female Lesser Kestrel is smaller and more slender. She has a moustachial stripe and pale underparts. Her tail and also that of the juvenile Rock Kestrel are brown with darker bars.) **Juv.** The juvenile resembles the adult, but has a dark eye. The flanks are streaked (not barred) and the tail is brown with narrow bars. The eye-ring and cere are bluish-white. It differs from the juvenile Rock Kestrel in that it has streaks (not spots) on the underparts. Again the female Lesser Kestrel is more slender, has a moustachial stripe and pale underparts.

Behaviour: Usually solitary or in pairs. Sometimes in small loose groups, but never as gregarious as the Lesser Kestrel. Mostly seen perched or hovering. The male displays by diving repeatedly with swerving flight while calling.

Feeding methods: Hunts mostly from a prominent perch. Regularly moves from one vantage point to the next, scanning the ground below. May also hover at a height of 10–15 m, especially in windy conditions. Prey is caught after a slow descent to the ground. Rarely makes long fast dashes to surprise prey or stoops at birds from soaring flight. Interesting is the behaviour of caching prey under grass tufts or stones.

Breeding: Season: July to January, peaking September to October. **Nest:** Breeds on old nests of crows or other raptors in tall trees or electricity pylons, rarely in tree cavities. **Clutch:** 1–7 eggs, usually 3–4. **Incubation:** 32–33 days, mostly by female. **Nestling:** 30–35 days, fed by female. Dependent on parents for another month.

Origin of name: *Falco* is Latin for 'falcon'. The suffix *-oides* means 'like'. *Rupicoloides* thus refers to the Greater Kestrel's resemblance to the Rock Kestrel (*Falco rupicolus*).

Adult

Juvenile

Rufous adult

Pale adult

Rufous adult

Pale adult

Juvenile

Juvenile

p. 42

p. 257

187

Measurements
Length: 18-20 cm
Wingspan: ±37 cm
Weight: ♂ 59-64 g
♀ 54-67 g

Distribution
Two populations: one in Southern and another in eastern Africa.

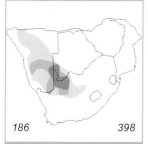

186   398

Habitat
Arid thornveld and semi-desert regions, especially where there are large thorn trees.

Food
Mostly large insects and small lizards. Also small mammals and small birds.

Status
Uncommon to locally common resident.

S: African Pygmy Falcon
A: Dwergvalk
F: Fauconnet d'Afrique
G: Halsband-Zwergfalke
P: Falcão-pigmeu

PYGMY FALCON
Polihierax semitorquatus

Field recognition: Very small. Southern Africa's smallest diurnal raptor and resembling a Common Fiscal or Lesser Grey Shrike in size and appearance. The upperparts are completely grey in the male, whereas the female has a chestnut back. The underparts are white. The eye is dark, but the red eye-ring, cere and legs are very conspicuous. In flight the white rump, black tail and flight feathers with prominent white spots are diagnostic. Cannot be confused with any other Southern African raptor. **Juv.** The juvenile resembles the adult but the back and chest are washed rufous. The juvenile female can already be recognised by her chestnut back. May start breeding when a year old.

Behaviour: Most common in the southern Kalahari. Vagrants from eastern Africa are sometimes seen in the eastern parts of Southern Africa. So closely associated with Sociable Weavers that the ranges of the two species closely approximate each other. Uses a chamber in the huge colonial nest of Sociable Weavers for roosting and nesting. The chicks' droppings whitewash the entrance and so indicate that the chamber is occupied. Pairs remain together throughout their lives. The female plays the leading role during the courtship display (hence her prominent chestnut back), consisting mostly of exaggerated tail wagging. The call is a high-pitched "kiki-KIK".

Feeding methods: Hunts from a perch. Scans the ground keenly, sometimes turning its head almost completely to look back over its tail. Drops down in a short swift swoop to catch prey on the ground. Occasionally pursues prey in a short aerial chase. Only rarely preys on Sociable Weavers or their chicks. Does not hunt during the heat of the day.

Breeding: Season: August to March, peaking September to December. May raise more than one brood in favourable years with an ample food supply. **Nest:** In Southern Africa a chamber in a Sociable Weaver nest. The nests of the White-headed Buffalo-Weaver are used in eastern Africa. **Clutch:** 1–4 eggs, usually 3. **Incubation:** 27–31 days, mostly by female. **Nestling:** ±30 days. Remains dependent on parents for up to 2 months.

Origin of name: *Polihierax* is derived from the Greek *polios*, 'pale grey', and *hierax*, 'hawk'. The Latin words *semi* and *torquatus* mean 'half' and 'collared' respectively and refer to the white half-collar stretching around the neck of this species.

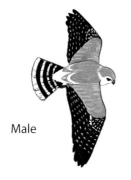

Male

Female

Male

Male

Juvenile females

Female

Female

p. 42

p. 257

189

BARN OWL
Tyto alba

Field recognition: Medium. Very similar to the slightly larger African Grass-Owl, both species have well-defined heart-shaped facial discs, small dark eyes, elongated bodies and long legs. The upperparts of the Barn Owl are mottled pale brown and grey with small white spots, the underparts are nearly white with darker spots and the white facial disc is distinctly heart-shaped. (The African Grass-Owl shows sharper contrast between the plain dark brown upperparts and the slightly buffy underparts. The spots on the underparts are horizontally elongated and the bottom of the facial disc is more rounded. The habitat preference is also an important distinguishing feature between the two species.) In flight it appears large-headed. The underwing is mostly white. **Juv.** The juvenile resembles the adult, but is darker above and buffy below.

Voice: Noisy when not actively hunting. A thin, eerie screech is given by both sexes at the perch or in flight. Hisses or snaps its bill in defence. A variety of screeching, snoring, wheezing and yelping sounds when breeding.

Behaviour: Occurs in pairs that use the same roost and nest for years. If disturbed during the day it elongates its body and closes its eyes to narrow slits. The silent flight and ghostly appearance have given rise to many superstitions, but the Barn Owl plays a valuable role in controlling rodents.

Feeding methods: Hunts at night by quartering up and down in alternate flapping and gliding flight while scanning the ground. May hover for short periods. Sometimes hunts by moving from one perch to another. Occasionally flaps its wings against bushes to disturb roosting birds. It can catch prey in total darkness by making use of its acute sense of hearing.

Breeding: Season: Throughout the year, peaking at times when the rearing of chicks coincides with the high rodent numbers after rains. May raise more than one brood in favourable years. **Nest:** Breeds in cavities in cliffs, buildings and similar sites. Also in Hamerkop or Sociable Weaver nests, tree holes or artificial nest boxes. **Clutch:** 2–13 eggs, usually 5. Dependent on the availability of prey. **Incubation:** 29–34 days, by female only. As incubation starts with the laying of the first egg, the chicks hatch over several days and differ in size. **Nestling:** Usually 45–55 days. When prey is abundant the first egg of the next clutch may be laid before all chicks of the current brood have left the nest.

Origin of name: The Greek word for 'night owl' is *tuto*. *Albus* is Latin for 'white'. (Some subspecies are very pale.)

Measurements
Length: 30-36 cm
Wingspan: ±91 cm
Weight: 219-470 g

Distribution
Almost worldwide. Virtually throughout Southern Africa.

392   160

Habitat
Generally associated with people in various habitats, from desert to woodland, but avoiding forest. A suitable nesting cavity is essential.

Food
Mainly rodents, but also other small animals such as shrews, birds, lizards and insects.

Status
Common resident, especially in urban areas.

A: Nonnetjie-uil
F: Effraie des clochers / Chouette effraie
G: Schleiereule
P: Coruja-das-torres

Sonogram

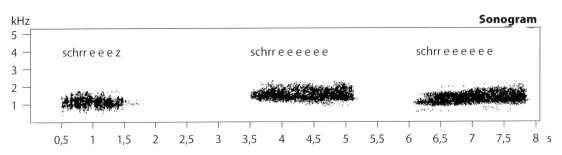

Possible confusion: African Grass-Owl p. 192, Marsh Owl p. 194

Albert Froneman

Adult

Trevor Hardaker

Adult in flight

Rip van Wyk

Chicks

Warwick Tarboton

Adult

Fanie Hendriks

Adult

p. 44

p. 268

AFRICAN GRASS-OWL
Tyto capensis

Measurements
Length: 34-40 cm
Wingspan: ±95 cm
Weight: 355-520 (419) g

Distribution
Occurs in suitable habitat
from South Africa to
Ethiopia and Cameroon.

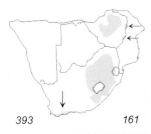

393   161

Habitat
Marshes, vleis, lush moist
grassland and even open,
dry grassland.

Food
Almost exclusively
rodents, especially vlei
rats.

Status
Uncommon to rare
resident. Numbers are
declining because of
the destruction of their
grassland habitat.

A: Grasuil
F: Effraie du Cap
G: Afrikanische Graseule /
   Kapgraseule
P: Coruja-do-capim

Field recognition: Medium. The African Grass-Owl and slightly smaller Barn Owl are similar: both have heart-shaped facial discs, small dark eyes, elongated bodies and long legs. Compared to the Barn Owl, the African Grass-Owl shows sharp contrast between the plain dark brown upperparts and the slightly buffy underparts. The spots on the underparts are horizontally elongated and the bottom of the facial disc is slightly rounded. (The Barn Owl has much paler upperparts and prefers a different habitat.) The African Grass-Owl may also be confused with the Marsh Owl with which it shares its grassland habitat. Although the Marsh Owl looks quite different with its uniform brown colour and round, buff or grey facial disc, these features may be difficult to see. In flight the upperparts of the African Grass-Owl appear uniform dark brown, while the Marsh Owl has pale ginger panels close to the tip of the wing. In contrast to Marsh Owls, African Grass-Owls have pale bills, are rare within their limited distribution, never occur in flocks and are very nocturnal. **Juv.** The juvenile resembles the adult, but is buff on the face and underparts.

Voice: A froglike ticking when flying, uttered repeatedly in bursts of about ten seconds. Also a muted screech like a Barn Owl's, but less strident.

Behaviour: Occurs singly or in pairs, although the offspring may stay with their parents for some time. Pairs use regular roosts in rank grass, allowing pellets to accumulate. It flushes reluctantly during the day, only to fly a short distance with legs dangling and dropping back into cover. (Marsh Owls usually circle to inspect the disturbance.) It is rarely seen during the day.

Feeding methods: Hunts by quartering low over the ground and suddenly dropping onto prey. Seldom hunts from a perch. As it is quite rare and very nocturnal its hunting techniques have not been studied in any detail, but the well-developed facial disc indicates that the sense of hearing is important.

Breeding: Season: October to July, peaking February to April. **Nest:** A sparse pad of dry grass on the ground at the end of a tunnel in tall grass. Usually this is connected to other chambers by tunnels. (These tunnels are lacking in Marsh Owl nests.) **Clutch:** 2–6 eggs, usually 3–4. **Incubation:** ±32 days, by female only. **Nestling:** ±42 days. Dependent for at least another month.

Origin of name: *Tuto* (Greek) means 'night owl'. *Capensis* means 'from the Cape', but often refers to the southern part of Africa.

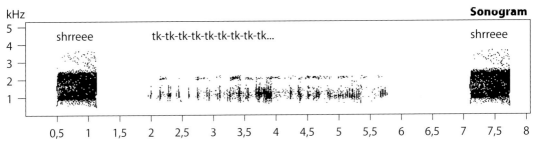

Fanie Hendriks

Adult

Ulrich Oberprieler

Adult

Rudi Erasmus (Photo Access)

Adult and chicks on nest

Niel Cillié

Adult

p. 44

p. 268

MARSH OWL
Asio capensis

Measurements
Length: 32-38 cm
Wingspan: 86,1-97 cm
Weight: ♂ 243-340 g
♀ 305-376 g

Distribution
Fragmented in Africa and
Madagascar. In Southern
Africa mostly absent from
the dry west except in
suitable small localities.

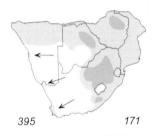

395   171

Habitat
Vleis, edges of marshes
and grassland, favouring
patches of long grass,
not necessarily in damp
situations.

Food
Mainly rodents, but also
a variety of other small
animals.

Status
Common resident.

A: Vlei-uil
F: Hibou du Cap
G: Kapohreule
P: Coruja-dos-pântanos

Field recognition: Medium. May be confused with the African Grass-Owl, which may occur in the same grassland habitat. The Marsh Owl appears plain dark brown at a distance, although the belly is paler brown and faintly barred. (The African Grass-Owl shows sharp contrast between the plain dark brown upperparts and the pale underparts.) The buff or greyish facial disc is round to oval (not heart-shaped) and is surrounded by a dark rim. The dark patches around the brown eyes give them a huge appearance. The small ear-tufts are close together, but are seldom seen in the field. Unlike African Grass-Owls, Marsh Owls have dark bills, have a wider distribution where they are quite common, often gather in flocks when not breeding and are regularly seen during the day. Seen from above in flight the Marsh Owl has pale ginger panels close to the wing tip, while the African Grass-Owl appears uniform dark brown. **Juv.** The juvenile is similar to the adult, but has a darker brown facial disc and some buff markings on the back.

Voice: A harsh, rasping, tearing croak 'krikkk', given singly or in rapid succession when disturbed or during courtship. Snaps bill in alarm. A loud, high-pitched squeal during the distraction display near the nest.

Behaviour: Southern Africa's only gregarious owl: flocks of a dozen or more birds gather when not breeding. Temporary depressions among grass are used as roosts during the day. When flushed while breeding it circles noisily, then suddenly drops into the grass and flops around as if injured.

Feeding methods: Hunts from a perch or by quartering low over its grassland habitat. Sometimes hovers briefly. Regularly hunts before sunset, but also at dawn or on overcast days. The facial disc indicates a well-developed sense of hearing. Surplus prey may be cached for later consumption.

Breeding: Season: Throughout the year, but primarily in the dry season, March to May. **Nest:** A hollow in long grass or weeds with a flat saucer of grass. Usually, but not always, built near water in marshes with dense grass cover which may be bent over to form a canopy. (It lacks the tunnels typical of African Grass-Owl nests.) **Clutch:** Usually 2–4 eggs, but up to 6. **Incubation:** 27–28 days, by female only. **Nestling:** Leaves the nest after 14–18 days, but only starts flying at 35–40 days.

Origin of name: The Greek word for 'horned owl' is *asio*. *Capensis* means 'from the Cape' but often refers to the southern part of Africa.

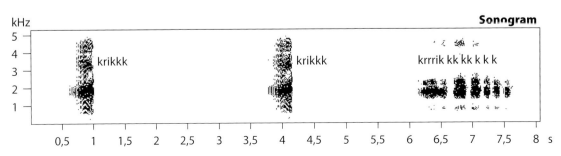

Clem Haagner

Adult and chicks on nest

Albert Froneman

Adult in flight

Albert Froneman

Adult

Bruce Ward-Smith

Adult

Mark Anderson

Adult

p. 44

p. 268

195

AFRICAN WOOD-OWL
Strix woodfordii

Measurements
Length: 30-36 cm
Wingspan: ±79 cm
Weight: ♂ 242-269 g
♀ 285-350 g

Distribution
Africa south of the Sahara.

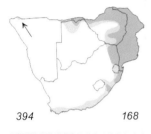

394   168

Habitat
Well-wooded areas:
forests, riverine and other
dense woodland, coastal
bush and even plantations
of alien trees.

Food
Mainly insects, but also
a variety of other small
animals, such as rodents,
shrews, small birds, frogs
and some invertebrates.

Status
Common but localised
resident.

A: Bosuil
F: Chouette africaine
G: Woodfordkauz /
   Afrikanischer Waldkauz
P: Coruja-da-floresta

Field recognition: Medium-small. An unmistakable and very attractive owl inhabiting forests or similar dense growths of trees. Appears large-headed. The large, brown eyes are surrounded by dark patches. These and the yellow bill contrast with the pale facial disc and white eyebrows. The underparts are barred russet and white. The colour of the upperparts varies from brown to russet, but the crown, nape, back and upperwing coverts are spotted with white. The long tail is marked with paler bars. **Juv.** The juvenile resembles the adult, but is paler on the head with a less pronounced facial disc. It acquires adult plumage after five months.

Voice: A pleasant series of hoots, 'WHOO-hu, WHOO-hu', that of the female probably higher pitched than the male's call. The male and female may duet, although they are not always co-ordinated. The female also utters a high 'wheeow' and is answered by a low 'hoo' from the male. Snaps its bill and hoots softly in alarm.

Behaviour: Seldom seen during the day, as it is well camouflaged when perched within the canopy of a tree. The main roost may be used for many years, while others are used infrequently. It is quite tame at the roost and watches an intruder with large eyes. Very nocturnal, only emerging to hunt after dark. Pairs are sedentary and highly territorial, and are easily located by their hooting call. Like most owls it is especially vocal in the period before settling down to breed.

Feeding methods: Hunts from a perch. Scans the ground intently and then drops down onto prey. May hawk insects in flight or snatch prey from vegetation. Most prey is swallowed whole.

Breeding: Season: July to November when insect prey is abundant. **Nest:** Natural hole in a tree such as a cavity or the top of a broken-off branch, usually 2–4 m above the ground. Rarely on the ground at the base of a tree or on an old raptor nest. The same nest is re-used over many years. **Clutch:** 1–3 eggs, usually 2. **Incubation:** 31 days, by female only. **Nestling:** 30–37 days. Starts flying at about 42 days. Dependent on parents for up to 4 months.

Origin of name: *Strix* is Latin for 'screech owl'. Col. E.J.A. Woodford (1761-1825) collected pictures and watercolours of birds in London. This owl was originally known as Woodford's Owl.

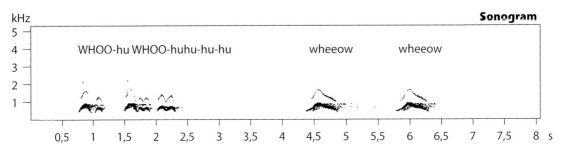

Sonogram

Possible confusion: A destinctive owl

Marietjie Oosthuizen

Adult

Albert Froneman

Adult

Nico Myburgh

Adult at nest

Ulrich Oberprieler

Adult

p. 44

p. 268

PEARL-SPOTTED OWLET
Glaucidium perlatum

Measurements
Length: 17-21 cm
Wingspan: 31,1-41,4 (37,1) cm
Weight: 61,5-123 (76,3) g

Distribution
Africa south of the Sahara. Widespread in Southern Africa, but absent from the south.

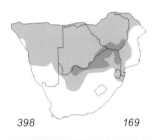

398   169

Habitat
Savanna, bushveld and open woodland.

Food
Mainly insects and other invertebrates; also a variety of other small animals, including rodents, bats, frogs, lizards and birds op to size of dove.

Status
Common resident. Often seen as partly diurnal.

S: Pearl-spotted Owl
A: Witkoluil
F: Chevêchette perlée
G: Perlkauz
P: Mocho-perlado

Field recognition: Very small. The rounded head without prominent ear-tufts distinguishes it from the African Scops-Owl and Southern White-faced Scops-Owl, although smaller ear-tufts may sometimes be seen on the side of the head. It is similar to, but smaller than the African Barred Owlet and occurs in a wider range of wooded habitats. The upperparts and head are marked with small white spots, those on the back, wings and tail being especially clear. A row of larger white spots on the wing is not always noticeable. The underparts are white with brown streaks. The face is white. (The upperparts of the African Barred Owlet are barred, whereas the white underparts bear brown spots. The row of large white spots on the wing is very prominent. The face is grey.) The eyes are bright yellow; the bill and strong feet yellow. Two large black spots surrounded by white feathers give the impression of eyes on the back of the head. **Juv.** The juvenile resembles the adult, but lacks the spots on the head and back.

Voice: Often heard, even during the day. An accelerated series of loud, penetrating whistles, first rising in pitch and volume, then becoming even louder, but more prolonged and falling slightly in pitch. The pair often duets. The female's call is higher pitched. Also a variety of soft calls when breeding.

Behaviour: Mainly nocturnal, but partly diurnal. Does not conceal itself well and is thus often seen. Unlike most other small owls it has the habit of staring at an intruder with eyes wide open. Wags its tail up and down or jerks it from side to side when alarmed or excited. The flight is fast and dipping, resembling that of a woodpecker, but not silent like most owls. Pairs are territorial.

Feeding methods: Usually hunts from a perch, intently scanning the ground and dropping onto prey. (The false eye-spots on the back of the head are especially prominent when it looks down and probably help to protect it from predators attacking from behind.) May catch insects, birds and even bats in flight. The strong feet enable it to handle fairly large prey.

Breeding: Season: August to February, peaking September to October when insect prey is abundant. **Nest:** Old woodpecker or barbet nest-hole in tree, rarely natural tree-hole or man-made nest box. **Clutch:** 2–4 eggs, usually 3. **Incubation:** 28–29 days, probably by both sexes. **Nestling:** 27–31 days.

Origin of name: *Glaukidion* is Greek for a very small owl, an owlet. The Latin *perlatum* means 'wearing pearls', and refers to the conspicuous white spots on the upperparts.

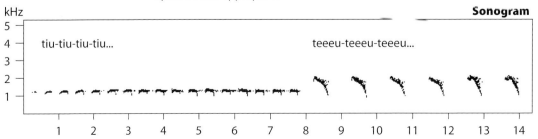

Sonogram

kHz

tiu-tiu-tiu-tiu...   teeeu-teeeu-teeeu...

Possible confusion: African Barred Owlet p. 200

Adult

Graham Kearney

Adult

Albert Froneman

Showing eye-spots on back of head

Niel Cillié

Adult

Niel Cillié

Adult in nest

Warwick Tarboton

Juvenile

Niel Cillié

p. 44

p. 268

AFRICAN BARRED OWLET
Glaucidium capense

Measurements
Length: 20-21 cm
Wingspan: ±40,5 cm
Weight: 100-130 g

Distribution
Mostly in south-central Africa with scattered populations elsewhere. In Southern Africa in the north and north-east with a small population in the Eastern Cape.

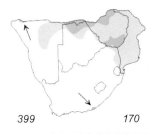

399   170

Habitat
Mature woodland, riparian and coastal forest.

Food
Mainly insects and other arthropods; also a variety of small animals.

Status
Locally common resident. Rare in the Eastern Cape.

S: African Barred Owl
A: Gebande Uil
F: Chevêchette du Cap / Chevêchette à poitrine barrée
G: Kapkauz
P: Mocho-barrado

Field recognition: Very small. The lack of ear-tufts distinguishes it from the African Scops-Owl and Southern White-faced Scops-Owl. The rounded head appears much larger in comparison to the body than that of the similar, but smaller, Pearl-spotted Owlet. The upperparts are barred, especially noticeable on the back, wings and tail. A row of large white spots on either wing is very prominent, forming a bold V when seen from behind. The underparts are white with bold brown spots, except for barring on the throat and upper chest. The face is grey. (The Pearl-spotted Owlet has spotted upperparts and white underparts with brown streaks. The row of white spots on the wing is less prominent. The face is white.) The eyes are bright yellow, whereas the bill is green-yellow and the feet dull yellow. It lacks the Pearl-spotted Owlet's false eyes on the back of the head. Birds of the Eastern Cape are darker above and have spots rather than bars on the head. This isolated population is sometimes regarded as a separate species, as the call is also slightly different. **Juv.** The juvenile resembles the adult, but the spots on the underparts are indistinct.

Voice: A repeated high-pitched series of Cape Turtle-Dove-like purring notes at the same pitch, but rising slightly in volume. Pattern somewhat like that of the Pearl-spotted Owlet, but softer and more mournful. Also a two-syllabled purring 'prr-purr' and other, softer calls.

Behaviour: Most active at dawn and dusk, less often during the day than the Pearl-spotted Owlet. Not too difficult to find as it does not conceal itself well, even when disturbed. The flight is fast and dipping, like that of the Pearl-spotted Owlet, but it rarely wags its tail. Prefers dense woodland with tall trees and a well-developed canopy. Pairs are territorial.

Feeding methods: Scans the ground from a perch and drops onto prey. The small feet indicate that it takes small prey, mostly insects.

Breeding: Season: August to January, peaking September to October when insect prey is most abundant. **Nest:** Natural hole in tree. Probably too large to fit through the entrance of old woodpecker or barbet nests like the Pearl-spotted Owlet. **Clutch:** 2–3 eggs. **Incubation:** 28–34 days. **Nestling:** 32–33 days.

Origin of name: *Glaukidion* is Greek for a very small owl, an owlet. *Capense* means 'from the Cape', but often refers to the southern part of Africa.

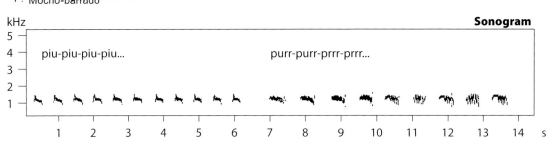

kHz   **Sonogram**
5
4 —   piu-piu-piu-piu...   purr-purr-prrr-prrr...
3
2
1 —

        1   2   3   4   5   6   7   8   9   10   11   12   13   14   s

Possible confusion: Pearl-spotted Owlet p. 198

Lex Hes

Adult

Lizeth Cillié

Adult

Richard du Toit

Adult

Geoff McIlleron

Adult (Eastern Cape)

p. 44

p. 268

201

AFRICAN SCOPS-OWL
Otus senegalensis

Field recognition: Very small: the smallest owl with ear-tufts in Southern Africa. Two colour forms occur: grey and brown, the grey form being the most common. The plumage is marked with the fine black streaks and blotches and white mottling, resembling tree bark. The tail is short and does not extend beyond the wingtips. (The Pearl-spotted and African Barred Owlets have longer tails.) The face is grey with a fine black rim. The eyes are yellow. (The larger Southern White-faced Scops-Owl has a white face with a broad black edge around the facial disc and orange eyes.) During the day the body is elongated and then the ear-tufts are very prominent. When active at night the owl appears heavier and the ear-tufts are often folded down. **Juv.** The juvenile is very similar to the adult, but often has a slight brown wash and shorter ear-tufts.

Voice: Often heard at night. A high-pitched, vibrant but monotonous 'prrrrup' repeated at 5–8 second intervals. Insect-like and hard to locate. A pair often answer each other, the female's call being softer and higher pitched. Various soft calls may be given at the nest.

Behaviour: Solitary or in pairs. Very nocturnal. Easily overlooked as it is extremely well camouflaged during the day, when it roosts pressed against a tree trunk. When disturbed it elongates its body, erects the ear-tufts and closes the eyes to narrow slits, resembling a dead branch. Does not flush easily. Uses the same perch day after day. Becomes active and starts calling at dusk. Prefers areas with tall scattered trees and open ground, especially mopane woodland.

Feeding methods: Hunts from a perch, dropping onto insects seen on the ground. May occasionally look for prey by walking around on the ground or hawk insects in flight.

Breeding: Season: June to December, mainly September to October when insect prey is abundant. **Nest:** Natural hole in tree, preferably open-topped such as the hollow created by a broken-off branch. Rarely in old woodpecker or artificial nest. **Clutch:** 2–4 eggs, usually 3. **Incubation:** 22–28 days, mainly by female. **Nestling:** 25–28 days.

Origin of name: The Latin word *otus* means 'horned or eared owl'. This owl was first described from Senegal. Sometimes regarded as conspecific with the Eurasian Scops-Owl (*Otus scops.*)

Measurements
Length: 15-18 cm
Wingspan: 41,5-49,3 (45,1) cm
Weight: 45,0-97,4 (64,5) g

Distribution
Africa south of the Sahara. In Southern Africa widely but patchily distributed. Absent from arid regions.

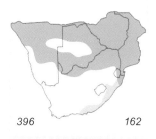

396   162

Habitat
Prefers drier savanna, but occurs widely in bushveld and woodland.

Food
Mainly insects and other arthropods. Occasionally also other small animals.

Status
Common resident, but absent from some regions where it might be expected.

A: Skopsuil
F: Hibou petit-duc africain / Petit-duc africain
G: Afrikanische Zwergohreule
P: Mocho-de-orelhas-africano

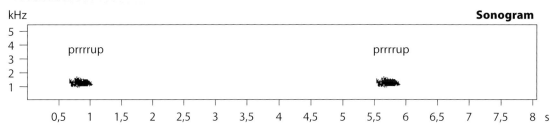

kHz   **Sonogram**

5
4   prrrrup   prrrrup
3
2
1

    0,5   1   1,5   2   2,5   3   3,5   4   4,5   5   5,5   6   6,5   7   7,5   8 s

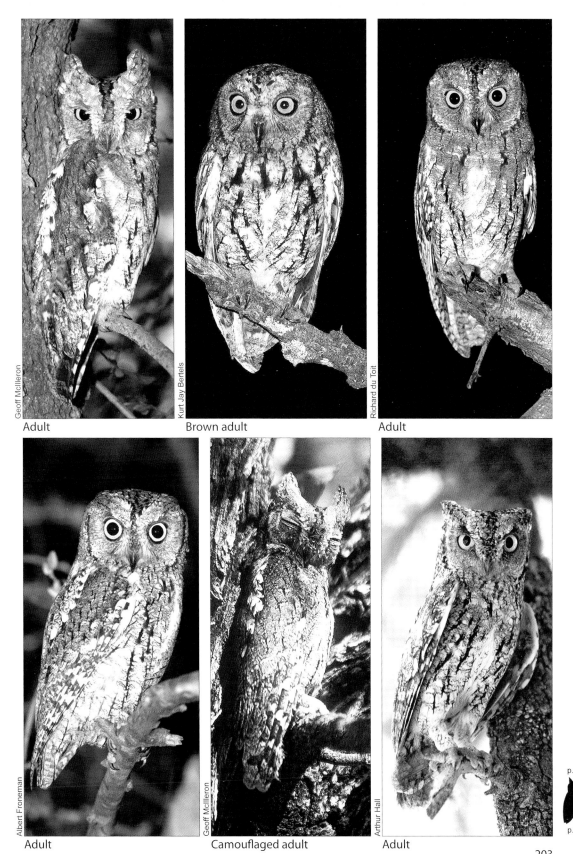

Adult

Brown adult

Adult

Adult

Camouflaged adult

Adult

p. 44

p. 268

203

SOUTHERN WHITE-FACED SCOPS-OWL
Ptilopsis granti

Field recognition: Small. A predominantly grey owl with conspicuous ear-tufts. (Larger than the African Scops-Owl, but much smaller than eagle-owls.) The underparts are pale grey with black streaks. There is a row of white spots on the wing. The white face with a broad black border and orange eyes distinguish it from the smaller African Scops-Owl, which has a grey face with a narrow black rim and yellow eyes. The tail is short and does not extend beyond the wingtips. (The smaller Pearl-spotted and African Barred Owlets have longer tails.) Elongates its body and narrows its eyes when disturbed, but is not as well camouflaged as the African Scops-Owl. The ear-tufts are less noticeable when it is active. **Juv.** The juvenile is very similar to the adult, but the eyes are yellow-orange and the face is grey, not white.

Voice: A rapidly repeated, somewhat dove-like bubbling hoot 'ho-ho-ho-ho-ho-WHOO-OO', the last two notes drawn out and higher pitched. Alarm call a cat-like snarl. Other soft calls at the nest.

Behaviour: Nocturnal. Seldom seen during the day, when it roosts in a tree. Pairs often roost close together and may use the same perch day after day. Draws itself into an elongate, slender form with erect ear-tufts and eyes narrowed to a slit when alarmed, but does not conceal itself as well as the African Scops-Owl. May start calling late afternoon, but only becomes active when it is dark. Resident in areas with a constant supply of prey, but nomadic in regions where rodent numbers fluctuate from year to year.

Feeding methods: Prey is caught by dropping onto it from a perch. Feeds mostly on rodents, especially multimammate mice.

Breeding: Season: May to February, peaking August to October. **Nest:** Two types are used: either old nests of other birds, mostly stick platforms such as those of small raptors, crows or the Grey Go-away-bird, or a natural hollow in a multiple fork of a tree. When prey is abundant, pairs may nest in close proximity to each other. **Clutch:** 1–4 eggs, usually 2–3. **Incubation:** 30 days, mostly by female. **Nestling:** At least 23 days. Flies at ±33 days.

Origin of name: The genus *Ptilopsis* is of Greek origin. *Ptilon* means 'feather' and *ops* means 'eye'. Captain Claude Grant (1878–1958) was a British ornithologist and author.

Measurements
Length: 25-28 cm
Wingspan: ±67,5 cm
Weight: 125-275 (193) g

Distribution
Africa south of the Sahara. In Southern Africa it is widely distributed in the northern regions with a sparser extension into the south-central and south-eastern parts.

397   163

Habitat
Prefers thornveld, but occurs in a wide variety of savanna, bushveld and woodland types.

Food
Mainly rodents, but also insects, birds and other small animals.

Status
Common resident.

S: White-faced Owl
A: Witwanguil
F: Petit-duc à face blanche
G: Weissgesicht-Ohreule / Buscheleule
P: Mocho-de-faces-brancas

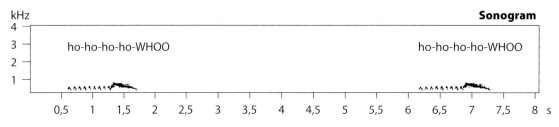

Adult

Adult

Adult on nest

Camouflaged adult

Adult

p. 44

p. 268

VERREAUX'S EAGLE-OWL
Bubo lacteus

Measurements
Length: 58-66 cm
Wingspan: ±143 cm
Weight: ♂ 1,62-1,96 (1,7) kg
♀ 2,48-3,12 (2,63) kg

Distribution
Africa south of the Sahara.
In Southern Africa absent
from the south except for
some isolated populations.

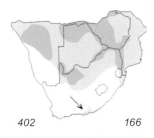

402   *166*

Habitat
Prefers open savanna;
also in bushveld and
woodland, especially
along floodplains.

Food
Small to medium
mammals, a variety of
birds and other small
animals and insects.

Status
Fairly common resident.

S: Giant Eagle-Owl / Milky
   Eagle-Owl
A: Reuse-ooruil
F: Grand-duc de Verreaux
G: Milchuhu / Blassuhu
P: Bufo-leltoso

Field recognition: Very large; Africa's largest owl. The plumage is grey with fine black-and-white barring which, however, is only visible at close quarters. The upperparts are slightly darker than the underparts and face. The eyes are dark, not yellow or orange as in other eagle-owls. When the eyes are closed the diagnostic pink eyelids may be seen. The grey face is bordered by a black rim. The ear-tufts are fairly short and broad. They are usually folded down and thus not always visible. Females are much larger than males. May be confused with the much smaller Southern White-faced Scops-Owl, which has a white face and orange eyes. The large size distinguishes it from the other two eagle-owls, except the northern subspecies of the Cape Eagle-Owl (i.e. Mackinder's Eagle-Owl), which has a brown appearance and orange eyes. **Juv.** The juvenile is paler than the adult with a less pronounced dark facial rim. It is no longer distinguishable from the adult by the age of five months. May start breeding when three years old.

Voice: Two main calls are given. One is a series of grunting hoots 'unnh-unnh-unnh-unnh' which may be in duet. The female's voice is deeper than the male's. The female and fledglings also utter a plaintive, far-carrying whistle that is difficult to locate. Other calls may also be given.

Behaviour: Usually seen singly or in pairs, but the juvenile may stay with its parents until the next breeding season. Nocturnal. Spends the day perched in the canopy of a large tree. May be approached quite closely, as it relies on the good camouflage of its plumage.

Feeding methods: Surveys its surroundings from a perch and swoops down to catch prey. May attack birds roosting in trees or catch insects in flight. Sometimes walks around on the ground in search of prey. Its large size and powerful feet allow it to catch large prey.

Breeding: Season: March to September, peaking June to August. **Nest:** Mostly old nests of other birds, especially stick platforms. Less often a hollow in a tree. **Clutch:** Usually 2 eggs, sometimes only 1. **Incubation:** 38–39 days, by both sexes. **Nestling:** Leaves the nest after about 1 month, but can fly properly only when ±3 months old. Stays with parents until the next season.

Origin of name: *Bubo* is Latin for 'eagle-owl', i.e. a large 'horned' owl. *Lacteus* means 'milky' and refers to the pale colour. Jules Verreaux (1808-1873) visited Southern Africa with his two brothers. He later became the director of the natural history museum in Paris.

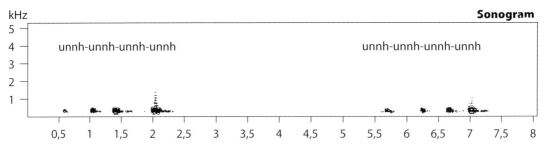

Ulrich Oberprieler

Adult

Niel Cillié

Adult

Burger Cillié

Juvenile

Niel Cillié

Adult

Albert Froneman

Adult

p. 44

p. 268

207

SPOTTED EAGLE-OWL
Bubo africanus

Measurements
Length: 43-50 cm
Wingspan: ±113 cm
Weight: 487-995 (696) g
Females are larger than males.

Distribution
Widespread in southern as well as the rest of Africa south of the Sahara.

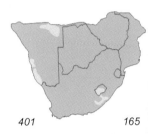

401   165

Habitat
Varied: from rocky outcrops in deserts to mature woodland, including urban areas.

Food
Mainly small mammals, birds and arthropods, but also other small animals.

Status
Resident. The most common owl in Southern Africa.

S: African Eagle-Owl
A: Gevlekte Ooruil
F: Grand-duc africain
G: Fleckenuhu / Berguhu
P: Bufo-malhado

Field recognition: Large. The upperparts are greyish with some white spots. The underparts are whitish with darker blotches on the chest and fine barring on the belly and flanks. The smaller size, yellow eyes and mottled appearance distinguish it immediately from Verreaux's Eagle-Owl. It is most easily confused with the slightly larger Cape Eagle-Owl, but differs from that species by its greyer plumage, yellow (not orange) eyes and the fine barring on the belly. A rarer rufous form occurs mostly in western arid regions. It varies from a pale sandy to a rufous colour, has orange eyes and is thus very similar to the Cape Eagle-Owl. The latter species, however, has some conspicuous, orange-brown feathers on the neck and chest, bold barring on the belly and larger feet. **Juv.** The juvenile is very similar to the adult, but browner below, less spotted above and has shorter ear-tufts.

Voice: A hooting call similar to that of the Cape Eagle-Owl, but softer and less penetrating. The male utters a two-syllabled 'hoo-hoo', while the female gives a three-syllabled 'hooho-hoo', the second note being very short ('who are you'). May call in duet. Other calls may also be given.

Behaviour: Nocturnal. Well camouflaged where it roosts during the day in a tree, on a rock face or on the ground. Elongates its body, raises its ear-tufts and narrows its eyes when disturbed. Pairs remain together for life. A common owl in gardens, where it becomes used to people. Often looks for insects on roads and many are killed by cars.

Feeding methods: An opportunistic and adaptable owl. Usually hunts from a perch, dropping or swooping down onto prey. May catch insects by pursuing them on the ground. May dash at roosting birds and even hawk insects and bats in flight.

Breeding: Season: July to January, peaking August to October. **Nest:** Varied. Mostly on the ground in a rocky outcrop or on a ledge of a cliff, donga or similar situations, even buildings. Also in trees, either on old nest of other birds, usually stick platforms, or in a tree hole or a hollow in a multiple fork. **Clutch:** 1–6 eggs, usually 2-3. **Incubation:** 29–33 days, by female only. **Nestling:** 40–42 days. Dependent on parents for another 5 weeks.

Origin of name: *Bubo* is the Latin for an 'eagle-owl', i.e. a large 'horned' owl. It is Africa's typical eagle owl, hence *africanus*.

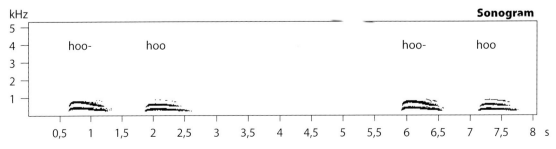

Possible confusion: Cape Eagle-Owl p. 210, Verreaux's Eagle-Owl p. 206

Ulrich Oberprieler

Adult

Richard du Toit

Rufous adult

Niel Cillié

Adult

Alan Knott-Craig

Adult

Clem Haagner

Adult and chicks on nest

Fanie Hendriks

Adult

p 44

p. 268

209

CAPE EAGLE-OWL
Bubo capensis

Measurements
Length: 48-54 cm
Wingspan: ±125 cm
Weight: 0,9-1,36 (1,12) kg
Females are larger than males.

Distribution
Southern to eastern Africa.

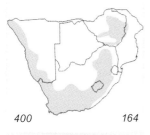

400   164

Habitat
Mostly in montane grassland especially where there are rocky outcrops, but also in fynbos and hilly woodland.

Food
Mostly small to medium-sized mammals and larger birds; also other small animals.

Status
Uncommon, localised resident.

S: Mountain Eagle-Owl / (Mackinder's Eagle-Owl for *B. c. mackinderi*)
A: Kaapse Ooruil
F: Grand-duc de montagne / Grand-duc de Cap
G: Kapuhu
P: Buto do Cabo

Field recognition: Large to very large. A brown, stockily built but very attractive eagle-owl inhabiting rocky terrain. It is distinguished from the slightly smaller Spotted Eagle-Owl by its orange eyes, bold black and rufous blotches on the chest, broad barring of black, tawny and white on the belly, tawny feathers on the neck and large feet. (Spotted Eagle-Owls are usually greyish with yellow eyes, fine barring on the belly and small feet. A rare rufous form has orange eyes but is still distinguished from the Cape Eagle-Owl by the finer barring on the belly, the absence of prominent tawny feathers on the neck and the small feet.) Females are larger than males. The subspecies occurring from Zimbabwe and Mozambique north to eastern Africa, known as Mackinder's Eagle-Owl (*B. c. mackinderi*), is much larger than the southern subspecies and approaches Verreaux's Eagle-Owl in size.
Juv. The juvenile is very similar to the adult, but has shorter ear-tufts.

Voice: A mellow two- or three-syllabled hooting 'hoo-hoo' or 'hoo-hoohooo', the last note being short or long. Similar to the call of the Spotted Eagle-Owl, but of a different quality and rhythm. Although male and female may call together, they have no regular duet like the Spotted Eagle-Owl.

Behaviour: Although it may be found in a variety of habitats, it is always associated with rocky areas. During the day it roosts in shade on the ground, hidden behind some cover or in a small cave, less often in a tree. The mottled colour makes it difficult to spot. Does not flush easily. May enter cities where it roosts on buildings and hunts Feral Pigeons (Rock Doves). Usually hunts during the early part of the night.

Feeding methods: Observes its surroundings from a perch and swoops down onto its prey. The large feet allow it to utilise fairly large prey, especially in the case of the larger Mackinder's Eagle-Owl.

Breeding: Season: May to August. **Nest:** Scrape on the ground, on a ledge or in a cave, well hidden by vegetation or rocks. **Clutch:** 1–3 eggs, usually 2. **Incubation:** 34–38 days, by female only. **Nestling:** Leaves nest after ±45 days. Able to fly when 70–77 days old.

Origin of name: *Bubo* is Latin for 'eagle-owl', i.e. a large 'horned' owl. *Capensis* means 'from the Cape', often referring to the southern part of Africa. Sir Halford Mackinder made the first ascent of Mount Kenya.

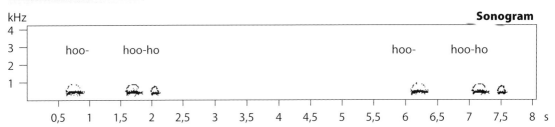

Sonogram

Possible confusion: Spotted Eagle-Owl p. 208, Verreaux's Eagle-Owl p. 206.

Ulrich Oberprieler

Adult

Warwick Tarboton

Adult with chick on nest

Chris van Rooyen

Adult

Ron Hartley

Adult (*B. c. mackinderi*)

p. 44

p. 268

PEL'S FISHING-OWL
Scotopelia peli

Measurements
Length: 61-63 cm
Wingspan: ±153 cm
Weight: 2,06-2,27 (2,14) kg

Distribution
Scattered populations occur in sub-Saharan Africa. In Southern Africa it is confined to large river systems in the north-east.

403   167

Habitat
Large, slow-flowing rivers and swamps with dense riverine woodland and forest with large overhanging trees, especially in lowlands.

Food
Mostly fish; sometimes other aquatic animals.

Status
Uncommon, localised resident.

A: Visuil / Pel-visuil
F: Chouette-pêcheuse de Pel
G: Bindenfischeule
P: Corujão-pesqueiro de Pel

Field recognition: Very large. Unmistakable. The plumage is rufous brown with some darker markings. The underparts are paler than the upperparts. The head is usually flattish with very slight, if any, ear-tufts. When alarmed or excited the feathers on the head are fluffed up, giving it a large rounded appearance. The eyes are dark. The legs and feet are unfeathered, but are usually hidden by the belly feathers. Females are larger than males. **Juv.** The juvenile is paler than the adult. It acquires full adult plumage by the age of 15 months.

Voice: A deep, resonant hoot sometimes preceded, but usually followed, by a low grunt: 'hooommm-hut'. Most often given before dawn and audible up to 3 km away. The male and female often call in duet, with the male having the higher-pitched voice. A high-pitched, penetrating trill is uttered during the distraction display.

Behaviour: Occurs in pairs, sometimes accompanied by their single offspring. Nocturnal. Prefers dense stands of large riverine trees in lowlands. Roosts inside the canopy of a shady tree during the day, where it is very easily overlooked. Suitable roosts are used repeatedly and may be revealed by barbel heads, pellets of fish scales or feathers lying below. When flushed, it flies a short distance to another tree and then watches the intruder intently. Pel's Fishing-Owls are most common in the Okavango Swamps. Elsewhere they are often threatened by destruction of their wooded habitat and damming of rivers.

Feeding methods: Hunts from a perch 1–2 m above the water or sometimes from a high riverbank. Prefers to hunt over quiet or shallow stretches of water. Swoops down like a fish-eagle to take fish from the surface. The long claws and spines on the soles help it to hold its slippery prey. The rudimentary facial disc indicates that hearing is not important in locating prey. Unlike other owls, fishing owls do not fly silently, as fish are not able to hear them under water.

Breeding: Season: January to June, peaking at the end of summer. **Nest:** Natural tree cavity or a hollow in a fork of a large, shady tree. Clutch: 1–2 eggs, usually 2. **Incubation:** Around 33–38 days, mostly by female. **Nestling:** 68–70 days. Only 1 chick survives. Dependent for at least another 4 months.

Origin of name: *Skotos* (Greek) means 'darkness', while *pelia* and *peli* refer to H.S. Pel, a Dutch naturalist and later Governor of the Gold Coast (Ghana) until 1850.

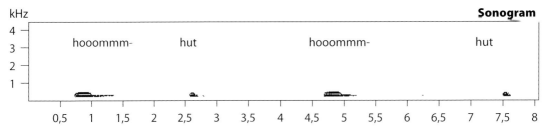

Sonogram

kHz

hooommm-   hut   hooommm-   hut

Anthony Bannister (Gallo Images)

Adult

Albert Froneman

Adult

Albert Froneman

Adult

Chris van Rooyen

Adult

p. 44

p. 268

Long-crested Eagle / Alan Knott-Craig

SECTION 4
CONFUSING BIRDS

HOW TO USE THIS SECTION

As stated previously, the key to raptor identification is the ability to place a bird in one of the 11 groups as indicated in Section 2. As this section (Section 4) is also based on these groups, it is of utmost importance to be familiar with their characteristics before attempting to identify a species in the section.

In this section similar species within each group are compared by means of illustrations in which the diagnostic features are indicated. Black-and-white drawings are used as colour plays a far less important role in the identification of raptors than the pattern, body shape, size, habitat, status and even some behaviours.

Each group starts with a short key which will lead you to a number of similar, confusing raptors within that group. If a raptor may be confused with a species falling within another group, this will be indicated at the end of the feature description.

Please note that not all Southern African raptors are described in this section. Unique species which cannot be confused with other raptors, such as the Secretarybird or adult African Fish-Eagle, have been omitted. It is advisable to use this section in combination with Section 3 by using the cross-references to find the relevant pages.

The illustrations are not to scale.

GROUP	page
Fish-eating raptors	217
Vultures	218
Eagles and hawk-eagles	224
Snake-eagles	232
Buzzards	236
Goshawks and sparrowhawks	241
Harriers	250
Kites	254
Falcons and kestrels	257
Owls	268

FISH-EATING RAPTORS
(p. 34)

The Osprey and African Fish-Eagle could be confused with true eagles from which they are distinguished by their unfeathered lower legs. Both catch fish and are therefore associated with water. They are often seen soaring overhead on long broad wings.

The adult African Fish-Eagle is unmistakable. The immature may be confused with the Osprey as both have a mainly white appearance. The juvenile African Fish-Eagle resembles a variety of other large brown raptors.

OSPREY (p. 50)

Field recognition:
- Size: Medium-large
1 Shaggy crest on back of head
2 Dark band through eye
3 Underparts white with streaks on chest
4 Wings very large with dark wrist patches and central
 bar on underwing
5 Tail longish
- Juvenile has slightly scaled upperparts

Other characteristics:
- Habitat: Mostly fresh water and estuaries
- Hunts in flight, hovers and plunge-dives to catch fish
- Status: Uncommon non-breeding summer visitor

AFRICAN FISH-EAGLE – immature (p. 52)

Field recognition:
- Size: Large
1 Head and chest white with brown markings
2 Dark eyebrow
3 Wings long and broad
4 Tail short

Other characteristics:
- Habitat: Mostly fresh water
- Hunts from a perch and swoops down to
 the water's surface to catch fish
- Status: Locally common resident

AFRICAN FISH-EAGLE – juvenile (p. 52)

Field recognition:
- Size: Large
1 Lower legs unfeathered; dirty yellow
2 Mainly brown with white markings on the neck and chest
- Wings long and broad in flight
- Tail short in flight

Other characteristics:
- See immature above
- Could be confused with various large brown raptors

VULTURES
(p. 35)

Vultures are large to very large scavenging birds. The shape of the bill varies from slender to very heavy. The head and neck of most species are partially or wholly naked and the weak feet are not suited to kill prey. Vultures have long broad wings and short tails for soaring flight. The Palm-nut and Bearded Vultures are not typical vultures.

1 White vultures (p. 218)
Only two vultures are predominantly white: the adult Palm-nut and Egyptian Vultures. They differ in body shape, colour pattern and behaviour.

2 Dark vultures (p. 219)
The colour of these vultures varies from brown to nearly black. The juvenile Bearded Vulture resembles the adult in body shape and behaviour. The juvenile Palm-nut Vulture may be confused with various other large brown raptors, but the shape of the head and bill is characteristic. The Hooded, White-headed and Lappet-faced Vultures differ not only in size but also in the shape of their bills.

3 Griffon vultures (p. 222)
The three griffons are large vultures with long snake-like necks devoid of feathers. They feed mostly on the soft flesh and internal organs of a carcass. Both the Cape Vulture and White-backed Vulture are quite common residents, whereas Rüppell's Vulture is a rare vagrant from East Africa.

1. White vultures

EGYPTIAN VULTURE – adult (p. 56)

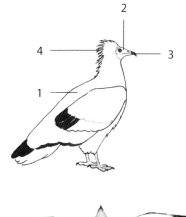

Field recognition:
• Size: Large
1 Plumage mainly white or buff
2 Face orange-yellow
3 Bill very slender
4 Long feathers on back of head
5 Flight feathers completely black
6 Tail wedge-shaped; completely white

Other characteristics:
• Habitat: Semi-desert, open plains and arid savanna
• Status: Rare vagrant

PALM-NUT VULTURE – adult (p. 54)

Field recognition:
- Size: Large
1 Plumage mainly white with some black areas
2 Face red to orange
3 Secondaries completely black, primaries with black tips only
4 Tail rounded; black with white tip

Other characteristics:
- Habitat: Associated with Raffia Palms
- Status: Rare, localised resident on the northern KwaZulu-Natal coast. Immatures may wander widely

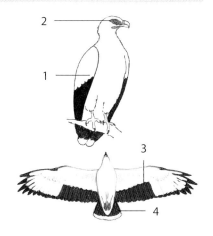

2. Dark vultures

PALM-NUT VULTURE – juvenile (p. 54)

Field recognition:
- Size: Large
1 Lower legs unfeathered; whitish
2 Shape of head and bill distinctive
3 Bare face yellowish to orange
4 All dark in flight

Other characteristics:
- See adult above

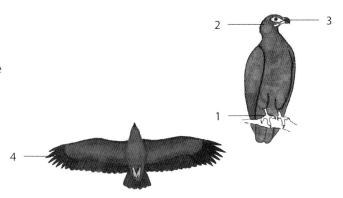

BEARDED VULTURE – juvenile (p. 70)

Field recognition:
- Size: Very large
1 Long body shape and beard like adult
2 Plumage brown with a darker head
3 Appears all dark in flight, but long narrow wings and wedge-shaped tail diagnostic

Other characteristics:
- Habitat: Mainly confined to Drakensberg
- Status: Rare and endangered resident

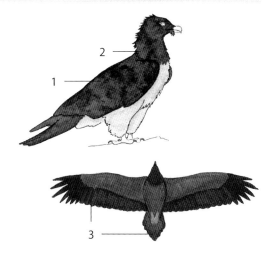

HOODED VULTURE – adult (p. 58)

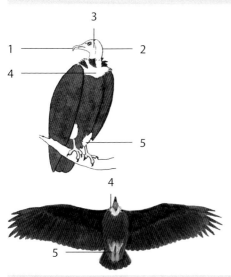

Field recognition:
- Size: Large
1 Bill very slender
2 Back of head covered with pale down
3 Face pink
4 Crop patch white
5 Leggings white

Other characteristics:
- Cannot compete with larger vultures at a carcass, but prefers to feed on smaller scraps
- Habitat: Woodland and savanna
- Status: Rare to locally common resident

HOODED VULTURE – juvenile (p. 58)

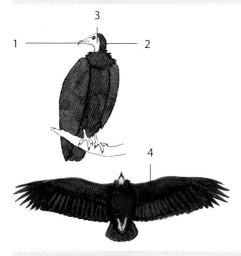

Field recognition:
- Size: Large
1 Bill very slender
2 Back of head covered with dark brown down
3 Face greyish
4 All dark in flight

Other characteristics:
- See adult above

EGYPTIAN VULTURE – juvenile (p. 56)

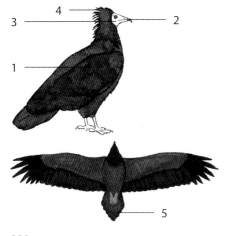

Field recognition:
- Size: Large
1 Plumage dark brown
2 Bill very slender
3 Face dull greyish
4 Long feathers on back of head
5 Tail wedge-shaped

Other characteristics:
- Habitat: Semi-desert, open plains and arid savanna
- Status: Rare vagrant

WHITE-HEADED VULTURE – adult (p. 60)

Field recognition:
- Size: Very large
1. Cere blue; bill red; face and throat pink
2. Back of head covered with white down
3. Crop patch white
4. Belly white
5. Legs red
6. Secondaries white in female, off-white or grey in male

Other characteristics:
- Pairs are territorial
- Habitat: Woodland and savanna
- Status: Uncommon to rare resident

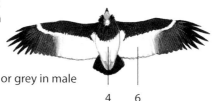

WHITE-HEADED VULTURE – juvenile (p. 60)

Field recognition:
- Size: Very large
1. Cere blue; bill red; face and throat pink
2. Back of head covered with brown down
3. Narrow white line along base of flight feathers on underwing

Other characteristics:
- See adult above

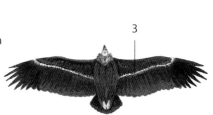

LAPPET-FACED VULTURE – adult (p. 62)

Field recognition:
- Size: Huge
1. Bill heavy and yellowish
2. Head red with conspicuous skin folds
3. Bold streaks on white underparts
4. Leggings white
5. White bar on underwing coverts

Other characteristics:
- Dominates other vultures at a carcass
- Habitat: Prefers semi-arid wooded regions
- Status: Uncommon to rare resident

LAPPET-FACED VULTURE – juvenile (p. 62)

Field recognition:
- Size: Huge
1. Bill heavy and horn-coloured
2. Head dull pink with conspicuous skin folds
3. Leggings brown
4. All dark in flight

Other characteristics:
- See adult above

3. Griffon vultures

WHITE-BACKED VULTURE – adult (p. 64)

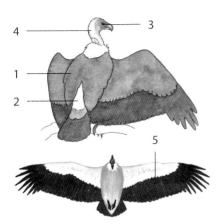

Field recognition:
- Size: Large; slightly smaller than Cape Vulture
1 Plumage usually buffy-brown, but becomes paler with age
2 White rump only seen when wings are spread
3 Eyes dark
4 Head and neck sparsely covered with white down; face appears dark, almost black
5 Dark flight feathers contrast with paler underwing coverts

Other characteristics:
- Habitat: Savanna and dry, open woodland
- Single pairs or loose colonies breed in trees
- Status: Locally common resident

CAPE VULTURE – adult (p. 66)

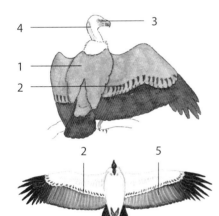

Field recognition:
- Size: Very large; slightly larger than White-backed Vulture
1 General appearance usually pale with darker flight feathers and tail
2 Dark spots on first row of wing coverts diagnostic
3 Eyes pale yellow
4 Head and neck sparsely covered with pale down; blue face and bare skin on back of neck
5 Secondaries appear paler than primaries

Other characteristics:
- Habitat: Prefers mountainous country and open veld
- Breeds colonially on cliffs
- Status: Rare to locally common resident

RÜPPELL'S VULTURE – adult (p. 68)

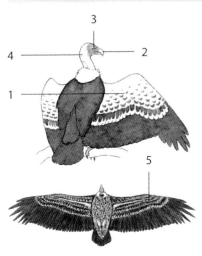

Field recognition:
- Size: Very large; between Cape and White-backed Vultures
1 General appearance speckled and scaled
2 Bill orange-yellow
3 Eyes pale yellow
4 Head and neck sparsely covered with white down; bare skin greenish-grey
5 Underwing coverts appear mottled

Other characteristics:
- Habitat: Prefers mountainous country, but also occurs in savanna
- Usually occurs near Cape Vulture colonies
- Status: Rare vagrant

WHITE-BACKED VULTURE – juvenile (p. 64)

Field recognition:
- Size: Large; slightly smaller than Cape Vulture
1. Plumage dark brown with paler streaks on underparts and wing coverts
2. Rump brown
3. Eyes dark
4. Head and neck densely covered with white down; only face is naked
5. Narrow white bar runs near leading edge of underwing

Other characteristics:
- See adult on previous page

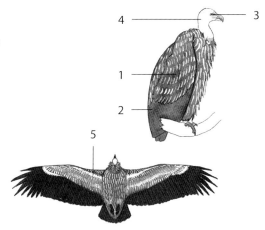

CAPE VULTURE – juvenile (p. 66)

Field recognition:
- Size: Very large; slightly larger than White-backed Vulture
1. Plumage warm rufous brown with paler streaks on underparts and wing coverts
2. Eyes dark
3. Head and neck sparsely covered with white down; bare skin on back of neck red
- In flight appears paler than juvenile White-backed Vulture, but difficult to separate

Other characteristics:
- See adult on previous page

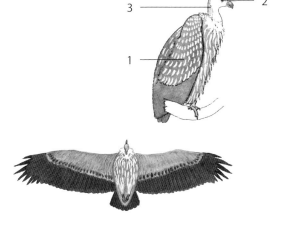

RÜPPELL'S VULTURE – juvenile (p. 68)

Field recognition:
- Size: Very large; between Cape and White-backed Vultures
- So similar to the juvenile Cape Vulture that the two may not be safely separated in the field (see above)

Other characteristics:
- See adult on previous page
- Status: Rare vagrant

EAGLES AND HAWK-EAGLES

(p. 36)

Eagles and hawk-eagles are medium to very large raptors. They are immediately distinguished from similar birds of prey by their fully feathered legs. They are powerful and aggressive hunters but also scavenge often. Their wings are long and broad, but the tails vary from shortish to medium, depending on the preferred hunting technique of the particular species.

1 Eagles with dark upperparts and distinctly spotted, streaked or barred underparts (p. 224)
The adult African Hawk-Eagle and Ayres's Hawk-Eagle have white underparts with darker markings. The adult Martial Eagle has a dark chest, while the rest of the underparts is white with dark spots. The underparts of the adult African Crowned Eagle are heavily barred with white, rufous and black.

2 Large pale eagles (p. 226)
The juvenile Martial and African Crowned Eagles have grey upperparts and white underparts. Although they resemble each other superficially, they prefer different habitats and also differ in wing and tail shape.

3 Eagles with dark brown upperparts and pale rufous underparts (p. 227)
The dark brown upperparts of the juvenile African Hawk-Eagle and Ayres's Hawk-Eagle contrast with their pale rufous underparts. They may be confused with the brown eagles of points 4 and 5 below and also resemble the rufous juvenile Black Sparrowhawk (p. 136).

4 Smaller, slenderly built brown eagles (p. 228)
These brown eagles are fairly small and slenderly built. They do not have the classical appearance of an eagle. Their dominant colours vary from pale brown to rufous brown to dark brown. Some have dark upperparts and pale underparts.

5 Large, powerful, classic brown eagles (p. 230)
These brown eagles are distinguished from similar species by their large powerful body shape giving them the classical appearance of an eagle. Their dominant colours vary from pale buff (blond) to rufous brown to chocolate brown.

1. Eagles with dark upperparts and distinctly spotted, streaked or barred underparts

AFRICAN CROWNED EAGLE – adult (p. 90)

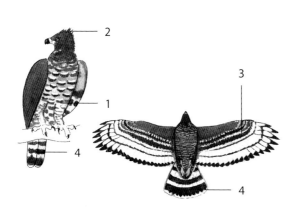

Field recognition:
- Size: Very large
1 Underparts and leggings heavily barred with rufous, black and white
2 Crest not always visible
3 Wings short and rounded; underwing coverts rufous and flight feathers boldly barred
4 Tail fairly long with three broad bars

Other characteristics:
- Habitat: Prefers forests, but also occurs in dense woodland or tall riverine growth
- Status: Locally common resident
- A fairly secretive species, difficult to locate in its wooded habitat

MARTIAL EAGLE – adult (p. 92)

Field recognition:
- Size: Very large
1. Upperparts, head and chest very dark brown, appearing black
2. Belly and leggings white with dark spots
3. Short crest not always visible
4. Underwing mostly dark
5. Tail fairly short and narrowly barred

Other characteristics:
- Habitat: Prefers savanna and woodland but also occurs in areas with scattered trees only
- Status: Uncommon to fairly common resident
- Differs from adult Black-chested Snake-Eagle (p. 94) in its larger size, fully feathered legs, spotted underparts and dark underwing

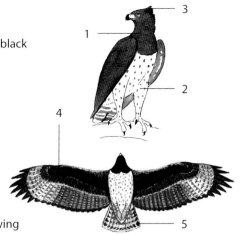

AFRICAN HAWK-EAGLE – adult (p. 86)

Field recognition:
- Size: Large; larger and more slenderly built than Ayres's Hawk-Eagle
1. Underparts white with black streaks (females are more heavily marked than males)
2. Leggings unmarked
3. Cap black with an ill-defined lower edge
4. Underwing coverts spotted
5. Flight feathers white with a black trailing edge
6. Tail faintly barred with a broad terminal band
- White windows near wingtips visible from above

Other characteristics:
- Habitat: Woodland and savanna
- Status: Uncommon to locally fairly common resident

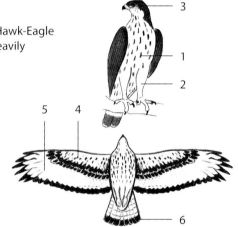

AYRES'S HAWK-EAGLE – adult (p. 88)

Field recognition:
- Size: Medium; smaller than African Hawk-Eagle but with broader shoulders
1. Underparts white with black blotches (females are more heavily marked than males)
2. Leggings with black streaks and blotches
3. Cap black with a well-defined lower edge
4. Forehead and eyebrow may be white
5. Underwing coverts heavily spotted
6. Flight feathers distinctly barred
7. Tail heavily barred

Other characteristics:
- Habitat: Dense woodland and forest edge
- Status: Uncommon to rare resident or non-breeding summer visitor

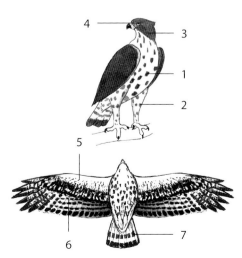

2. Large pale eagles

AFRICAN CROWNED EAGLE – juvenile (p. 90)

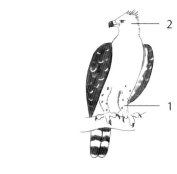

Field recognition:
- Size: Very large
1 Legs fully feathered with dark spots
2 Head mainly white with a darker crest
3 Flight feathers boldly barred; underwing coverts pale rufous
4 Tail fairly long and boldly barred

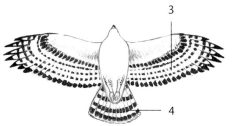

Other characteristics:
- Habitat: Prefers forests, but also occurs in dense woodland or tall riverine growth
- Status: Locally common resident
- A fairly secretive species, difficult to locate in its wooded habitat

MARTIAL EAGLE – juvenile (p. 92)

Field recognition:
- Size: Very large
1 Legs fully feathered; plain white
2 Crown and neck grey
3 Flight feathers finely barred; underwing coverts white
4 Tail relatively short; finely barred

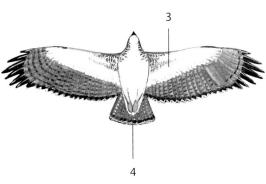

Other characteristics:
- Habitat: Prefers savanna and woodland but also occurs in areas with scattered trees only
- Status: Uncommon to fairly common resident

3. Eagles with dark brown upperparts and pale rufous underparts

AFRICAN HAWK-EAGLE – juvenile (p. 86)

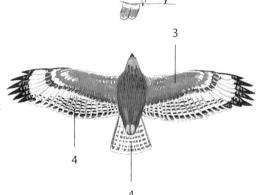

Field recognition:
- Size: Large; larger and more slenderly built than Ayres's Hawk-Eagle
1 Underparts rich rufous with dark streaks on the chest
2 Eyes brown
3 Underwing coverts rufous
4 Flight feathers and tail faintly barred

Other characteristics:
- Habitat: Woodland and savanna
- Status: Uncommon to locally fairly common resident
- See rufous juvenile Black Sparrowhawk p.136

AYRES'S HAWK-EAGLE – juvenile (p. 88)

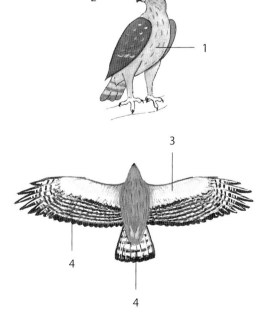

Field recognition:
- Size: Medium; smaller than African Hawk-Eagle but with broader shoulders
1 Underparts rich rufous (rarely pale) with dark streaks on the chest
2 Eyes yellow
3 Underwing coverts rufous
4 Flight feathers and tail heavily barred

Other characteristics:
- Habitat: Dense woodland and forest edge
- Status: Uncommon to rare resident or non-breeding summer visitor
- See rufous juvenile Black Sparrowhawk p.136

4. Smaller, slenderly built brown eagles

LONG-CRESTED EAGLE – adult (p. 84)

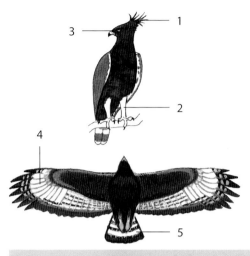

Field recognition:
- Size: Medium-large
1 Long crest of loose feathers
2 Leggings are white in males, dirty white to mottled brown in females
3 Eyes yellow to golden
4 Large white windows near wingtip
5 Boldly barred tail
- Juveniles resemble adults but have a slightly shorter crest, grey eyes and white leggings, irrespective of sex

Other characteristics:
- Habitat: Prefers mosaic of wooded habitats and wetlands
- Status: Locally common resident

LESSER SPOTTED EAGLE – adult (p. 78)

Field recognition:
- Size: Large, but slender, more buzzard-like
1 Plumage uniform brown, rarely pale yellow-brown
2 Thin 'stove-pipe' leggings diagnostic
3 Eyes yellowish
4 Trailing edge of wing nearly straight
5 Tail not barred; usually spread in flight

Other characteristics:
- Habitat: Woodland and savanna
- Status: Locally common but regular non-breeding summer visitor

LESSER SPOTTED EAGLE – juvenile (p. 78)

Field recognition:
- Size: Large, but slender, more buzzard-like
1 Pale patch on the nape
2 Two pale bands on the folded wing
3 Pale spots on the wing coverts and pale streaks on the head and underparts
4 Thin 'stove-pipe' legs diagnostic
5 Eyes brown
6 Pale line on trailing edge of wing and on base of flight feathers visible from above and below
7 Trailing edge of wing nearly straight in flight
8 Tail not barred; usually spread in flight
- White U-shaped rump seen from above in flight

Other characteristics:
- See adult above

WAHLBERG'S EAGLE – adult and juvenile (p. 80)

Field recognition:
- Size: Medium-large, slenderly built
1 Plumage varies from dark chocolate brown to nearly white
2 Head small and pointed; often with a slight crest
3 Eyes dark; dark patch in front of eye
4 Looks like two crossed planks in flight: leading and trailing edges of wings are nearly parallel and the long square tail is usually held closed
- Young birds resemble adults

Other characteristics:
- Habitat: Woodland and savanna
- Status: Common breeding summer resident

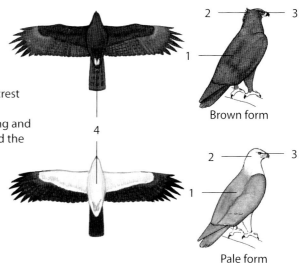

Brown form

Pale form

BOOTED EAGLE – adult (p. 82)

Field recognition:
- Size: Medium
1 Two colour forms: a dark form with brown underparts and a pale form with pale underparts
2 Pale band on wing diagnostic
3 Pale 'landing lights' on base of wing
4 Wings fairly broad
5 Tail fairly short; usually spread in flight
- Pale U-shaped rump seen from above in flight
- The dark form juvenile resembles the adult; see juvenile pale form below

Other characteristics:
- Habitat: Occurs widely from desert to woodland; most common in karoo and fynbos
- Status: Fairly common breeding resident and non-breeding summer visitor

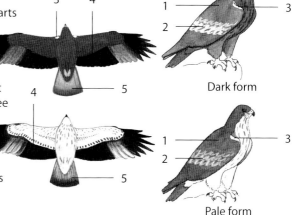

Dark form

Pale form

BOOTED EAGLE – juvenile pale form (p. 82)

Field recognition:
- Size: Medium
1 Resembles pale form adult, but the underparts and underwing coverts are washed rufous

Other characteristics:
- See adult above

5. Large, powerful, classic brown eagles

VERREAUXS' EAGLE – juvenile (p. 72)

Field recognition:
- Size: Very large and powerful: the body shape of a classic eagle
1 Plumage mottled pale and dark brown
2 Crown and nape rufous; cheeks and chest black
3 Wing shape with narrow base and broad tip

Other characteristics:
- Habitat: Mountainous regions
- Status: Locally fairly common resident

TAWNY EAGLE – adult (p. 74)

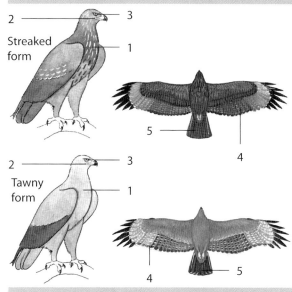

Streaked form

Tawny form

Field recognition:
- Size: Large and powerful: the body shape of a classic eagle
1 Plumage usually tawny, but varies from streaked dark brown to pale buff
2 Gape ends below the centre of the eye (see opposite page)
3 Eyes dull yellow to pale brown
4 Trailing edge of wing S-shaped in flight
5 Tail not or only faintly barred; usually spread in flight

Other characteristics:
- Habitat: Prefers woodland and savanna, but also occurs in more open habitats
- Status: Common to rare resident

STEPPE EAGLE – adult (p. 76)

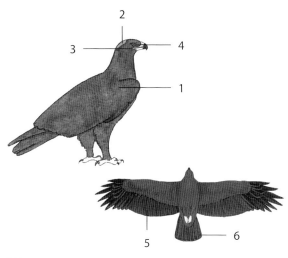

Field recognition:
- Size: Large and powerful: the body shape of a classic eagle
1 Plumage chocolate brown
2 May have a ginger patch on the nape
3 Gape ends below the back of the eye (see opposite page)
4 Eyes dark brown
5 Trailing edge of wing S-shaped in flight
6 Tail barred; usually spread in flight

Other characteristics:
- Flocks often feed on the ground
- Habitat: Woodland, thornveld and savanna
- Status: Common but erratic non-breeding summer visitor

TAWNY EAGLE – juvenile (p. 74)

Field recognition:
- Size: Large and powerful: the body shape of a classic eagle
1 Plumage usually tawny at first, then fading to pale buff when sub-adult
2 Gape ends below the centre of the eye (see below)
3 Eyes brown
4 Faint white line on trailing edge of wing and on base of flight feathers visible from above and below
5 Trailing edge of wing S-shaped in flight
6 Tail not or only faintly barred; usually spread in flight

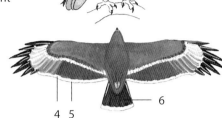

Other characteristics:
- See adult on previous page

STEPPE EAGLE – juvenile (p. 76)

Field recognition:
- Size: Large and powerful: the body shape of a classic eagle
1 Plumage clay-brown
2 Two pale bands on folded wing
3 Gape ends below the back of the eye (see below)
4 Eyes dark brown
5 Pale line on trailing edge of wing and on base of flight feathers visible from above and below
6 Trailing edge of wing S-shaped in flight
- White U-shaped rump seen from above in flight
- Tail barred on top with a white tip; usually spread in flight

Other characteristics:
- See adult on previous page

Steppe Eagle
A. n. nipalensis
(rare)

Steppe Eagle
A. n. orientalis
(common)

Tawny Eagle
A. rapax
(common)

SNAKE-EAGLES
(p. 37)

These medium-large to large raptors resemble true eagles, but are easily distinguished by their large heads, large yellow eyes and unfeathered lower legs. As the name indicates, many species feed primarily on snakes.

As they soar often and well, their wings are broad and long, while the tail is of medium length. The Bateleur is not a typical snake-eagle as indicated by its dark eyes.

1. Snake-eagles with white or pale underparts (p. 232)
The adult Black-chested Snake-Eagle is a characteristic raptor that may only be confused with the adult Martial Eagle. The juveniles of the two banded snake eagles do not only have pale underparts but also pale heads.

2. Brown, rufous-brown or grey-brown snake-eagles (p. 234)
These snake-eagles have a brownish appearance. The juvenile Bateleur is immediately distinguished by its characteristic body shape and dark eyes. The juvenile Black-chested Snake-Eagle is characterised by its rufous underparts, while the two banded snake-eagles have broad pale bars across their tails.

1. Snake-eagles with white or pale underparts

BLACK-CHESTED SNAKE-EAGLE – adult (p. 94)

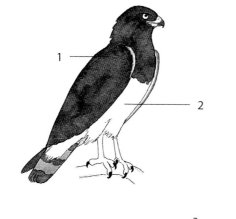

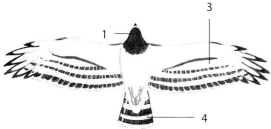

Field recognition
- Size: Large
1 Upperparts, head and chest blackish
2 Rest of underparts plain white
3 Underwing mostly white with bold barring on flight feathers
4 Tail broadly barred

Other characteristics:
- Habitat: Prefers arid regions with scattered trees, but occurs from desert to open woodland
- Status: Nomadic resident and non-breeding summer visitor
- Differs from adult Martial Eagle (p. 92) in its smaller size, unfeathered lower legs, plain white underparts and mainly white underwing

SOUTHERN BANDED SNAKE-EAGLE – juvenile (p. 96)

Field recognition
- Size: Medium-large
1 Upperparts dark brown
2 Head and underparts very pale; some brown streaks on head and chest; brown barring on the flanks
3 Three dark and two white bars on tail
4 Eyes and cere yellow
5 Underwing barred with dark trailing edge
- The sub-adult has a browner head with some white streaks and whiter underparts than the juvenile

Other characteristics:
- Habitat: Prefers dense woodland and forest in the eastern lowlands
- Distribution does not overlap with that of Western Banded Snake-Eagle
- Status: Rare, localised resident

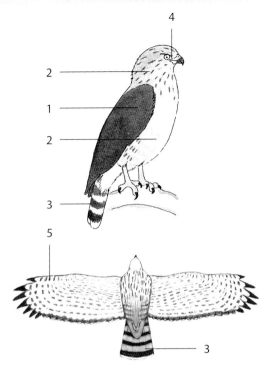

WESTERN BANDED SNAKE-EAGLE – juvenile (p. 98)

Field recognition
- Size: Medium-large
1 Upperparts brown
2 Crown whitish with darker streaks
3 Underparts buffy white; darker on the chest
4 Eyes and cere yellow
5 Tail pale brown with a dark terminal band
6 Underwing barred with dark trailing edge
- Immatures are mottled brown
- Sub-adults are all dark brown

Other characteristics:
- Habitat: Riverine woodland in northern Botswana, Namibia and Zimbabwe
- Distribution does not overlap with that of Southern Banded Snake-Eagle
- Status: Uncommon resident

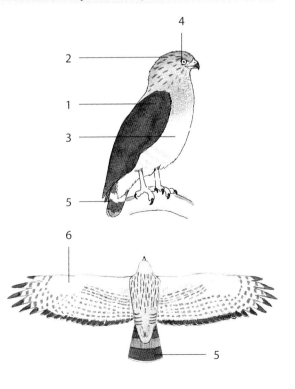

2. Brown, rufous-brown or grey-brown snake-eagles

BROWN SNAKE-EAGLE – adult and juvenile (p. 100)

Field recognition
- Size: Large
1 Plumage dark brown, sometimes with white speckling on the underparts
2 Legs grey-white
3 Underwing coverts brown
4 Flight feathers silvery-grey
5 Three narrow pale bars on brown tail
- Juvenile mostly like adult, but may be pale brown or have white mottling on the underparts

Other characteristics:
- Habitat: Savanna, bushveld and woodland
- Status: Rare to common resident

BLACK-CHESTED SNAKE-EAGLE – juvenile (p. 94)

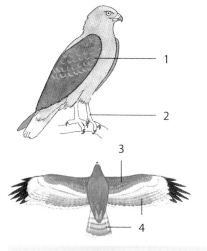

Field recognition
- Size: Large
1 Plumage rufous brown; underparts pale tawny to dark rufous, but more richly coloured than upperparts
2 Legs grey-white
3 Underwing coverts rich rufous or tawny brown like underparts
4 Flight feathers and tail pale; indistinctly barred

Other characteristics:
- Habitat: Prefers arid regions with scattered trees, but occurs from desert to open woodland
- Status: Nomadic resident and non-breeding summer visitor

BATELEUR – juvenile (p. 102)

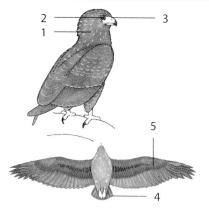

Field recognition
- Size: Large
1 Head large compared to brown eagles
2 Eyes dark
3 Bare face greenish-grey
4 Tail short
5 Wings long and tapering

Other characteristics:
- Rocks slowly from side to side while soaring
- Habitat: Woodland and savanna
- Status: Rare to common resident

SOUTHERN BANDED SNAKE-EAGLE – adult (p. 96)

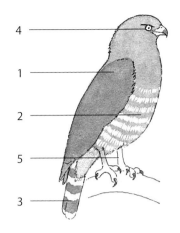

Field recognition
- Size: Medium-large
1 Plumage greyish-brown
2 White barring on lower chest, belly and thighs
3 Three dark and two white bars on tail
4 Eyes and cere yellow
5 Legs pale yellow
6 Underwing heavily barred with dark trailing edge

Other characteristics:
- Habitat: Prefers dense woodland and forest in the eastern lowlands
- Distribution does not overlap with that of Western Banded Snake-Eagle
- Status: Rare, localised resident

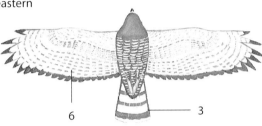

WESTERN BANDED SNAKE-EAGLE – adult (p. 98)

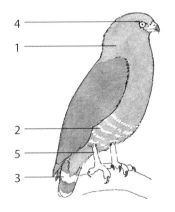

Field recognition
- Size: Medium-large
1 Plumage ashy brown
2 Faint white barring on belly and thighs only
3 One broad white band across dark tail
4 Eyes yellow; cere yellow-orange
5 Legs pale yellow
6 Underwing barred with dark trailing edge

Other characteristics:
- Habitat: Riverine woodland in northern Botswana, Namibia and Zimbabwe
- Distribution does not overlap with that of Southern Banded Snake-Eagle
- Status: Uncommon resident

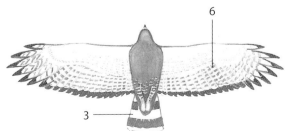

235

BUZZARDS
(p. 38)

These medium to medium-large robustly built raptors resemble small eagles, but have unfeathered lower legs. They hunt mostly from a perch, but soar well as the wings are long and broad while the tail is shortish to medium in length. The European Honey-Buzzard is not a typical buzzard.

1. Brown buzzards (p. 236)
The European Honey-Buzzard is distinguished from all true buzzards by its pigeon-shaped head. The adult has bright yellow or orange eyes. The robustly built juvenile Jackal Buzzard has rufous underparts. Steppe and Forest Buzzards are very similar, but differ in status and preferred habitat. The Long-legged Buzzard is unlikely to be seen in Southern Africa as it is a rare vagrant.

2. Buzzards that are not brown (p. 240)
The Jackal and Augur Buzzards are large, robustly built buzzards that prefer mountainous country. Their areas of distribution only overlap in Namibia.

1. Brown buzzards

JACKAL BUZZARD – juvenile (p. 106)

Field recognition
- Size: Medium-large
1 Upperparts brown
2 Underparts rufous
3 Tail grey-brown with indistinct bars
4 Underwing coverts rufous like underparts
5 Flight feathers white with a dark trailing edge

Other characteristics:
- Habitat: Mountains and hills, but may occur in open regions
- Status: Locally common resident

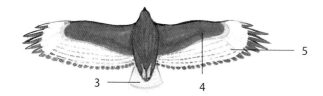

Field recognition
- Size: Medium
1 Head pigeon-shaped
2 Eyes bright yellow or orange
3 Cere grey
4 Underparts variable, but three forms are recognised. In the barred form the underparts are barred brown on white. The pale form has white underparts which are either plain or streaked and spotted to a varying degree. The dark form has pale to dark brown underparts.
5 Legs yellow
6 Tail with two dark bands at its base and a dark terminal band
7 Head small and protruding
8 Wrist patches dark

Dark form

Other characteristics:
- Habitat: Woodland and forest edge
- Status: Uncomon but regular non-breeding summer visitor

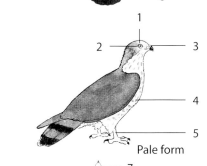

Pale form

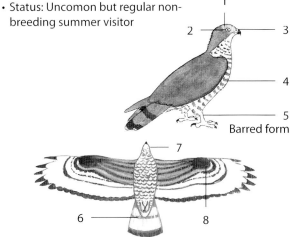

Barred form

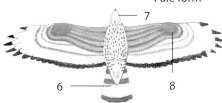

Field recognition
- Size: Medium
- The juvenile differs from the adult in the following ways:
1 Eyes brown
2 Cere yellow
3 Tail with four evenly spaced but indistinct bands

Other characteristics:
- See adult above

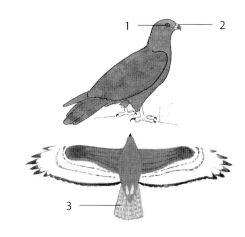

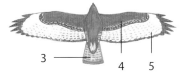

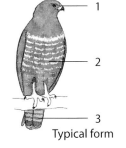

Dark form

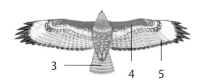

Field recognition
- Size: Medium
1 Eyes brown
2 Underparts variable. The darkest form has completely chocolate brown underparts. Most individuals have the following markings to varying degrees: the upper chest is blotched or mottled, there is a pale band across the lower chest, and the belly is barred
3 Tail barred with a broad terminal band
4 Underwing coverts match the colour of the upper chest
5 Flight feathers barred with a dark trailing edge

Other characteristics:
- Habitat: Prefers open habitats from fynbos to open woodland
- Status: Common non-breeding summer visitor
- Resembles the adult Forest Buzzard except for the barred belly, preferred habitat and status. Juvenile Steppe and Forest Buzzards differ from the adult Steppe Buzzard in having pale eyes and a narrow band at the tip of the tail

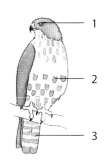

Typical form

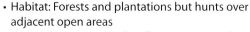

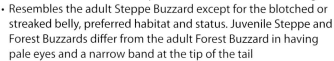

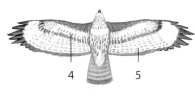

Field recognition
- Size: Medium
1 Eyes brown
2 Belly blotched or streaked like upper chest; pale band across lower chest
3 Tail barred with a broad terminal band
4 Underwing coverts match the colour of the upper chest
5 Flight feathers barred with a dark trailing edge

Other characteristics:
- Habitat: Forests and plantations but hunts over adjacent open areas
- Status: Uncommon to locally common resident and local migrant
- Resembles the adult Steppe Buzzard except for the blotched or streaked belly, preferred habitat and status. Juvenile Steppe and Forest Buzzards differ from the adult Forest Buzzard in having pale eyes and a narrow band at the tip of the tail

STEPPE BUZZARD – juvenile (p. 108)

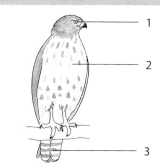

Field recognition
- Size: Medium
- The juvenile is similar to the adult but differs in the following ways:
1 Eyes pale
2 Upper chest and belly streaked with a pale band across the lower chest
3 Tail barred with a narrow terminal band

Other characteristics:
- Virtually indistinguishable from the juvenile Forest Buzzard, which is slightly smaller
- See adult on opposite page

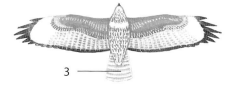

FOREST BUZZARD – juvenile (p. 110)

Field recognition
- Size: Medium
- The juvenile is similar to the adult but differs in the following ways:
1 Eyes pale
2 Tail barred with a narrow terminal band

Other characteristics:
- Virtually indistinguishable from the juvenile Steppe Buzzard, which is slightly larger
- See adult on opposite page

LONG-LEGGED BUZZARD – adult (p. 112)

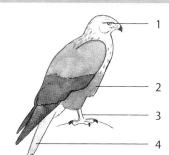

Field recognition
- Size: Medium-large
1 Eyes brown
2 Underparts variable with streaks, mottling or bars, but the belly is darker than the chest and head
3 Long legs
4 Tail pale
- The juvenile is similar to the adult but has pale eyes and a pale tail with numerous dark bands

Other characteristics:
- Habitat: Savanna to semi-desert
- Status: Rare summer vagrant
- Extremely difficult to distinguish from the Steppe Buzzard, except by its larger size, longer legs and pale tail

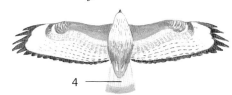

2. Buzzards that are not brown

JACKAL BUZZARD – adult (p. 106)

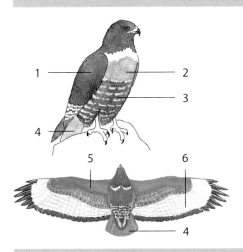

Field recognition
- Size: Medium-large
1 Plumage mostly slaty black
2 Chest rufous
3 White barring or blotches on belly
4 Tail rufous
5 Underwing coverts dark
6 Flight feathers white with a dark trailing edge

Other characteristics:
- Habitat: Mountains and hills
- Status: Locally common resident

AUGUR BUZZARD – adult (p. 104)

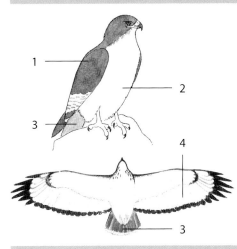

Field recognition
- Size: Medium-large
1 Upperparts slaty black
2 Underparts completely white in male; female has a black throat
3 Tail rufous
4 Underwing white with a dark trailing edge

Other characteristics:
- Habitat: Mountains and hills
- Status: Locally fairly common resident
- See adult Black Sparrowhawk p. 136

AUGUR BUZZARD – juvenile (p. 104)

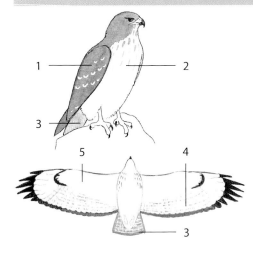

Field recognition
- Size: Medium-large
1 Upperparts grey-brown
2 Underparts buff with streaks on sides of throat and chest
3 Tail rufous brown with indistinct bars
4 Underwing coverts buff like underparts
5 Flight feathers white with a dark trailing edge

Other characteristics:
- See adult above

GOSHAWKS AND SPARROWHAWKS

(p. 39)

These very small to medium-sized raptors prefer well-wooded habitats. Their secretive life styles and similar colours make them difficult to identify. Their wings are short, while the tail is long: an adaptation for fast but manoeuvrable flight. The legs are long. The two chanting goshawks, the Lizard Buzzard and the African Harrier-Hawk are not typical goshawks.

1. Juvenile African Harrier-Hawk (p. 241)
The juvenile African Harrier-Hawk is often confused with various medium-sized brown raptors, but the body shape makes it unmistakable.

2. Melanistic (black) goshawks and sparrowhawks (p. 242)
Three species have black colour forms: Gabar Goshawk, Ovambo Sparrowhawk and Black Sparrowhawk.

3. Goshawks and sparrowhawks with completely barred underparts (p. 243)
The chests and bellies of four adult hawks are completely barred: Shikra, Ovambo Sparrowhawk, Little Sparrowhawk and African Goshawk.

4. Goshawks and sparrowhawks with grey chests and barred bellies (p. 244)
Its characteristic bodyshape makes the African Harrier-Hawk unmistakable. The two adult chanting goshawks, the adult Gabar Goshawk and the Lizard Buzzard have grey upperparts and chests, barred bellies, red legs, red ceres and dark eyes.

5. Goshawks and sparrowhawks with streaked or blotched chests and barred bellies (p. 246)
These four juvenile birds, namely the two chanting goshawks, the Gabar Goshawk and the Shikra, have an overall brown appearance.

6. Goshawks and sparrowhawks with rufous underparts (p. 247)
The underparts may be plain (adult Rufous-chested Sparrowhawk) or variously marked (juvenile Rufous-chested Sparrowhawk and rufous juveniles of Ovambo and Black Sparrowhawks).

7. Goshawks and sparrowhawks with pale underparts (p. 248)
The underparts are variously marked on a pale background. These include both the adult and pale juvenile Black Sparrowhawk, the pale juvenile Ovambo Sparrowhawk, the juvenile Little Sparrowhawk as well as the juvenile African Goshawk.

1. Juvenile African Harrier-Hawk

AFRICAN HARRIER-HAWK – juvenile (p. 118)

Field recognition
- Size: Medium
1 Plumage varies from pale to dark brown
2 Head slender and elongated
3 Legs yellow
4 Underwing coverts brown
5 Flight feathers and tail faintly barred

Other characteristics:
- Habitat: Prefers woodland
- Status: Locally common resident

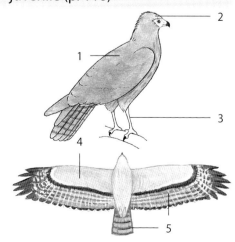

2. Melanistic (black) goshawks and sparrowhawks

GABAR GOSHAWK – melanistic adult (p. 124)

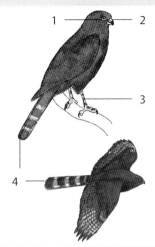

Field recognition
- Size: Small
1 Eyes dark red-brown, usually appear black
2 Cere red
3 Legs red with black markings on the front
4 Tail black with paler bars

Other characteristics:
- Habitat: Prefers open woodland and savanna
- Status of melanistic form: Not uncommon

OVAMBO SPARROWHAWK – melanistic adult (p. 128)

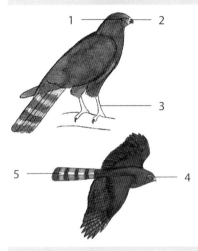

Field recognition
- Size: Medium-small
1 Eyes dark red, usually appear black
2 Cere varies from orange-yellow to orange to orange-red
3 Legs vary from orange-yellow to orange to orange-red
4 Head small with a large bill
5 White central lines on pale bars of upper tail

Other characteristics:
- Habitat: Woodland and savanna, favouring mosaic of trees and open areas
- Status of melanistic form: Very rare

BLACK SPARROWHAWK – melanistic adult (p. 136)

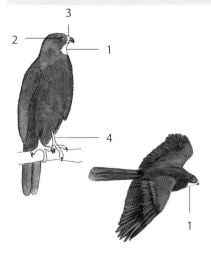

Field recognition
- Size: Medium
1 White patch on throat
2 Eyes wine-red but usually appear dark
3 Cere yellow
4 Legs yellow

Other characteristics:
- Habitat: Dense vegetation such as mature woodland, dense riverine growth and forests
- Status of melanistic form: Rare

3. Goshawks and sparrowhawks with completely barred underparts

OVAMBO SPARROWHAWK – adult (p. 128)

Field recognition
- Size: Medium-small
1 Underparts barred grey
2 Eyes dark red, usually appear black
3 Cere and legs vary from orange-yellow to orange to orange-red
4 Head small with a large bill
5 Upperparts grey
6 White central lines on pale bars of upper tail

Other characteristics:
- Habitat: Woodland and savanna, favouring mosaic of trees and open areas
- Status: Rare to locally common resident

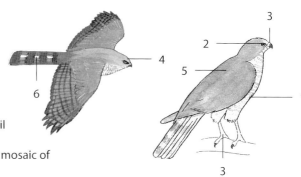

SHIKRA – adult (p. 126)

Field recognition
- Size: Small
1 Eyes bright red
2 Cere yellow
3 Legs orange-yellow
4 Upperparts completely grey

Other characteristics:
- Habitat: Woodland and savanna
- Status: Common to scarce resident

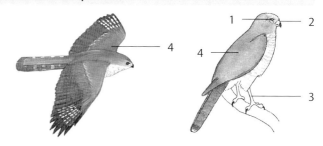

LITTLE SPARROWHAWK – adult (p. 130)

Field recognition
- Size: Very small
1 Underparts barred grey-brown in males, rufous in females
2 Eyes yellow to yellow-orange; cere yellow
3 Legs yellow
4 Rump white
5 Tail with two white eye-spots and narrow white tip

Other characteristics:
- Habitat: Woodland and bushveld
- Status: Common to scarce resident

AFRICAN GOSHAWK – adult (p. 132)

Field recognition
- Size: Medium-small
1 Upperparts bluish-grey in male, brown in female
2 Underparts barred rufous in male, barred brown in female
3 Eyes yellow, may appear dark
4 Cere grey
5 Legs yellow
6 Tail with two white eye-spots in male, plain brown in female

Other characteristics:
- Habitat: Dense vegetation such as forests, mature woodland, riverine growth and thickets
- Status: Scares to locally common resident
- See adult African Cuckoo-Hawk p. 150

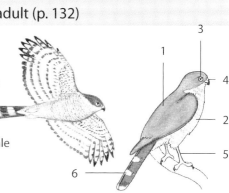

4. Goshawks and sparrowhawks with grey chests and barred bellies

AFRICAN HARRIER-HAWK – adult (p. 118)

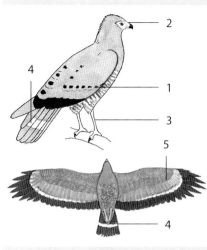

Field recognition
- Size: Medium
1 Black spots on wing coverts
2 Head elongated; face and cere yellow but may blush red
3 Legs yellow
4 Broad white bar on tail
5 Wing with black trailing edge and tip
- Rump white

Other characteristics:
- Habitat: Prefers woodland, but may occur in other regions
- Status: Locally common resident

DARK CHANTING GOSHAWK – adult (p. 120)

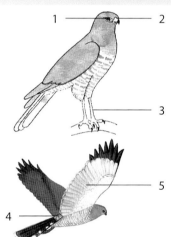

Field recognition
- Size: Medium
1 Eyes dark brown, often appear black
2 Cere red
3 Legs red
4 Rump barred
5 Secondaries grey

Other characteristics:
- Differs in distribution and habitat from the similar Southern Pale Chanting Goshawk
- Habitat: Eastern well-developed woodland or savanna
- Status: Fairly common resident

SOUTHERN PALE CHANTING GOSHAWK – adult (p. 122)

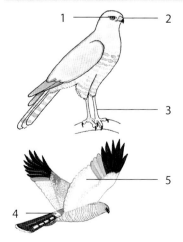

Field recognition
- Size: Medium
1 Eyes dark brown, often appear black
2 Cere red
3 Legs red
4 Rump white
5 Secondaries white

Other characteristics:
- Differs in distribution and habitat from the similar Dark Chanting Goshawk
- Habitat: Western arid regions with trees
- Status: Locally common resident

GABAR GOSHAWK – adult (p. 124)

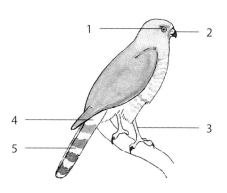

Field recognition
- Size: Small
1 Eyes dark red-brown but often appear black
2 Cere red
3 Legs red
4 Rump white
5 Pale bars on tail

Other characteristics:
- Much smaller than similar chanting goshawks
- Habitat: Prefers open woodland and savanna
- Status: Locally common resident

LIZARD BUZZARD – adult and juvenile (p. 116)

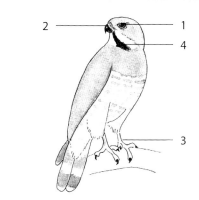

Field recognition
- Size: Medium
1 Eyes dark red-brown but often appear black
2 Cere red
3 Legs red
4 Black streak on centre of throat
5 Rump white
6 One (or rarely two) broad white bars on tail
- Juvenile slightly browner than adult with buff edges to upperwing coverts

Other characteristics:
- Habitat: Woodland and savanna
- Status: Fairly common resident; somewhat nomadic

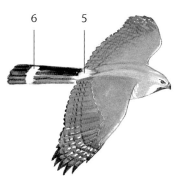

5. Goshawks and sparrowhawks with streaked or blotched chests and barred bellies

DARK CHANTING GOSHAWK – juvenile (p. 120)

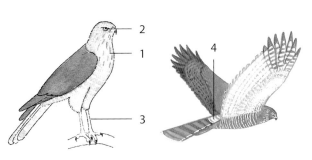

Field recognition
- Size: Medium
1 Chest streaked
2 Eyes yellow, cere orange
3 Legs orange
4 Rump barred

Other characteristics
- Differs in distribution and habitat from the similar Southern Pale Chanting Goshawk
- See adult on p. 244

SOUTHERN PALE CHANTING GOSHAWK – juvenile (p. 122)

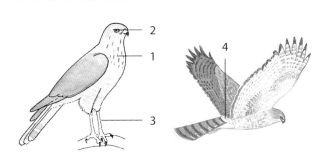

Field recognition
- Size: Medium
1 Chest streaked
2 Eyes yellow, cere orange
3 Legs orange
4 Rump white

Other characteristics:
- Differs in distribution and habitat from the similar Dark Chanting Goshawk
- See adult on p. 244

GABAR GOSHAWK – juvenile (p. 124)

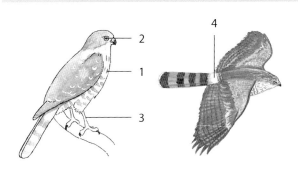

Field recognition
- Size: Small
1 Chest streaked
2 Eyes yellow, cere orange-red
3 Legs orange-red
4 Rump white

Other characteristics:
- Much smaller than similar chanting goshawks
- See adult on p. 245

SHIKRA – juvenile (p. 126)

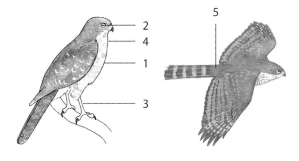

Field recognition
- Size: Small
1 Chest blotched
2 Eyes and cere yellow
3 Legs yellow
4 Dark line on centre of throat
5 Rump dark brown like rest of upperparts

Other characteristics:
- See adult on p. 243

6. Goshawks and sparrowhawks with rufous underparts

RUFOUS-CHESTED SPARROWHAWK – adult (p. 134)

Field recognition
- Size: Medium-small
1 Upperparts slate grey
2 Underparts plain rufous
3 Eyes and cere yellow
4 Legs yellow
5 Underwing coverts plain rufous

Other characteristics:
- Habitat: Mosaic of forest patches in montane grassland and fynbos
- Status: Locally common to scarce resident

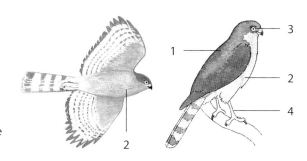

RUFOUS-CHESTED SPARROWHAWK – juvenile (p. 134)

Field recognition
- Size: Medium-small
1 Underparts usually rufous with fine dark streaks and faint white barring
2 Eyes and cere yellow
3 Legs yellow
4 Faint white eyebrow

Other characteristics:
- See adult above

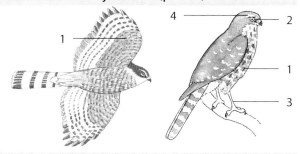

OVAMBO SPARROWHAWK – rufous juvenile (p. 128)

Field recognition
- Size: Medium-small
1 Underparts may be plain rufous but are usually well streaked
2 Eyes brown and cere yellow-orange to orange
3 Legs yellow-orange to orange
4 Bold white eyebrow
5 Dark patch on ear coverts
6 White central lines on pale bars of upper tail

Other characteristics:
- Habitat: Woodland and savanna, favouring mosaic of trees and open areas
- Status: Rare to locally common resident

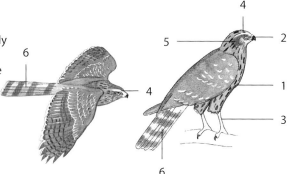

BLACK SPARROWHAWK – rufous juvenile (p. 136)

Field recognition
- Size: Medium
1 Underparts rufous with bold streaks
2 Eyes grey-brown and cere greenish-yellow
3 Legs yellow

Other characteristics:
- Habitat: Dense vegetation such as mature woodland, dense riverine growth and forests
- Status: Scares to locally common resident
- See juvenile African Hawk-Eagle p. 86, and juvenile Ayres's Hawk-Eagle p. 88

7. Goshawks and sparrowhawks with pale underparts

BLACK SPARROWHAWK – adult (p. 136)

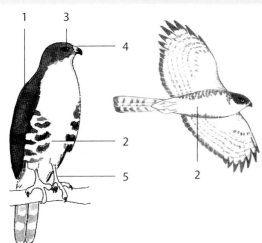

Field recognition
- Size: Medium
1 Upperparts black
2 Underparts white with barring on the flanks
3 Eyes wine-red but usually appear dark
4 Cere yellow
5 Legs yellow

Other characteristics:
- Habitat: Dense vegetation such as mature woodland, dense riverine growth and forests
- Status: Scarce to locally common resident

BLACK SPARROWHAWK – pale juvenile (p. 136)

Field recognition
- Size: Medium
1 Underparts white with bold streaks
2 Eyes grey-brown
3 Cere greenish-yellow
4 Legs yellow

Other characteristics:
- See adult above

OVAMBO SPARROWHAWK – pale juvenile (p. 128)

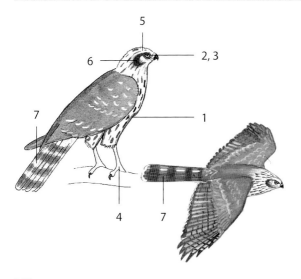

Field recognition
- Size: Medium-small
1 Underparts well streaked
2 Eyes brown
3 Cere yellow-orange to orange
4 Legs yellow-orange to orange
5 Bold white eyebrow
6 Dark patch on ear coverts
7 White central lines on pale bars of upper tail

Other characteristics:
- Habitat: Woodland and savanna, favouring mosaic of trees and open areas
- Status: Rare to locally common resident

LITTLE SPARROWHAWK – juvenile (p. 130)

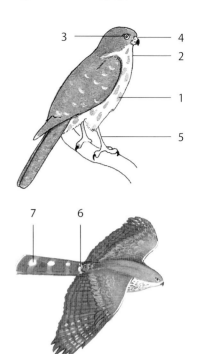

Field recognition
- Size: Very small
1 Underparts white with prominent teardrop-shaped brown spots
2 Dark line on centre of throat either faint or absent
3 Eyes yellow
4 Cere yellow
5 Legs yellow
6 White rump very faint
7 Tail with two white eye-spots

Other characteristics:
- Habitat: Woodland and bushveld
- Status: Common to scarce resident

AFRICAN GOSHAWK – juvenile (p. 132)

Field recognition
- Size: Medium-small
1 Underparts white with prominent teardrop-shaped brown spots
2 Dark line on centre of throat
3 Cere grey
4 Eyebrow white
5 Legs yellow
6 No white rump or white spots on tail

Other characteristics:
- Habitat: Dense vegetation such as forests, mature woodland, riverine growth and thickets
- Status: Scares to locally common resident
- See juvenile African Cuckoo-Hawk p. 150

HARRIERS
(p. 40)

Harriers are medium-sized raptors. They are characterised by their slender bodies, long narrow wings, long tails and long legs. These are adaptations to fly low over the ground, quartering to and fro, and dropping onto prey on the ground. Harriers occur in marshes or open habitats such as grassland, Karoo, fynbos and open savanna.

1. Black-and-white harriers (p. 250)
The only harrier in this category is the adult Black Harrier. Although the bird appears mainly black when perched, its flight pattern is boldly black and white.

2. Grey-and-white harriers (p. 251)
The males of Montagu's and Pallid Harriers are grey above and white below. Both are fairly uncommon summer visitors.

3. Brown harriers (p. 252)
A number of harriers have a predominantly brown appearance. The Western and African Marsh-Harriers prefer moist environments such as marshes. Female and juvenile Montagu's and Pallid Harriers occur in grasslands and open savanna, while juvenile Black Harriers are confined to Southern Africa's southwestern regions.

1. Black-and-white harriers

BLACK HARRIER – adult (p. 138)

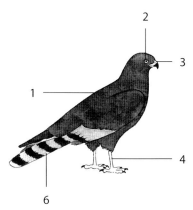

Field recognition
- Size: Medium
1 Plumage mostly black
2 Eyes yellow
3 Cere yellow
4 Legs yellow
5 Rump white
6 Paler bars on tail
7 Underwing boldly black and white

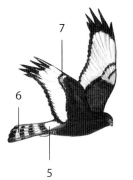

Other characteristics:
- Habitat: Arid open areas such as fynbos, grassland, Karoo and semi-desert
- Status: Uncommon resident in the southwest, non-breeding visitor elsewhere
- See adult Black Sparrowhawk p. 136

2. Grey-and-white harriers

MONTAGU'S HARRIER – adult male (p. 144)

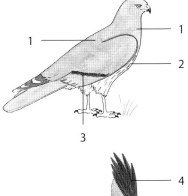

Field recognition
- Size: Medium-small
1 Upperparts and chest grey
2 Belly white with chestnut streaks
3 Black bar on upperwing
4 Large black wingtip
5 Underwing with two black bars on the secondaries
  and brown spots on the coverts

Other characteristics:
- Habitat: Mostly open grassland and marshy areas
- Status: Scarce to locally common non-breeding summer visitor
- See Black-shouldered Kite p. 148

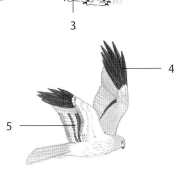

PALLID HARRIER – adult male (p. 146)

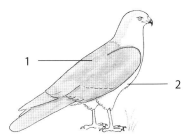

Field recognition
- Size: Medium-small
1 Upperparts plain grey
2 Chest and belly white
3 Small black wingtip
4 Rest of underwing white

Other characteristics:
- Habitat: Open grassland and sometimes
  savanna or agricultural lands
- Status: Locally common to rare non-breeding summer
  visitor
- See Black-shouldered Kite p. 148

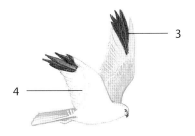

3. Brown harriers

WESTERN MARSH-HARRIER – adult male (p. 140)

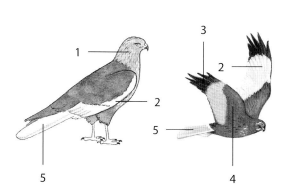

Field recognition
- Size: Medium
1 Head appears greyish, contrasting with the rest of the body
2 Flight feathers and last row of upperwing coverts grey
3 Wingtips black
4 Underwing coverts rufous
5 Tail plain grey

Other characteristics:
- Habitat: Marshes and adjacent moist grassland
- Satus: Rare non-breeding summer visitor

WESTERN MARSH-HARRIER – adult female and juvenile (p. 140)

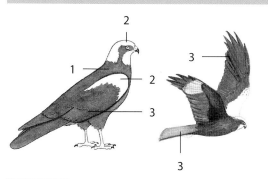

Field recognition
- Size: Medium
1 Plumage mostly chocolate brown
2 Crown, nape, throat and 'shoulder' creamy white
3 Wings and tail brown
- The female has yellow eyes; those of the juvenile are brown

Other characteristics:
- See male above

AFRICAN MARSH-HARRIER – adult (p. 142)

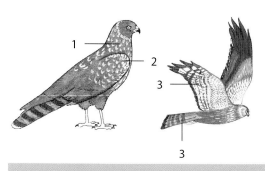

Field recognition
- Size: Medium-small
1 Head, back, chest and flanks brown with pale streaks
2 Pale dappling on 'shoulders'
3 Flight feathers and tail boldly barred

Other characteristics:
- Habitat: Marshes and adjacent moist grassland
- Status: Locally common resident

AFRICAN MARSH-HARRIER – juvenile (p. 142)

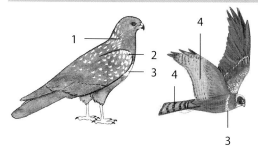

Field recognition
- Size: Medium-small
1 Plumage mostly chocolate brown
2 Buff patches on nape, throat and 'shoulders'
3 Pale band across chest
4 Flight feathers and tail barred

Other characteristics:
- See adult above

MONTAGU'S HARRIER – adult female (p. 144)

Field recognition
- Size: Medium-small
1 Underparts streaked
2 Rump pale
3 Tail barred
4 Narrow pale collar behind ear coverts
5 Narrow dark stripe at back of eye
6 Broad pale eyebrow
- The juvenile is plain rufous below and has dark (not yellow) eyes

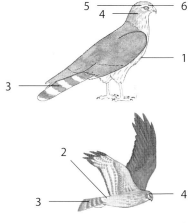

Other characteristics:
- Extremely difficult to distinguish from the female Pallid Harrier in the field
- Habitat: Mostly open grassland and marshy areas
- Status: Scarce to locally common non-breeding summer visitor

PALLID HARRIER – adult female (p. 146)

Field recognition
- Size: Medium-small
1 Underparts streaked
2 Rump pale
3 Tail barred
4 Broader and more obvious pale collar behind ear coverts
5 Broader dark stripe at back of eye
6 Narrow pale eyebrow
- The juvenile is plain rufous below and has dark (not yellow) eyes

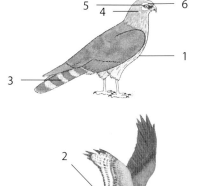

Other characteristics:
- Extremely difficult to distinguish from the female Montagu's Harrier in the field
- Habitat: Open grassland and sometimes savanna or agricultural lands
- Status: Locally common to rare non-breeding summer visitor

BLACK HARRIER – juvenile (p. 138)

Field recognition
- Size: Medium
1 Upperparts dark brown with buff markings on wing coverts, nape, cheeks and eyebrow
2 Underparts buff with bold dark brown markings on chest and flanks
3 Eyes yellow
4 Rump white
5 Tail boldly barred brown and white
6 Underwing coverts buff with brown markings
7 Flight feathers mainly white with a dark trailing edge

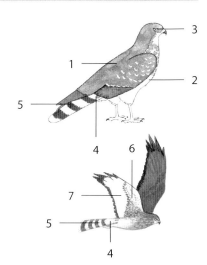

Other characteristics:
- Habitat: Arid open areas such as fynbos, grassland, Karoo and semi-desert
- Status: Uncommon resident in the southwest, non-breeding visitor elsewhere

KITES
(p. 41)

Kites are a diverse collection of small to medium-sized raptors with long, rather pointed wings. They are excellent flyers. In spite of their names, the African Cuckoo-Hawk and Bat Hawk also belong to this group. As most kites may be confused with species belonging to other groups, it is best to familiarise oneself with the five species.

1. The Black-shouldered Kite (p. 254)
This characteristic kite may be confused with Montagu's and Pallid Harrier males or possibly with the two chanting goshawks.

2. Brown kites with long, forked tails (p. 255)
These medium-sized raptors, the so-called *Milvus* kites, are a familiar sight during the summer months. They are excellent fliers. The long wings are slightly angled and the long, forked tail is continually twisted in flight.

3. Kites with a slight crest on the back of the head (p. 256)
The African Cuckoo-Hawk may be confused with the African Goshawk, while the Bat Hawk resembles a large falcon in flight.

1. The Black-shouldered Kite

BLACK-SHOULDERED KITE – adult (p. 148)

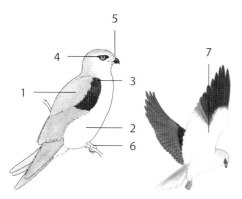

Field recognition
• Size: Small
1 Upperparts mostly grey
2 Underparts and head white
3 'Shoulders' black
4 Eyes red
5 Cere yellow
6 Legs yellow
7 Underwing mostly white with a black tip

Other characteristics:
• Habitat: Varied: from desert to open woodland
• Status: Common to very common resident; nomadic
• See male Montagu's p. 144 and Pallid Harriers p. 146

BLACK-SHOULDERED KITE – juvenile (p. 148)

Field recognition
• Size: Small
1 Upperparts brownish with pale feather edges giving a scaled appearance
2 Underparts washed rufous with fine brown streaks on the chest
3 'Shoulder' patch dark
4 Eyes pale brown at first, then changing to orange

Other characteristics:
• See adult above

2. Brown kites with long, forked tails

BLACK KITE – adult (p. 152)

Field recognition
- Size: Medium
1. Bill black with a yellow cere
2. Head greyish
3. Body dark brown
4. Tail long and forked
5. Wings angled at the wrist joint

Other characteristics:
- Habitat: Prefers open woodland and savanna but also occurs in other habitats
- Status: Locally common non-breeding summer visitor

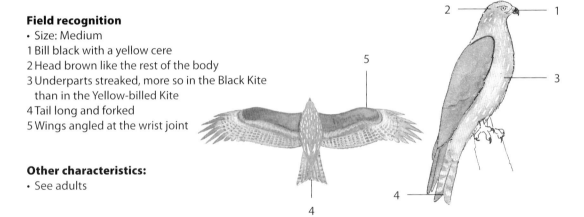

BLACK AND YELLOW-BILLED KITES – juveniles (pp. 152 and 154)

Field recognition
- Size: Medium
1. Bill black with a yellow cere
2. Head brown like the rest of the body
3. Underparts streaked, more so in the Black Kite than in the Yellow-billed Kite
4. Tail long and forked
5. Wings angled at the wrist joint

Other characteristics:
- See adults

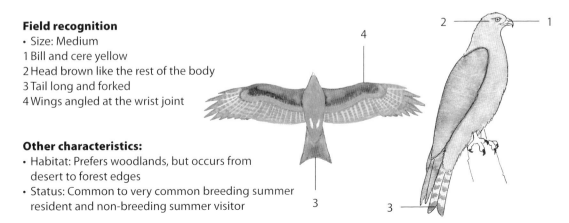

YELLOW-BILLED KITE – adult (p. 154)

Field recognition
- Size: Medium
1. Bill and cere yellow
2. Head brown like the rest of the body
3. Tail long and forked
4. Wings angled at the wrist joint

Other characteristics:
- Habitat: Prefers woodlands, but occurs from desert to forest edges
- Status: Common to very common breeding summer resident and non-breeding summer visitor

3. Kites with a slight crest on the back of the head

AFRICAN CUCKOO-HAWK – adult (p. 150)

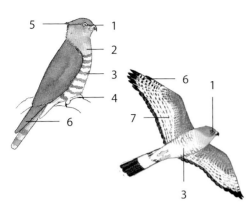

Field recognition
- Size: Medium-small
1 Eyes dark brown in males and orange in females
2 Chest grey
3 Belly barred rufous
4 Legs short and yellow
5 Small crest with a rufous patch below
6 Wings long and pointed
7 Underwing coverts barred rufous

Other characteristics:
- Habitat: Densely wooded areas
- Status: Uncommon resident
- See adult African Goshawk p. 132

AFRICAN CUCKOO-HAWK – juvenile (p. 150)

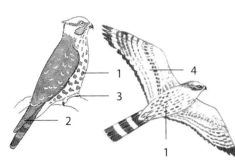

Field recognition
- Size: Medium-small
1 Underparts white with dark brown blotches
2 Wings long and pointed
3 Legs short
4 Underwing mainly white with blotches on the coverts and barring on the flight feathers

Other characteristics:
- See adult above
- See juvenile African Goshawk p. 132

BAT HAWK – adult (p. 156)

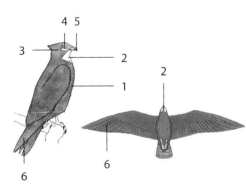

Field recognition
- Size: Medium-small
1 Plumage mostly dark brown
2 Throat white
3 Head slim and slightly crested
4 Eyes large and yellow
5 Bill small and slender
6 Wings long and pointed

Other characteristics:
- Usually hunts at dusk; catches bats in flight
- Habitat: Mostly moist woodland and tall riverine growth
- Status: Rare resident

BAT HAWK – juvenile (p. 156)

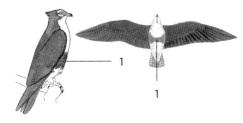

Field recognition
- Size: Medium-small
1 The juvenile resembles the adult, but the underparts are white with a brown band across the lower chest

Other characteristics:
- See adult above

FALCONS AND KESTRELS
(p. 42)

These very small to medium-small raptors inhabit open habitats and are adapted for fast (falcons) or hovering (kestrels) flight. Their wings are long and pointed while the tail is long. The powerful jaw muscles give the head a characteristic pug-faced appearance. The eyes are dark except in the adult Greater Kestrel.

1. A very small falcon: the Pygmy Falcon (p. 257)
This smallest of Southern African diurnal raptors is easily identified by its tiny size and grey-and-white plumage.

2. Grey falcons and kestrels (p. 258)
Three of these, namely the Sooty Falcon, Grey Kestrel and Eleonora's Falcon, have an overall grey appearance. Dickinson's Kestrel has a pale grey head and rump. The male Red-footed and Amur Falcons are characterised by their rufous lower bellies.

3. Rufous kestrels (p. 260)
Greater, Rock and Lesser Kestrels are often confused. Noting their body shape, colour pattern, habitat and behaviour will aid identification.

4. Falcons and kestrels with dark upperparts and rufous underparts (p. 262)
The African Hobby (adult and juvenile), Eleonora's Falcon (typical adult and juvenile), Taita Falcon (adult and juvenile), Red-footed Falcon (female) and Red-necked Falcon (juvenile) differ in body shape, colour pattern, habitat and behaviour.

5. Falcons with pale, well-marked underparts and rufous lower bellies (p. 265)
The adult Eurasian Hobby may be confused with the female Amur Falcon.

6. Falcons with pale underparts, either plain, barred or blotched (p. 266)
The adult Lanner Falcon has plain pinkish-buff to whitish underparts. The adult Red-necked Falcon's lower chest and belly are white with black bars, whereas those of the adult Peregrine Falcon are variously barred and spotted. The underparts of juvenile Peregrine, Lanner and Sooty Falcons and Eurasian Hobby are boldly blotched.

1. A very small falcon: the Pygmy Falcon

PYGMY FALCON – male and female (p. 188)

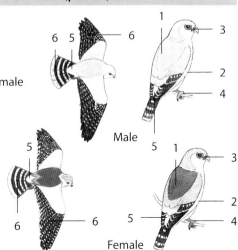

Male

Female

Field recognition
- Size: Very small
1 Upperparts completely grey in male; back chestnut in female
2 Underparts white
3 Cere and eye-ring red
4 Legs red
5 Rump white
6 Flight feathers and tail black with white spots
- The juvenile resembles the adult, but the back and chest are washed rufous

Other characteristics:
- Habitat: Arid thornveld and semi-desert regions
- Status: Uncommon to locally common resident

2. Grey falcons and kestrels

AMUR FALCON – male (p. 180)

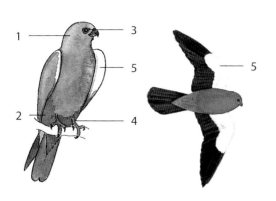

Field recognition
- Size: Small
1 Plumage mostly grey
2 Lower belly and leggings rufous
3 Eye-ring and cere red
4 Legs red
5 Underwing coverts white

Other characteristics:
- Occurs in flocks consisting of both sexes
- Hunts on the wing and hovers often
- Habitat: Open grassland; sometimes lightly wooded areas
- Status: Common non-breeding summer visitor

RED-FOOTED FALCON – male (p. 178)

Field recognition
- Size: Small
1 Plumage mostly grey
2 Lower belly and leggings rufous
3 Eye-ring and cere red
4 Legs red
5 Underwing coverts dark

Other characteristics:
- Occurs in flocks consisting of both sexes
- Hunts on the wing and hovers often
- Habitat: Semi-arid savanna and open grassland
- Status: Common to rare non-breeding summer visitor

DICKINSON'S KESTREL – adult (p. 176)

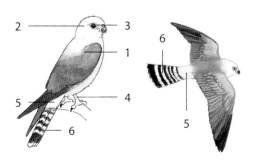

Field recognition
- Size: Small
1 Stockily built with shortish wings
2 Head pale grey
3 Eye-ring and cere yellow
4 Legs yellow
5 Rump pale grey
6 Tail boldly barred

Other characteristics:
- Hunts mostly from a perch
- Habitat: Tropical savanna woodland and swampy floodplains
- Status: Uncommon to rare resident

SOOTY FALCON – adult (p. 172)

Field recognition
- Size: Small
1 Slender bodyshape with long wings and tail
2 Plumage mostly pale grey, but may be dark grey
3 Eye-ring and cere yellow
4 Dark moustachial stripe may be seen at close range
5 Legs yellow
6 Underwing and tail plain grey
7 Tail wedge-shaped

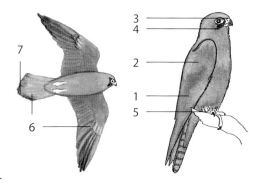

Other characteristics:
- Spends most of the day perched quietly in a tree and hunts at dawn and dusk, catching insects in flight
- Habitat: Eastern well-wooded areas; usually near water
- Status: Rare non-breeding summer visitor and vagrant

ELEONORA'S FALCON – dark adult (p. 170)

Field recognition
- Size: Medium-small
1 Slender bodyshape with very long wings and a long tail
2 Entire plumage dark sooty brown or even black
3 Cere and eye-ring yellowish in male and bluish in female
4 Legs dull yellow-greenish
5 Underwing and tail dark
- Very similar to the Sooty Falcon, but larger with a longer tail

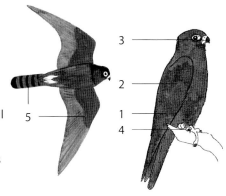

Other characteristics:
- Spends most of the day perched quietly in a tree and hunts at dawn and dusk, catching insects in flight
- Habitat: Broadleaved woodland and adjoining grassland
- Status: Rare non-breeding summer vagrant

GREY KESTREL – adult (p. 174)

Field recognition
- Size: Small
1 Stockily built with shortish wings
2 Plumage uniform grey
3 Large-headed with a large bill
4 Eye-ring and cere yellow
5 Legs yellow
6 Flight feathers and tail faintly barred
- The juvenile resembles the adult, but the plumage has a slight brown wash

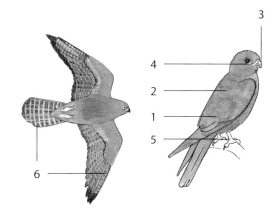

Other characteristics:
- Usually hunts from a perch
- Habitat: Palm savanna, trees along watercourses and artificially cleared areas in adjacent dry woodland; northern Namibia
- Status: Rare and localised resident

3. Rufous kestrels

GREATER KESTREL – adult (p. 186)

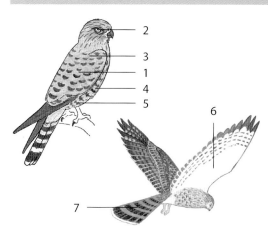

Field recognition
- Size: Medium-small
1 Overall colour varies from pale tawny to rufous
2 Eyes pale
3 Upperparts coarsely barred
4 Underparts streaked
5 Flanks barred
6 Underwing nearly completely white
7 Tail grey with darker bars

Other characteristics:
- Hunts from a prominent perch, sometimes hovers
- Habitat: Prefers arid, open country such as savanna and grassland
- Status: Fairly common resident

ROCK KESTREL – adult (p. 184)

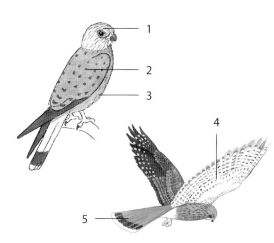

Field recognition
- Size: Small
1 Head grey with dark streaks
2 Upperparts spotted
3 Underparts the same shade of rufous as the upperparts
4 Underwing mostly white with conspicuous barring on the flight feathers
5 Tail plain grey in male and narrowly barred in female. Both sexes have a broad dark band just beyond the white tip of the tail

Other characteristics:
- Hovers frequently
- Habitat: Occurs widely from desert to forest edges wherever there are rocky outcrops for breeding
- Status: Common resident

LESSER KESTREL – male (p. 182)

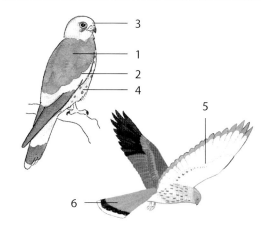

Field recognition
- Size: Small
1 Slender body shape
2 Upperparts plain rufous with a grey wing-bar
3 Head plain grey
4 Underparts buffy, contrasting with the darker back
5 Underwing white
6 Tail plain grey with a broad bar just beyond the white tip

Other characteristics:
- Occurs in flocks consisting of both sexes
- Hunts on the wing and hovers often
- Habitat: Prefers semi-arid grassland and Karoo
- Status: Locally common non-breeding summer visitor

GREATER KESTREL – juvenile (p. 186)

Field recognition
- Size: Medium-small
- The juvenile resembles the adult, but differs in the following ways:
1 Eyes dark
2 Flanks streaked
3 Tail brown with darker bars

Other characteristics:
- See adult on opposite page

ROCK KESTREL – juvenile (p. 184)

Field recognition
- Size: Small
- The juvenile resembles the adult female, but differs in the following ways:
1 Head brown with darker streaks
2 Tail brown with darker bars

Other characteristics:
- See adult on opposite page

LESSER KESTREL – female (p. 182)

Field recognition
- Size: Small
1 Slender body shape
2 Upperparts coarsely barred
3 Underparts buff with darker streaks
4 Small moustachial stripe
5 Underwing buff with darker spots
6 Tail brown with fine bars and a broad bar just beyond the tip
- The juvenile resembles the female, but is paler and duller

Other characteristics:
- Usually in flocks consisting of both sexes
- See male on opposite page

4. Falcons with dark upperparts and rufous underparts

AFRICAN HOBBY – adult (p. 168)

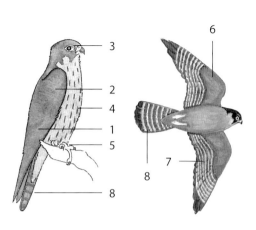

Field recognition
- Size: Small
1. Slender body shape with long wings and a long tail
2. Upperparts slaty black
3. Cere and eye-ring yellow
4. Underparts rufous with fine black streaks which are hardly visible
5. Legs yellow
6. Underwing coverts rufous
7. Flight feathers barred rufous
8. Tail barred rufous

Other characteristics:
- Spends most of the day perched quietly in a tree and hunts at dawn and dusk, usually catching insects in flight
- Habitat: Palm savanna, broadleaved woodland and adjoining open country
- Status: Rare breeding summer resident and non-breeding summer vagrant

AFRICAN HOBBY – juvenile (p. 168)

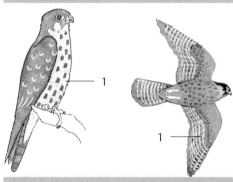

Field recognition
- Size: Small
1. Resembles the adult but the underparts and underwing coverts are distinctly streaked

Other characteristics:
- See adult above

RED-NECKED FALCON – juvenile (p. 164)

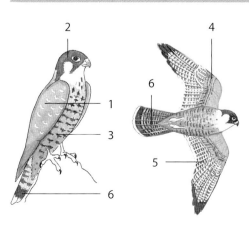

Field recognition
- Size: Small
1. Upperparts dark grey with darker bars and paler scales
2. Cap and nape brown
3. Underparts dull rufous with bars on the lower chest and belly
4. Underwing coverts rufous
5. Flight feathers barred
6. Tail barred with a broad subterminal bar

Other characteristics:
- Employs a perch-and-chase hunting technique
- Habitat: Prefers palm savanna and floodplains; also around water-holes in arid regions
- Status: Uncommon to rare resident

TAITA FALCON – adult (p. 162)

Field recognition
- Size: Small
1 Stocky body shape with a short tail
2 Two rufous patches on nape
3 Cere and eye-ring yellow
4 Throat and cheeks white
5 Underparts rufous with fine black streaks which are hardly visible
6 Legs yellow
7 Underwing coverts rufous with darker streaks
8 Flight feathers faintly barred
9 Tail faintly barred

Other characteristics:
- Stoops at its avian prey
- Habitat: Cliffs, gorges and adjacent woodland
- Status: Rare resident

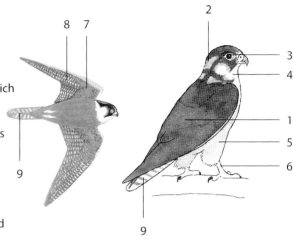

TAITA FALCON – juvenile (p. 162)

Field recognition:
- Size: Small
1 Resembles the adult but is distinctly streaked on the underparts

Other characteristics:
- See adult above

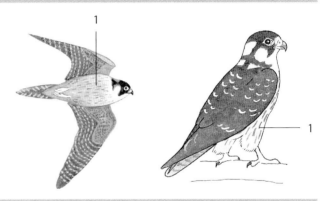

RED-FOOTED FALCON – female (p. 178)

Field recognition
- Size: Small
1 Upperparts grey with coarse black barring
2 Cere and eye-ring orange
3 Underparts and head rufous with faint streaks
4 Dark mask through eye
5 Throat and cheeks whitish
6 Legs orange
7 Underwing coverts rufous with darker streaks
8 Flight feathers boldly barred
9 Tail boldly barred

Other characteristics:
- Occurs in flocks consisting of both sexes
- Hunts on the wing and hovers often
- Habitat: Semi-arid savanna and open grassland
- Status: Common to rare non-breeding summer visitor

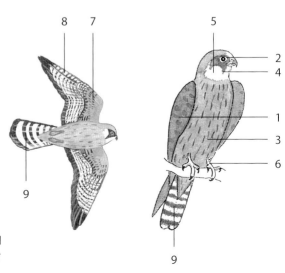

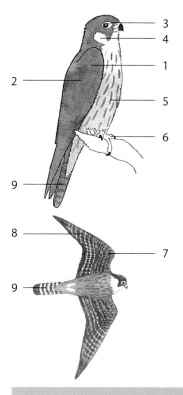

Field recognition
- Size: Medium-small
1 Slender body shape with very long wings and a long tail
2 Upperparts dark sooty brown
3 Cere and eye-ring yellowish in male and bluish in female
4 Throat and cheeks white
5 Underparts pale to dark rufous with heavy black streaks
6 Legs dull yellow
7 Underwing coverts dark brown
8 Flight feathers dark grey
9 Tail barred

Other characteristics:
- Spends most of the day perched quietly in a tree and hunts at dawn and dusk, catching insects in flight
- Habitat: Broadleaved woodland and adjoining grassland
- Status: Rare non-breeding summer vagrant

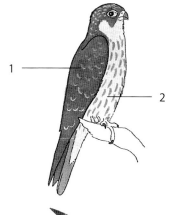

Field recognition
- Size: Medium-small
1 Upperparts dark brown with buff scales
2 Underparts pale rufous with dark streaks
3 Underwing and tail dark

Other characteristics:
- Very difficult to distinguish from juvenile Eurasian Hobby and Sooty Falcon in the field
- See adult above
- Status: Rare non-breeding summer vagrant

5. Falcons and kestrels with pale, well-marked underparts and rufous lower bellies

EURASIAN HOBBY – adult (p. 166)

Field recognition
- Size: Small
1 Slender body shape with long wings and a long tail
2 Upperparts slaty black
3 Cere and eye-ring yellow
4 Underparts buff with heavy black streaks
5 Lower belly and leggings rufous
6 Legs yellow
7 Underwing coverts streaked
8 Flight feathers barred
9 Tail barred

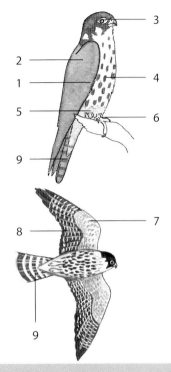

Other characteristics:
- Spends most of the day perched quietly in a tree and hunts at dawn and dusk, feeding mainly on flying termites
- Habitat: Broadleaved woodland and savanna, often near water
- Status: Uncommon non-breeding summer visitor

AMUR FALCON – female (p. 180)

Field recognition
- Size: Small
1 Upperparts grey with faint black barring and a paler crown
2 Cere and eye-ring orange
3 Underparts white with distinct barring and blotching
4 Lower belly and leggings pale rufous
5 Legs orange
6 Underwing coverts white with darker streaks
7 Tail barred

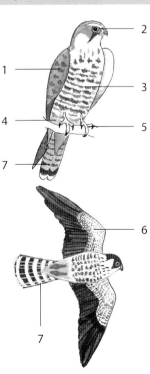

Other characteristics:
- Occurs in flocks consisting of both sexes
- Hunts on the wing and hovers often
- Habitat: Open grassland, sometimes lightly wooded areas
- Status: Common non-breeding summer visitor

6. Falcons with pale underparts, either plain, barred or blotched

LANNER FALCON – adult (p. 160)

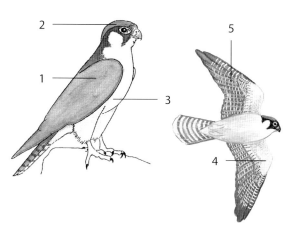

Field recognition
- Size: Medium-small
1 Upperparts bluish-grey
2 Rufous crown
3 Underparts plain pinkish
4 Underwing coverts plain as underparts
5 Flight feathers barred
- Appears paler and less stocky in flight than the Peregrine Falcon

Other characteristics:
- A versatile hunter which often stoops at its avian prey
- Habitat: Various habitats from woodland to desert
- Status: Fairly common resident

PEREGRINE FALCON – adult (p. 158)

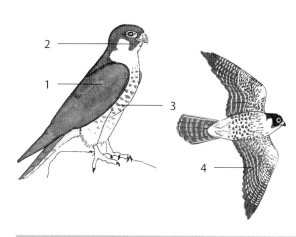

Field recognition
- Size: Medium-small
1 Upperparts dark slate grey
2 Broad moustachial stripe resembling a 'hangman's hood'
3 Lower chest and belly barred and spotted
4 Underwing barred
- Appears darker and stockier in flight with more dynamic movements than the Lanner Falcon

Other characteristics:
- Typically hunts by stooping at its avian prey
- Habitat: Mainly cliffs, mountains and gorges, but hunts over adjacent habitats
- Status: Scarce resident and rare non-breeding summer visitor

RED-NECKED FALCON – adult (p. 164)

Field recognition
- Size: Small
1 Crown and nape chestnut
2 Upperparts blue-grey with fine black bars
3 Lower chest and belly white with conspicuous black bars
4 Underwing barred
5 Tail barred with a broad bar near the tip

Other characteristics:
- Employs a perch-and-chase hunting technique
- Habitat: Prefers palm savanna and floodplains; also around water-holes in arid regions
- Status: Uncommon to rare resident

LANNER FALCON – juvenile (p. 160)

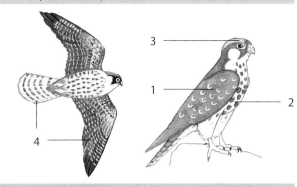

Field recognition
- Size: Medium-small
1. Upperparts dark brown with buff scales
2. Underparts buff with heavy streaks
3. Crown mostly rufous, but may be buff with some rufous blotches
4. Underwing and tail appear dark
- Appears paler and less stocky in flight than the juvenile Peregrine Falcon

Other characteristics:
- See adult on opposite page

PEREGRINE FALCON – juvenile (p. 158)

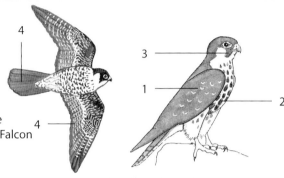

Field recognition
- Size: Medium-small
1. Upperparts dark brown with buff scales
2. Underparts buff with heavy dark streaks
3. Broad moustachial stripe resembling 'hangman's hood'
4. Underwing and tail appear dark
- Appears darker and stockier in flight with more dynamic movements than the juvenile Lanner Falcon

Other characteristics:
- See adult on opposite page

EURASIAN HOBBY – juvenile (p. 166)

Field recognition
- Size: Small
1. Upperparts brown with buff scales
2. Underparts buff with heavy dark streaks
3. Underwing coverts streaked
4. Flight feathers barred
5. Tail barred

Other characteristics:
- Very difficult to distinguish from juvenile Eleonora's and Sooty Falcons in the field
- Habitat: Broadleaved woodland and savanna, often near water
- Status: Uncommon non-breeding summer visitor

SOOTY FALCON – juvenile (p. 172)

Field recognition
- Size: Small
1. Upperparts grey with buff scales
2. Underparts buff with poorly defined grey blotches
3. Underwing coverts faintly mottled
4. Flight feathers and tail faintly barred

Other characteristics:
- Very difficult to distinguish from juvenile Eurasian Hobby and Eleonora's Falcon in the field
- Habitat: Well-wooded areas; usually near water
- Status: Rare non-breeding summer visitor and vagrant

OWLS
(p. 44)

Owls are well-known. They are very small to very large raptors adapted to a nocturnal lifestyle. Their eyes are large and their flight is silent.

1. Small owls without ear-tufts (p. 268)
The Pearl-spotted Owlet and African Barred Owlet are very similar, but differ in colour pattern and habitat preference.

2. Small owls with ear-tufts (p. 269)
The cryptically coloured African Scops-Owl is Southern Africa's smallest owl. The Southern White-faced Scops-Owl is easily recognised by its larger size, white face and orange eyes.

3. Medium owls with well-defined facial discs (p. 270)
The Barn Owl is often confused with the similar African Grass-Owl, but the two species differ in their habitat preference. Although African Grass-Owls and Marsh Owls occur in similar habitats, they are distinguished by their colour pattern and behaviour.

4. Eagle-owls: large owls with ear-tufts (p. 271)
Its dark eyes and grey appearance distinguish the Verreaux's Eagle-Owl. The Cape and Spotted Eagle-Owls differ in eye colour, colour pattern and habitat preference.

1. Small owls without ear-tufts

PEARL-SPOTTED OWLET – adult (p. 198)

Field recognition
• Size: Very small
1 Upperparts and tail marked with small white spots
2 Underparts white with brown streaks
3 Face white
• Two large dark spots on the back of the head give the impression of eyes

Other characteristics:
• Often seen during the day
• Habitat: Savanna, bushveld and open woodland
• Status: Common resident

AFRICAN BARRED OWLET – adult (p. 200)

Field recognition
• Size: Very small
1 Upperparts and tail barred
2 Row of large white spots on the wings
3 Underparts white with bold brown spots
4 Face grey

Other characteristics:
• Habitat: Mature woodland, riparian and coastal forest
• Status: Locally common resident; rare in the Eastern Cape

2. Small owls with ear-tufts

AFRICAN SCOPS-OWL – adult (p. 202)

Field recognition
- Size: Very small
1 Overall colour usually grey, but sometimes brown
2 Fine black streaks and blotches and white markings resemble tree bark
3 Eyes yellow

Other characteristics:
- Elongates body and closes its eyes when disturbed, thus resembling a dead branch
- Habitat: Prefers drier savanna, but occurs widely in bushveld and woodland
- Status: Common resident

SOUTHERN WHITE-FACED SCOPS-OWL – adult (p. 204)

Field recognition
- Size: Small
1 Eyes orange
2 Face white with a black border
3 Underparts pale grey with black streaks
4 Row of white spots on the wing

Other characteristics:
- Habitat: Prefers thornveld, but occurs widely in wooded areas
- Status: Common resident

3. Medium owls with well-defined facial discs

BARN OWL – adult (p. 190)

Field recognition
- Size: Medium
1 Well-defined heart-shaped facial disc
2 Upperparts mottled pale brown and grey with small white spots
3 Underparts very pale
- There is little contrast between the colour of the upper- and underparts

Other characteristics:
- Habitat: Widespread from desert to woodland; often associated with human habitation
- Status: Common resident

AFRICAN GRASS-OWL – adult (p. 192)

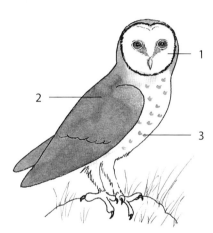

Field recognition
- Size: Medium
1 Well-defined heart-shaped facial disc
2 Upperparts plain brown
3 Underparts buff
- There is a distinct contrast between the darker upperparts and the paler underparts

Other characteristics:
- Strictly nocturnal
- Habitat: Prefers marshes, vleis and lush grassland
- Status: Uncommon to rare resident

MARSH OWL – adult (p. 194)

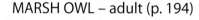

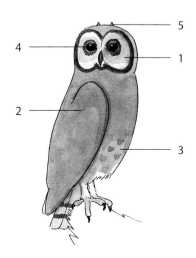

Field recognition
- Size: Medium
1 Facial disc oval and not well defined
2 Upperparts dark brown
3 Underparts slightly paler than upperparts
4 Dark patches around eyes
5 Small ear-tufts seldom seen in the field
- There is little contrast between the colour of the upper- and underparts
- Shows pale patches near the wing tips in flight

Other characteristics:
- Often occurs in flocks
- Regularly hunts at dawn or dusk or on overcast days
- Habitat: Prefers patches of long grass in vleis, marshes and grassland
- Status: Common resident

4. Eagle-owls: large owls with ear-tufts

SPOTTED EAGLE-OWL – adult (p. 208)

Field recognition
- Size: Large
1 Eyes yellow, rarely orange
2 Plumage usually mottled greyish-brown, rarely rufous
3 Fine barring on belly
4 Feet small
- A rare western form may be rufous with orange eyes, but is distinguished from the Cape Eagle-Owl by fine barring on the belly

Other characteristics:
- Habitat: From desert to woodland
- Status: Very common resident

CAPE EAGLE-OWL – adult (p. 210)

Field recognition
- Size: Large to very large
1 Eyes orange
2 Plumage a mottled rufous brown
3 Bold black and rufous blotches on chest
4 Broad black, tawny and white barring on belly
5 Feet large

Other characteristics:
- The subspecies in Zimbabwe and Mozambique, known as Mackinder's Eagle Owl, is very large
- Habitat: Mostly montane grassland with rocky outcrops; also fynbos and hilly woodland
- Status: Uncommon, localised resident

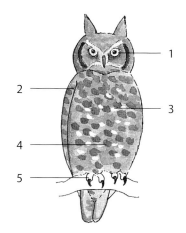

VERREAUX'S EAGLE-OWL – adult (p. 206)

Field recognition
- Size: Very large
1 Eyes dark with pink eyelids
2 Face pale grey with a black border
3 Plumage grey with very fine black and white barring

Other characteristics:
- Habitat: Prefers open savanna, but occurs widely in bushveld and woodland
- Status: Fairly common resident

Verreaux's Eagle / Philip van den Berg

SECTION 5

REFERENCES

RAPTORS IN FLIGHT

SECRETARYBIRD (p. 48)

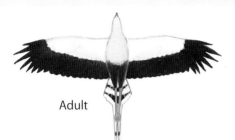

Adult

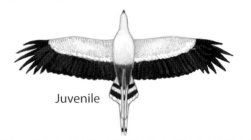

Juvenile

OSPREY (p. 50)

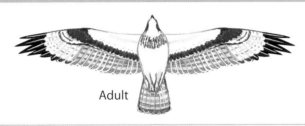

Adult

AFRICAN FISH-EAGLE (p. 52)

Adult

Immature

PALM-NUT VULTURE (p. 54)

Adult

Juvenile

EGYPTIAN VULTURE (p. 56)

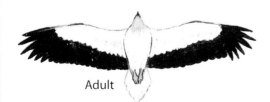

Adult

Juvenile

HOODED VULTURE (p. 58)

Adult

Juvenile

WHITE-HEADED VULTURE (p. 60)

Female   Male

Juvenile

LAPPET-FACED VULTURE (p. 62)

Adult

Juvenile

WHITE-BACKED VULTURE (p. 64)

Adult

Juvenile

CAPE VULTURE (p. 66)

Adult

Juvenile

RÜPPELL'S VULTURE (p. 68)

Adult

Juvenile

BEARDED VULTURE (p. 70)

Adult

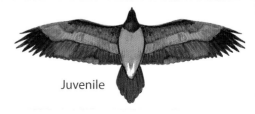

Juvenile

VERREAUXS' EAGLE (p. 72)

Adult

Juvenile

TAWNY EAGLE (p. 74)

Tawny adult

Pale adult

Streaky adult

Juvenile

STEPPE EAGLE (p. 76)

Adult

Juvenile

LESSER SPOTTED EAGLE (p. 78)

Adult

Juvenile

WAHLBERG'S EAGLE (p. 80)

Brown form

Pale form

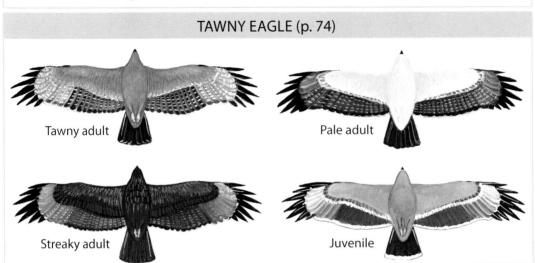

BOOTED EAGLE (p. 82)

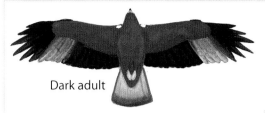

Dark adult

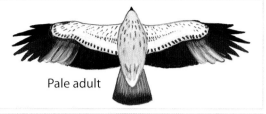

Pale adult

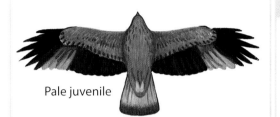

Pale juvenile

LONG-CRESTED EAGLE (p. 84)

Adult

AFRICAN HAWK-EAGLE (p. 86)

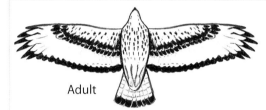

Adult

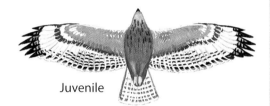

Juvenile

AYRES'S HAWK-EAGLE (p. 88)

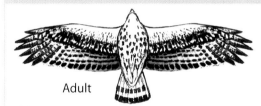

Adult

Rufous juvenile

AFRICAN CROWNED EAGLE (p. 90)

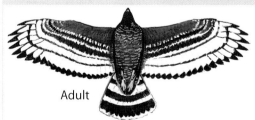

Adult

Juvenile

MARTIAL EAGLE (p. 92)

Adult

Juvenile

BLACK-CHESTED SNAKE-EAGLE (p. 94)

Adult

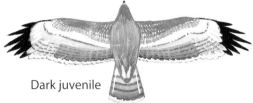

Dark juvenile

SOUTHERN BANDED SNAKE-EAGLE (p. 96)

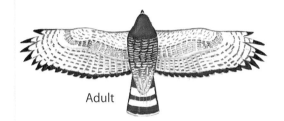

Adult

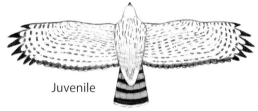

Juvenile

WESTERN BANDED SNAKE-EAGLE (p. 98)

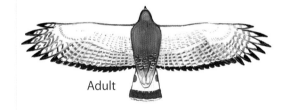

Adult

Juvenile

BROWN SNAKE-EAGLE (p. 100)

BATELEUR (p. 102)

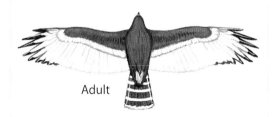

Adult

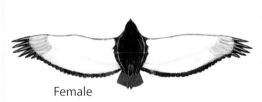

Female

Male

Juvenile

AUGUR BUZZARD (p. 104)

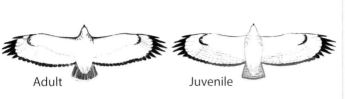

Adult

Juvenile

JACKAL BUZZARD (p. 106)

Adult

STEPPE BUZZARD (p. 108)

Typical
adult

Dark
adult

Juvenile

Juvenile

FOREST BUZZARD (p. 110)

Adult

Juvenile

LONG-LEGGED BUZZARD (p. 112)

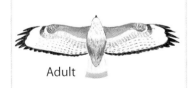

Adult

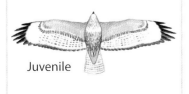

Juvenile

EUROPEAN HONEY-BUZZARD (p. 114)

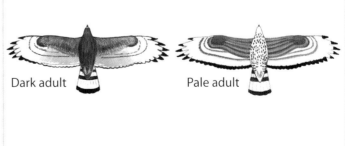

Dark adult

Pale adult

Barred adult

Juvenile

LIZARD BUZZARD (p. 116)

Adult

AFRICAN HARRIER-HAWK (p. 118)

Adult

Dark juvenile

SOUTHERN PALE CHANTING GOSHAWK (p. 122)

Adult

Juvenile

DARK CHANTING GOSHAWK (p. 120)

Adult

Juvenile

GABAR GOSHAWK (p. 124)

Adult

Melanistic adult

SHIKRA (p. 126)

Adult

Juvenile

Juvenile

OVAMBO SPARROWHAWK (p. 128)

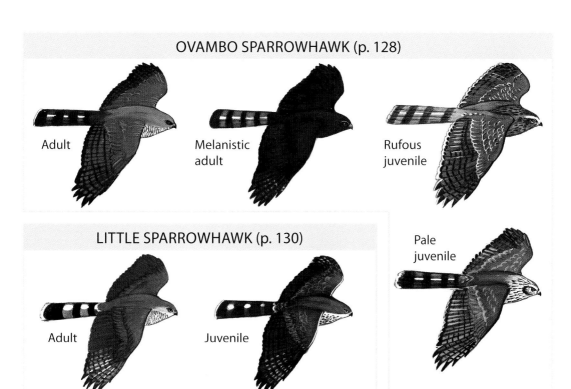

Adult

Melanistic adult

Rufous juvenile

LITTLE SPARROWHAWK (p. 130)

Adult

Juvenile

Pale juvenile

AFRICAN GOSHAWK (p. 132)

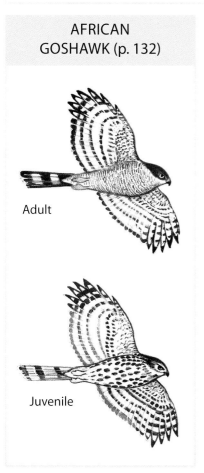

Adult

Juvenile

RED-CHESTED SPARROWHAWK (p. 134)

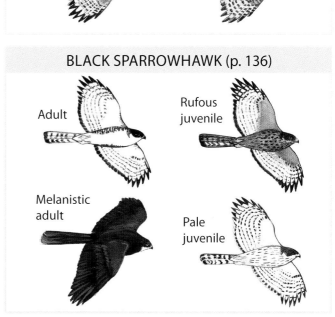

Adult

Juvenile

BLACK SPARROWHAWK (p. 136)

Adult

Rufous juvenile

Melanistic adult

Pale juvenile

BLACK HARRIER (p. 138)

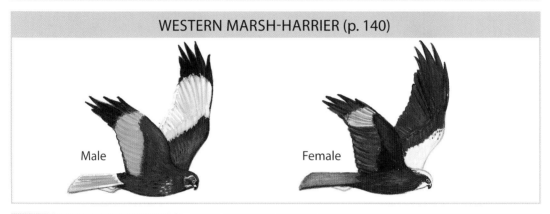

Adult

Juvenile

WESTERN MARSH-HARRIER (p. 140)

Male

Female

AFRICAN MARSH-HARRIER (p. 142)

Adult

Juvenile

MONTAGU'S HARRIER (p. 144)

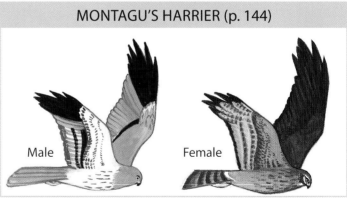

Male

Female

PALLID HARRIER (p. 146)

Male

Female

AFRICAN CUCKOO-HAWK (p. 150)

Adult

Juvenile

BLACK-SHOULDERED KITE (p. 148)

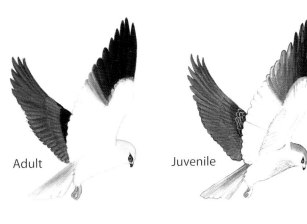

Adult

Juvenile

BLACK KITE (p. 152)

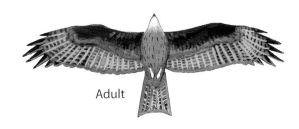

Adult

YELLOW-BILLED KITE (p. 154)

Adult

Juvenile

BAT HAWK (p. 156)

Adult

Juvenile

PEREGRINE FALCON (p. 158)

Adult   Juvenile

LANNER FALCON (p. 160)

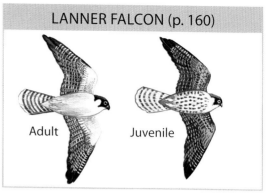

Adult   Juvenile

TAITA FALCON (p. 162)

Adult   Juvenile

RED-NECKED FALCON (p. 164)

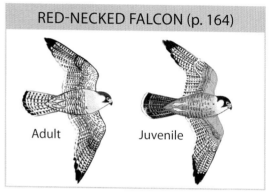

Adult   Juvenile

EURASIAN HOBBY (p. 166)

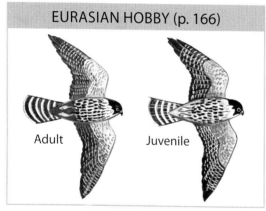

Adult   Juvenile

AFRICAN HOBBY (p. 168)

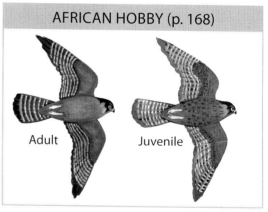

Adult   Juvenile

ELEONORA'S FALCON (p. 170)

Adult   Dark adult   Juvenile

SOOTY FALCON (p. 172)

Adult

Juvenile

GREY KESTREL (p. 174)

Adult

DICKINSON'S FALCON (p. 176)

Adult

RED-FOOTED FALCON (p. 178)

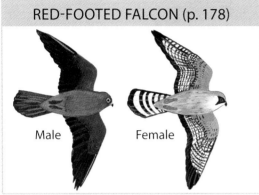

Male

Female

AMUR FALCON (p. 180)

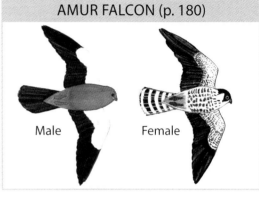

Male

Female

LESSER KESTREL (p. 182)

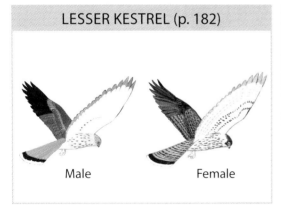

Male

Female

ROCK KESTREL (p. 184)

Male

Juvenile

GREATER KESTREL (p. 186)

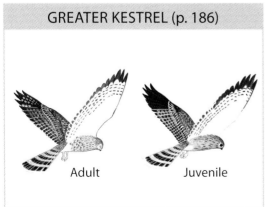

Adult

Juvenile

PYGMY FALCON (p. 188)

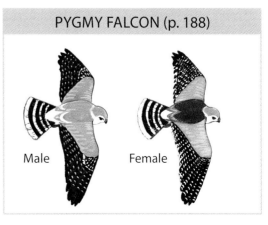

Male

Female

Selected photographs of raptors in flight

SECRETARYBIRD
Adult (p.48)

Johann Knobel

SECRETARYBIRD
Adult (p.48)

Trevor Hardaker

OSPREY
Adult (p. 50)

Markus Varesvuo

OSPREY
Adult (p. 50)

Markus Varesvuo

OSPREY
Adult (p. 50)

Markus Varesvuo

AFRICAN FISH-EAGLE
Adult (p. 52)

Chris van Rooyen

AFRICAN FISH-EAGLE
Adult (p. 52)

Albert Froneman

AFRICAN FISH-EAGLE
Immature (p. 52)

Richard du Toit

AFRICAN FISH-EAGLE
Immature (p. 52)

Chris van Rooyen

PALM-NUT VULTURE
Adult (p. 54)

Steve Garvie

EGYPTIAN VULTURE
Adult (p. 56)

Markus Varesvuo

EGYPTIAN VULTURE
Adult (p. 56)

Markus Varesvuo

EGYPTIAN VULTURE
Juvenile (p. 56)

Markus Varesvuo

HOODED VULTURE
Adult (p. 58)

Albert Froneman

HOODED VULTURE
Juvenile (p. 58)

Sue Robinson

WHITE-HEADED VULTURE
Male (p. 60)

Albert Froneman

WHITE-HEADED VULTURE
Female (p. 60)

Marius van Zyl

WHITE-HEADED VULTURE
Juvenile (p. 60)

Chris van Rooyen

LAPPET-FACED VULTURE
Adult (p. 62)

Chris van Rooyen

LAPPET-FACED VULTURE
Adult (p. 62)

Albert Froneman

LAPPET-FACED VULTURE
Juvenile (p. 62)

Chris van Rooyen

WHITE-BACKED VULTURE
Pale adult (p. 64)

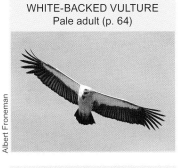

Albert Froneman

WHITE-BACKED VULTURE
Typical adult (p. 64)

Chris van Rooyen

WHITE-BACKED VULTURE
Juvenile (p. 64)

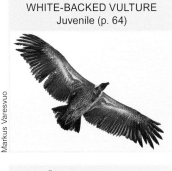

Markus Varesvuo

CAPE VULTURE
Dirty adult (p. 66)

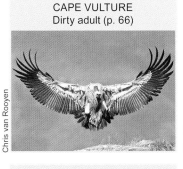

Chris van Rooyen

CAPE VULTURE
Adult (p. 66)

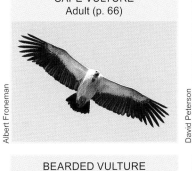

Albert Froneman

RÜPPELL'S VULTURE
Adult (p. 68)

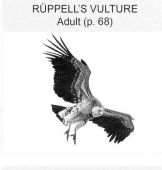

David Peterson

RÜPPELL'S VULTURE
Immature (p. 68)

Markus Varesvuo

BEARDED VULTURE
Adult (p. 70)

Chris van Rooyen

BEARDED VULTURE
Adult (p. 70)

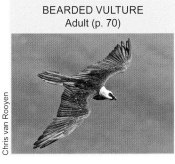

Chris van Rooyen

BEARDED VULTURE
Juvenile (p. 70)

Marietjie Oosthuizen

BEARDED VULTURE
Juvenile (p. 70)

Albert Froneman

VERREAUXS' EAGLE
Adult (p. 72)

Niel Cillié

VERREAUXS' EAGLE
Adult (p. 72)

Chris van Rooyen

VERREAUXS' EAGLE
Juvenile (p. 72)

Albert Froneman

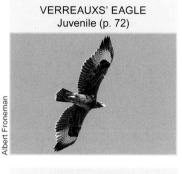

TAWNY EAGLE
Moulting adult (p. 74)

Albert Froneman

TAWNY EAGLE
Tawny adult (p. 74)

Albert Froneman

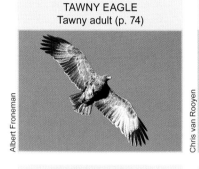

TAWNY EAGLE
Streaky adult (p. 74)

Chris van Rooyen

TAWNY EAGLE
Tawny adult (p. 74)

Johann Knobel

TAWNY EAGLE
Pale adult (p. 74)

Johann Knobel

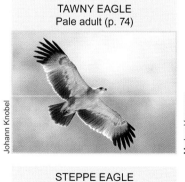

STEPPE EAGLE
Juvenile (p. 76)

Markus Varesvuo

STEPPE EAGLE
Juvenile (p. 76)

Markus Varesvuo

STEPPE EAGLE
Juvenile (p. 76)

Markus Varesvuo

LESSER SPOTTED EAGLE
Adult (p. 78)

Johann Knobel

LESSER SPOTTED EAGLE
Adult (p. 78)

Bruce Ward-Smith

LESSER SPOTTED EAGLE
Immature (p. 78)

Markus Varesvuo

WAHLBERG'S EAGLE
Pale adult (p. 80)

Albert Froneman

WAHLBERG'S EAGLE
Dark adult (p. 80)

Graham Kearney

WAHLBERG'S EAGLE
Brown adult (p. 80)

Chris van Rooyen

BOOTED EAGLE
Pale adult (p. 82)

Chris van Rooyen

BOOTED EAGLE
Pale juvenile (p. 82)

Markus Varesvuo

BOOTED EAGLE
Pale adult (p. 82)

Johann Knobel

BOOTED EAGLE
Dark adult (p. 82)

Chris van Rooyen

LONG-CRESTED EAGLE
Adult (p. 84)

Albert Froneman

LONG-CRESTED EAGLE
Adult (p. 84)

Johan Stenlund

LONG-CRESTED EAGLE
Adult (p. 84)

Johan Stenlund

AFRICAN HAWK-EAGLE
Adult (p. 86)

Johann Knobel

AFRICAN HAWK-EAGLE
Adult (p. 86)

Chris van Rooyen

AYRES'S HAWK-EAGLE
Adult (p. 88)

Tisha Greyling

AYRES'S HAWK-EAGLE
Pale juvenile (p. 88)

Niel Cillié

AYRES'S HAWK-EAGLE
Adult (p. 88)

Geoffrey Einon

AFRICAN CROWNED
EAGLE Adult (p. 90)

Albert Froneman

AFRICAN CROWNED
EAGLE Adult (p. 90)

Chris van Rooyen

MARTIAL EAGLE
Adult (p. 92)

Mark Anderson

MARTIAL EAGLE
Adult (p. 92)

Chris van Rooyen

MARTIAL EAGLE
Juvenile (p. 92)

Albert Froneman

MARTIAL EAGLE
Juvenile (p. 92)

Warwick Tarboton

BLACK-CHESTED
SNAKE-EAGLE Adult (p. 94)

Chris van Rooyen

BLACK-CHESTED SNAKE-
EAGLE Sub-adult (p. 94)

Albert Froneman

BLACK-CHESTED SNAKE-
EAGLE Immature (p. 94)

Johann Knobel

BLACK-CHESTED SNAKE-
EAGLE Juvenile (p. 94)

Albert Froneman

SOUTHERN BANDED
SNAKE-EAGLE Adult (p. 96)

Johan van Rensburg

BROWN SNAKE-EAGLE
Adult (p. 100)

Chris van Rooyen

BROWN SNAKE-EAGLE
Adult (p. 100)

Chris van Rooyen

BATELEUR
Juvenile (p. 102)

Albert Froneman

BATELEUR
Sub-adult (p. 102)

Albert Froneman

BATELEUR
Female (p. 102)

Niel Cillié

BATELEUR
Male (p. 102)

Brendan Ryan

AUGUR BUZZARD
Juvenile (p. 104)

Richard du Toit

JACKAL BUZZARD
Adult (p. 106)

Chris van Rooyen

JACKAL BUZZARD
Pale adult (p. 106)

Niel Cillié

JACKAL BUZZARD
Adult (p. 106)

Chris van Rooyen

JACKAL BUZZARD
Immature (p. 106)

Warwick Tarboton

STEPPE BUZZARD
Adult (p. 108)

Warwick Tarboton

STEPPE BUZZARD
Adult (p. 108)

Trevor Hardaker

STEPPE BUZZARD
Juvenile (p. 108)

Niel Cillié

FOREST BUZZARD
Adult (p. 110)

Warwick Tarboton

FOREST BUZZARD
Adult (p. 110)

Trevor Hardaker

LONG-LEGGED BUZZARD
Adult (p. 112)

Brendan Ryan

LONG-LEGGED BUZZARD
Juvenile (p. 112)

M Mendi

EUROPEAN HONEY-
BUZZARD Dark adult (p. 114)

Markus Varesvuo

EUROPEAN HONEY-
BUZZARD Barred adult (p. 114)

Markus Varesvuo

AFRICAN HARRIER-
HAWK Adult (p. 118)

Warwick Tarboton

AFRICAN HARRIER-
HAWK Adult (p. 118)

Richard du Toit

SOUTHERN PALE CHANTING
GOSHAWK Adult (p. 122)

Chris van Rooyen

SOUTHERN PALE CHANTING
GOSHAWK Adult (p. 122)

Chris van Rooyen

SOUTHERN PALE CHANTING
GOSHAWK Juvenile (p. 122)

Chris van Rooyen

GABAR GOSHAWK
Adult (p. 124)

Chris van Rooyen

GABAR GOSHAWK
Melanistic adult (p. 124)

Richard du Toit

GABAR GOSHAWK
Juvenile (p. 124)

Chris van Rooyen

GABAR GOSHAWK
Juvenile (p. 124)

Chris van Rooyen

OVAMBO SPARROWHAWK
Adult (p. 128)

Warwick Tarboton

OVAMBO SPARROWHAWK
Adult (p. 128)

Albert Froneman

RUFOUS-CHESTED
SPARROWHAWK Adult (p. 134)

Graham Kearney

RUFOUS-CHESTED
SPARROWHAWK Adult (p. 134)

Albert Froneman

BALCK SPARROWHAWK
Adult (p. 136)

Warwick Tarboton

BLACK HARRIER
Adult (p. 138)

Basil Boer

BLACK HARRIER
Sub-adult (p. 138)

Bruce Ward-Smith

BLACK HARRIER
Juvenile (p. 138)

Trevor Hardaker

WESTERN MARSH-HARRIER
Male (p. 140)

Markus Varesvuo

WESTERN MARSH-HARRIER
Male (p. 140)

Markus Varesvuo

WESTERN MARSH-HARRIER
Very old male (p. 140)

Markus Varesvuo

WESTERN MARSH-HARRIER Female (p. 140)

Glenice Ebedes

AFRICAN MARSH-HARRIER
Adult (p. 142)

Albert Froneman

AFRICAN MARSH-HARRIER
Adult (p. 142)

Richard du Toit

MONTAGU'S HARRIER
Male (p. 144)

Richard du Toit

MONTAGU'S HARRIER
Female (p. 144)

Tomi Muukkonen

MONTAGU'S HARRIER
Sub-adult male (p. 144)

Chris van Rooyen

PALLID HARRIER
Male (p. 146)

Arie Ouwerkerk

BLACK-SHOULDERED KITE
Adult (p. 148)

Chris van Rooyen

BLACK-SHOULDRED KITE Adult (p. 148)

Alan Knott-Craig

AFRICAN CUCKOO-HAWK Adult (p. 150)

Warwick Tarboton

AFRICAN CUCKOO-HAWK Adult (p. 150)

Johan van Rensburg

AFRICAN CUCKOO-HAWK Juvenile (p. 150)

Richard du Toit

BLACK KITE Adult (p. 152)

Michel Geven

BLACK KITE Juvenile (p. 152)

Trevor Hardaker

YELLOW-BILLED KITE Adult (p. 154)

Albert Froneman

YELLOW-BILLED KITE Adult (p. 154)

Fanie Hendriks

YELLOW-BILLED KITE Juvenile (p. 154)

Trevor Hardaker

PEREGRINE FALCON Adult (p. 158)

Mark Anderson

PEREGRINE FALCON Juvenile (p. 158)

Trevor Hardaker

LANNER FALCON Adult (p. 160)

Marietjie Oosthuizen

LANNER FALCON Juvenile (p. 160)

Brendan Ryan

RED-NECKED FALCON Adult (p. 164)

Chris van Rooyen

RED-NECKED FALCON Adult (p. 164)

Chris van Rooyen

294

EURASIAN HOBBY
Adult (p. 166)

Brendan Ryan

EURASIAN HOBBY
Adult (p. 166)

Markus Varesvuo

RED-FOOTED FALCON
Male (p. 178)

Markus Varesvuo

RED-FOOTED FALCON
Female (p. 178)

Niel Cillié

AMUR FALCON
Male (p. 180)

Chris van Rooyen

AMUR FALCON
Male (p. 180)

Lizeth Cillié

AMUR FALCON
Juvenile (p. 180)

Warwick Tarboton

AMUR FALCON
Female (p. 180)

Brendan Ryan

LESSER KESTREL
Male (p. 182)

Mark Anderson

LESSER KESTREL
Male (p. 182)

Trevor Hardaker

LESSER KESTREL
Female (p. 182)

Trevor Hardaker

ROCK KESTREL
Adult (p. 184)

Trevor Hardaker

ROCK KESTREL
Juvenile (p. 184)

Chris van Rooyen

GREATER KESTREL
Pale adult (p. 186)

Trevor Hardaker

GREATER KESTREL
Rufous adult (p. 186)

Mark Anderson

SELECTED BIBLIOGRAPHY

Allen, D. 1996. **A photographic guide to birds of prey of southern, Central and East Africa**. New Holland, Cape Town.

Allen, D. 1997. **Africa's barred hawks, a guide to their identification**. Africa Birds & Birding 2 (6): 31–36.

Barnes, K. (ed.). 2000. **The Eskom red data book of South Africa, Lesotho and Swaziland**. BirdLife South Africa, Johannesburg.

Bekker, F., Bowland, T., Brand, D., Davies, R. & Steyn, P. Undated. **Innocent until proven guilty**. EWT, Johannesburg.

Bennet, G. 1991. **Looking at kestrels**. Birding in SA 43 (4): 111–113.

Brown, L.H. 1970. **African birds of prey**. Collins, London.

Brown, L.H. & Amandon, D. 1968. **Eagles, hawks and falcons of the world**, Vols. 1 & 2. Country Life Books, Hamlyn Publishing Group, Feltham.

Brown, L.H., Urban, E.K. & Newman, K.B. (eds.). 1982. **The Birds of Africa**, Vol. 1. Academic Press, London.

Burton, P. 1989. **Birds of prey of the world**. Dragon's World, Limpsfield.

Butchard, D. (ed.). 1985. **Vultures & farmers**. Vulture Study Group, Johannesburg.

Butchard, D. (ed.). 1987. **Eagles & farmers**. EWT & SAOS, Johannesburg.

Butchard, D. 1988. **Give a bird a bone; a brief account of vulture 'restaurants' in southern Africa**. African Wildlife 42 (6): 316–322.

Cade, T.J. 1982. **The falcons of the world**. Collins, London.

Campbell, B. & Lack, E. (eds.). 1985. **A dictionary of birds**. T & AD Poyser, Calton.

Chittenden, H. & Myburgh, N. 1996. **Vultures in the village**. Africa Birds & Birding 1 (1): 20–27.

Clancey, P.A. 1996. **The birds of southern Mozambique**. African Bird Book Publishing, Westville.

Clinning, C. 1989. **Southern African bird names explained**. SAOS, Johannesburg.

Cohan, C., Spottiswoode, C. & Rossouw, J. 2006. **Southern African bird finder**. Struik, Cape Town.

Del Hoyo, J., Elliot, A. & Sargatal, J. (eds.). 1994. **The birds of the world**, Vol 2. Lynx Edicions, Barcelona.

Ferguson-Lees, J. & Christie, D.A. 2001. **Raptors of the world**. Christopher Helm, London.

Finch-Davies, C.G. & Kemp, A.C. 1980. **The birds of prey of southern Africa**. Winchester Press, Johannesburg.

Fry, C.H., Keith, S. & Urban, E.K. (eds.). 1988. **The birds of Africa**, Vol. 3. Academic Press, London.

Ginn, P.J., McIlleron, W.G. & Milstein, P. le S. 1989. **The complete book of southern African birds**. Struik Winchester, Cape Town.

Gotch, A.F. 1981. **Birds – their Latin names explained**. Bladford Press, Poole.

Grossman, M.L. & Hamlet, J. 1965. **Birds of prey of the world**. Cassell, London.

Harris, A., Tucker, L. & Vinicombe, K. 1989. **The Macmillan guide to bird identification**. Macmillan, London.

Harrison, J.A., Allen, D.G., Underhill, L.G., Herremans, M., Tree, A.J., Parker, V. & Brown, C.J. (eds.). 1997. **The atlas of Southern African birds**, Vol. 1. BirdLife South Africa, Johannesburg.

Hockey, P.A.R., Dean, W.R.J. & Ryan, P.G. 2005. **Roberts Birds of Southern Africa**. John Voelcker Bird Book Fund, Cape Town.

Hollom, P.A.D., Porter, R.F., Christensen, S. & Willis, I. 1988. **Birds of the Middle East and North Africa**. T & AD Poyser, Calton.

Hume, R. & Boyer, T. 1991. **Owls of the world**. Dragon's World, Limpsfield.

Kemp, A. & Calburn, S. 1987. **The owls of southern Africa**. Struik, Cape Town.

Kemp, A. & Kemp, M. 1998. **Sasol birds of prey of Africa and its islands**. New Holland, Cape Town.

Kemp, A. 2001. **Fly-by-night operators**. Africa Birds & Birding 6 (1): 27–32.

König, C., Weick, F. & Becking, J-H. 1999. **Owls, a guide to the owls of the world**. Pica Press, Sussex.

Maclean, G.L. 1993. **Robert's birds of southern Africa**. John Voelcker Bird Book Fund, Cape Town.

Mundy, P., Butchart, D., Ledger, J. & Piper, S. 1992. **The vultures of Africa**. Acorn Books & Russel Friedman Books, Randburg & Halfway House.

Newman, K. (ed.). 1979. **Birdlife in southern Africa**. Macmillan South Africa, Johannesburg.

Newman, K. 1983. **Newman's birds of southern Africa**, 7th edition. Southern Book Publishers, Halfway House.

Newman, K. & Solomon, D. 1988. **Confusing Birds**. Southern Book Publishers, Halfway House.

Newton, I. (ed.). 1990. **Birds of prey**. Merehurst, London.

Oatley, T.B., Oschadleus, H.D., Navarro, R.A. & Underhill, L.G. 1998. **Review of ring recoveries of birds of prey of southern Africa**: 1948–1998. EWT, Johannesburg.

Parker, V. 1999. **The atlas of the birds of Sul do Save, southern Mozambique**. Avian Demography Unit, Cape Town, and Endangered Wildlife Trust, Johannesburg.

Pickford, P., Pickford, B. & Tarboton, W. 1989. **Southern African birds of prey**. Struik, Cape Town.

Piper, S.E., Mundy, P.J. & Vernon, C.J. 1989. **An ageing guide for the Cape Vulture**. Madoqua 1 (2): 105–110.

Siegfried, W.R. 1968. **The Mountain Buzzard**. Bokmakierie 20 (3): 58–59.

Simmons, R. 2004. **Blood brothers; the mystery of killing kin in the nest**. Africa Birds & Birding 9 (3): 43–48.

Sinclair, I. & Hockey, P. 2005. **Sasol, the larger illustrated guide to birds of Southern Africa**. Struik Publishers, Cape Town.

Sinclair, I. & Ryan, P. 2003. **Birds of Africa south of the Sahara**. Struik, Cape Town.

Steyn, P. 1973. **Eagle days; a study of African eagles at the nest**. Purnell & Sons South Africa. Johannesburg.

Steyn, P. 1982. **Birds of prey of Southern Africa**. David Phillip, Cape Town.

Steyn, P. 1984. **A delight of owls; African owls observed**. David Phillip, Cape Town.

Svenson, L., Grant, P.S., Mullarney, K. & Zetterström, D. 1999. **Der neue Kosmos Vogelführer**. Franckh-Kosmos, Stuttgart.

Tarboton, W. 1979. **Eagles of the Transvaal**. Transvaal Nature Conservation Division, Pretoria.

Tarboton, W. 1991. **Identifying small accipiters and their look-alikes**. Birding in SA 43 (1): 15–17.

Tarboton, W. & Allen, D. 1984. **The status and conservation of birds of prey in the Transvaal**. Transvaal Museum, Pretoria.

Tarboton, W. & Erasmus, R. 1988. **Sasol owls and owling in southern Africa**. Struik, Cape Town.

Van Perlo, B. 1999. **Collins illustrated checklist, birds of Southern Africa**. Harper Collins, London.

Zimmerman, D.A., Turner, D.A. & Pearson, D.J. 1996. **Birds of Kenya and northern Tanzania**. Russel Friedman Books, Halfway House.

By the same authors:

Cillié, B. 1997. **The mammal guide of Southern Africa**. Briza Publications, Pretoria.

Cillié, B. 2003. **The pocket photoguide to mammals of Southern Africa**. Sunbird Publishing, Cape Town.

Cillié, B. & Oberprieler, U.B. 2009. **Pocket-guide to Birds of Southern Africa**. Sunbird Publishing, Cape Town.

Cillié, B., Oberprieler, U.B. & Joubert, C. 2004. **Animals of Pilanesberg, an identification guide**. Game Parks Publishing, Pretoria.

Joubert, C., Oberprieler, U.B. & Cillié, B. 2007. **Field guide to the animals of the Greater Kruger Park**. Game Parks Publishing, Pretoria.

Joubert, C., Oberprieler, U.B. & Cillié, B. 2007. **Identification guide to the animals of the Greater Kruger Park**. Game Parks Publishing, Pretoria.

Oberprieler, U.B. & Cillié, B. 2001. **Southern African garden birds**. Lapa Publishers, Pretoria.

Oberprieler, U.B. & Cillié, B. 2002. **Raptor identification guide for Southern Africa**. Rollerbird Press & Random House, Johannesburg.

Oberprieler, U.B. & Cillié, B. 2008. **The bird guide of Southern Africa**. Game Parks Publishing, Pretoria.

INDEX

The preferred English names are indicated in **bold**, while scientific names are given in *italics*.

FALCONS AND KESTRELS

These very small to medium-small raptors inhabit open country and are adapted for fast (falcons) or hovering (kestrels) flight. Their wings are long and pointed while the tail is long.

(pp. 42, 158, 257)

OWLS

Owls are very small to very large raptors adapted to a nocturnal lifestyle.

(pp. 44, 190, 268)

KITES

Kites are a diverse collection of small to medium-sized raptors with long wings, and are excellent flyers. In spite of their names, the African Cuckoo-Hawk and Bat Hawk also belong to this group.

(pp. 41, 148, 254)

HARRIERS

Harriers are medium-sized, slenderly built raptors with long narrow wings, long tails and long legs. They occur in marshes or open habitats where they fly low over the ground, quartering to and fro, and dropping onto their prey on the ground.

(pp. 40, 138, 250)

10

9

8

7

GOSHAWKS AND SPARROWHAWKS

These very small to medium-sized raptors usually occur in well-wooded habitats where their secretive lifestyle makes them difficult to observe. Their wings are short, while the tail is long; an adaptation for fast but manoeuvrable flight. They have long legs. The two chanting goshawks, the Lizard Buzzard and the African Harrier-Hawk are not typical goshawks.

(pp. 39, 116, 241)

BUZZARDS

Buzzards resemble small eagles, but have unfeathered lower legs. They are medium to medium-large, robustly built raptors which hunt mostly from a perch. They soar well as the wings are long and broad while the tail is shortish to medium in length. The European Honey-Buzzard is not a typical buzzard.

(pp. 38, 104, 236)

SECRETARYBIRD

This is the only very large raptor with very long legs. It is further characterised by its crest of long feathers on the back of the head and long central tailfeathers. The plumage is grey and black.

(pp. 33, 48)

FISH-EATING RAPTORS

The Osprey and African Fish-Eagle are both large raptors which catch fish and are therefore associated with water. Both have long broad wings which enable them to carry even heavy fish. The unfeathered lower legs distinguish them from the true eagles and hawk-eagles.

(pp. 34, 50, 217)

VULTURES

These large to very large raptors are adapted to a scavenging lifestyle. The head and neck of most species are partially or wholly naked and the weak feet are not suited to killing prey. Vultures have long broad wings and short tails for soaring flight. The Palm-nut and Bearded Vultures are not typical vultures.

(pp. 35, 54, 218)

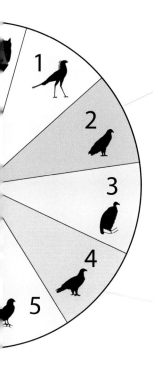

SNAKE-EAGLES

Although resembling true eagles, snake-eagles are easily distinguished by their large heads, large yellow eyes and unfeathered lower legs. As the name indicates, they feed mostly on snakes. As they soar often and well, their wings are broad and long, while the tail is of medium length. The Bateleur is not a typical snake-eagle as indicated by its dark eyes.

(pp. 37, 94, 232)

EAGLES AND HAWK-EAGLES

These medium to very large raptors are immediately distinguished by their fully feathered legs. They are powerful and aggressive hunters but are not averse to carrion. Their wings are long and broad, but the tails vary from shortish to medium, depending on the preferred hunting technique of the particular species.

(pp. 36, 72, 224)

QUICK INDEX

DAY ONE